# THE ULTIMATE GUIDE TO BREEDING BEETLES

## COLEOPTERA LABORATORY CULTURE METHODS

## ORIN MCMONIGLE

**COACHWHIP PUBLICATIONS**
CoachwhipBooks.com

ACKNOWLEDGEMENTS

I thank the greatest coleopterist in the universe, God, for creating such a large number of incredible and fascinating beetles and for giving me the interest and ability to work with and write about them. Special thanks go to Steven Barney for help writing the chapter on breeding dung beetles. Thanks to my wife Sylvia and daughters Kree and Gwynevere for their input and support in my beetle endeavors. Thanks also to Peter Clausen, Annie Lastar, Cameron Campbell, Tony Palmer, Christian Elowsky, James Smolka, Tom Larsen, Don Ahart, Hatari Invertebrates, Jonathan Lai, Takao Suzuki, Randy Morgan, Wade Harrell, Susan Gruner, Ryan Minard, Aaron Dossey, Oldrich Jahn, Dave Hawks, Barney Tomberlin, Michael Barney, John Lorbiecke, Tatiana Luzan, Travis Huval, Lary Reeves, Marita De La Pena, Zack Lemann, Jayme Necaise, Jen-Pan Huang, Dan Sundberg, Ray Dryer, Karl Meier, various keepers at the Cleveland Zoo, and many others.

DEDICATION
To my mother, who would let me stay up
past my bedtime to catch June beetles.

LEGAL NOTICE
Please note that the possession, exhibition, purchase, or sale of certain native or exotic invertebrates may be illegal or require permits in some states and other localities. Please check applicable codes and state departments (wildlife, agriculture, etc.). Some beetles in this book were photographed by permission at permitted institutions.

ISBN-13 978-1-61646-132-4
*The Ultimate Guide to Breeding Beetles*, © 2012 Orin McMonigle
Coachwhip Publications (Landisville, Pennsylvania), CoachwhipBooks.com

Front Cover: *Lucanus elaphus* and *Dynastes tityus*
Back Cover: (Top) *Eudicella gralli hubini*
(Bottom) *Mantichora* species

# CONTENTS

*PSEUDOLUCANUS CAPREOLUS* PAIR

# INTRODUCTION

This book is a compilation of the *Complete Guides to Rearing Beetles* series with updates, additional information, and a new section that provides culture details for rarely kept groups that will probably never merit their own book. The species presented throughout are primarily those that are easily maintained in laboratory culture following the prescribed husbandry parameters. However, a small number are easily maintained and long-lived display specimens that are difficult to successfully reproduce, including *Zarhipis* and *Calosoma*. The largest and most spectacular beetle species native to the United States are the main focus of this book. Some non-native beetles commonly kept in insect zoos and by hobbyists in other countries are also presented.

When *The Complete Guide to Rearing Grant's Rhinoceros Beetle* was first published in 1999, it was created for a hobby that did not exist. At that time the few people keeping *Dynastes granti* were concerned primarily with keeping the adults alive for a few weeks for temporary exhibits. The name *Complete Guide* referred to the text's details on care and information for captive husbandry that included all stages of the beetle's life cycle, complete from egg to beetle. A second edition was published in 2001 which included expanded information on other native rhinoceros beetles. The *Complete Guide to Rearing the Elephant Stag Beetle* was written in 2004 after the complete life cycle of *Lucanus elaphus* was worked out into multiple generations. With no

other comparable U.S. beetles in other groups the series seemed to be at an end. In 2006 *The Complete Guide to Rearing Flower and Jewel Scarabs* was a greatly expanded and updated version of two chapters written in 1999 for the text of *For*

*PHALACROGNATHUS MUELLERI*

the Love of Rhinoceros and Stag Beetles*, published in 2001. That book was printed in combined Chinese and English text and has been credited with mainstreaming the Taiwanese beetle hobby. The book went out of print after a few years, which was why the flower and jewel scarab book was published. In 2008 the first guide on rhinoceros beetle breeding was rewritten to concentrate on *Dynastes tityus* over *Dynastes granti*, since the adults are much longer-lived and wide-ranging. The Eastern Hercules was the original species meant for the

*CHALCOSOMA ATLAS* PUPA

publication. Again it seemed the series was at a dead-end, but in 2011 *The Complete Guide to Rearing Darkling Beetles* was published, since there was finally enough material for this group. (*Eleodes* were one of my first beetles and were the subject of an article in the premiere issue of *Invertebrates-Magazine* 2001.) In 2012, inspired by an *Invertebrates-Magazine* article submission, *The Complete Guide to Rearing the Rainbow Scarab* was published. The compiled and updated text you now hold is in large format, full color, and is the ultimate expression of the complete guide to rearing beetles series.

The flower and jewel beetle chapters are not listed near each other in this text. Both subfamilies include large, brightly-colored scarabs that can appear similar to hobbyists but are extremely different. The most important difference from the beetle culturist's perspective is the dichotomy of husbandry requirements. Flower beetle larvae consume a mix of decaying materials, just as do the popular rhinoceros beetles, while jewel scarab larvae feed almost exclusively on rotten wood (in earlier stages of decay) and so are kept like stag beetles. They are grouped accordingly.

The final chapter includes a jumble of different beetle groups, including an additional scarab subfamily, the Euchirinae, as well as the families Passalidae, Cerambycidae, Carabidae, Silphidae, Phengodidae, Dermestidae, Dytiscidae, Hydrophilidae, Bruchidae, and Elateridae. These range from predators to scavengers, and generalists to specialists, while a few are reared similarly to species in the earlier chapters. Some are valuable display specimens that have never been reared through a generation in captivity, while others have been cultured for uncountable generations in mass and have no individual specimen value.

The main stars of this book are a few large, beautiful beetles that are easily reared in captivity and are native to large areas of the United States. This book is intended primarily for U.S. hobbyists who can find many of the listed species in their own states. A small part of the audience will be keepers working for various permitted institutions who will hopefully find the short sections on exotics useful. However, those sections are mainly included for English-speaking beetle enthusiasts in other countries. Photographs included here of exotic species taken at institutions are for the most part wild-caught specimens.

*CANTHON CHALCITES* PAIR (© STEVEN BARNEY)

Collection of zero eggs from a female is something that will happen to every beetle culturist and, for the majority of species, is a thousand times more likely than collecting over a hundred. Nevertheless, zero is not included in the averages. In the first edition of *For the Love of Rhinoceros and Stag Beetles*, an average range of eggs counts I provided for an array of different species was based on reported captive culture experiences. In the second edition, the number of eggs per female was changed by another contributor to "over a hundred" for most species. While the absolute theoretical maximum is not necessarily a false number (such as, "a human female will have 45 children"), it is not very useful and tends to be misleading. Many ova count changes are highly dubious even as absolute maximums, such as *Golofa* at over 150. The only definitely false statement was the *Strategus antaeus* egg count, changed from 20 to over a 100, that was made by a person who never saw that species alive, let alone bred it. Average number of eggs per female listed in this text are those commonly encountered in laboratory culture. A primary reason for providing this range is to allow culturists to gauge culture methods. If beetles produce eggs below average rates, husbandry parameters are likely not being met.

Breeding beetles is a science and an art. While all aspects can be described and repeated, tiny details can make a big difference. Rotten wood and leaves are the primary food for all the commonly reared species. There will always be variation in quality depending on source, batch, and season. Identification of the degree of decay and treatment for pests are important to prevent problems of substrate variation but it is often not possible to determine the species of tree, let alone species of associated fungus. Close personal attention will help grow monstrous, beautiful beetles, but excessive disturbance can damage eggs and pupal cells. Overzealous hobbyists may be prone to overfeeding or excessive watering. The methods outlined in the following chapters have been used to rear countless beetles by many hobbyists. There may be more than one good rearing method, but there are certainly limitless wrong ways.

## A LITTLE HISTORY

Interest in beetle husbandry to some extent has existed since man first dug up dung beetle pupae in Egypt four or five thousand years ago. My own interest in beetles, I was born with. As early as five or six I would beg my mother to let me stay up past eight to catch the large June beetles that flew into our porch light. (My mother was never a lover of insects, though she did tell my father she wanted to buy my childhood home upon finding a toad in the yard.)

In addition to the *Magicicada* 17-year emergence of 1982, catching large June beetles is a favorite childhood memory. As I grew older I was able to find a bit of available information on identifying and killing dead insects to place in cigar boxes. While I tried my hand at this gruesome endeavor, my joy was never in dead creatures and funeral trays. I tried my hand at keeping the uncommon large click beetle or small stag over the years, but desired greatly to find a large rhinoceros beetle like the *Dynastes tityus* listed in my identification books.

My uncle mentioned that he found rhinoceros beetles "all the time" in the Orlando area—it took me a year or two but by early 1988 I had saved up for a plane ticket. Over a few weeks of collecting I discovered where *Strategus antaeus* lived and how to collect them in numbers. From this I formulated a methodology successfully used to rear this species, which hatched in 1988 and eclosed in 1989.

Among others, in 1992 I picked up some *Scarabaeus sacer* from a local pet shop—they lived for nearly two years but attempts at rearing were unsuccessful. In 1995 I finally collected my first *Dynastes tityus*, my dream beetle (a single female). It is native to my state but from further south, and it's not easy to find. After various successes rearing different native beetles, I published an article with rearing details for *Dynastes tityus*, *Dynastes granti*, *Cotinis*, and *Odontotaenius* in *Invertebrata*, vol. 1, no. 2, in 1996. (The same issue mentions a presentation at the Invertebrates in Captivity Conference by

Cameron Campbell of the Fort Worth Zoo on attempts at breeding *Chalcosoma*.)

Up to this point I had still never met a single person with an interest in breeding beetles, and certainly not someone who wasn't being paid to do it. In late summer of 1996 I was contacted by Jonathan Lai, who was looking for information on raising *Dynastes granti*. He came here from Taiwan for schooling. When we spoke he told me how he fell in love with beetles during a trip to a department store in Japan. I learned beetle enthusiasts had been raising their native *Allomyrina dichotoma* for years (Kishida, 1971). He had reared *A. dichotoma*, but *D. granti* were different. *Dynastes* didn't do well on the pure rotten wood normally used to keep the Asian species. We discussed beetle breeding in depth and between then and 1999 I provided various species details and wrote a few chapters for a book we hoped to publish to share our love of beetles with others in the United States and Taiwan. (The book would be published in English and Chinese.) The late '90s brought about a big change in Japan as previously they had only been allowed to keep native beetles, but evidence provided to their agriculture department allowed the import of various harmless exotic species.

Breeding beetles in the U.S. has a long history and may have helped spur the beginnings of German interest in rhinoceros beetles. There are some very old references to beetle culture, such as documentation of the life cycle for *Hydrophilus triangularis* in relation to fisheries management (Wilson, 1923), but only in the last few decades has beetle culture been for the sake of the animals themselves. In response to the decline of the endangered American burying beetle, attempts at breeding this and related species began at a few permitted institutions. In 1992 *Natural History, Husbandry, and Display of Carrion Beetles* and in 1993 *Husbandry and Display Techniques of the American Burying Beetle Nicrophorus Americanus* were presented at AAZPA regional conferences (Creamer, 1992; Creamer, 1993), based partly on unpublished husbandry manuscripts by Andrea Kozol from 1990 and 1992. In 1995 the curator of invertebrates from the Cincinnati Zoo gave a presentation at the Invertebrates in Captivity Conference on the history of *Dynastes hercules* in captivity at Insect World. Not long ago even zoos had to catch their own beetles. Collected stock from Trinidad in June 1981 was reared to adulthood and in 1983 captive-reared adults were sent to the Lobbecke-Museum and Aquarium in Dusseldorf, Germany, and the Wilhelma Zoologischer-Botonischer Garten in Stuttgart, Germany (Busching, 1995).

THE FUTURE . . .

There seems to be a strong push to concern our young people with observing and keeping only those insects that are made out of plastic or that can be fed or petted in a video game. The idea is that Earth's creatures are not our legacy or gift, but rather we are their curse. They are something to be preserved somewhere with no one allowed to see them. They are to be equal to the human species but separate. Sadly the very organizations we animal lovers support to save animals commonly work hard to eliminate them from public life. Eventually nobody knows what the lockbox contains. If we continue down this path, not a soul will notice when they disappear. Hopefully more books and further interest in keeping beetles will offer a slight diversion from the path we are presently on.

# 1
# RHINOCEROS BEETLES

## INTRODUCTION

This chapter is written to provide beetle enthusiasts in the USA and abroad with all the common breeding knowledge and special tricks for rearing this incredible animal. Only recently has *Dynastes tityus* become available to nearly everyone. Many new beetle hobbyists are trying their hand at rearing rhinoceros beetles and many have little or no practical information. Outside this series, insect-rearing books and manuals written in English and available today do not even begin to offer information that details the techniques necessary for rearing beetles other than mealworms and mundoworms. Every aspect from egg care to adult care is covered here. This text is designed to provide understandable rearing techniques to the serious breeder, but is also written for anyone with an interest in development and natural history. Photographs accompany text whenever possible to clarify descriptions.

Despite the number of steps, requirements, and techniques involved with the rearing of *D. tityus*, this rhinoceros beetle truly requires less time and financial upkeep than most other pets. For periods while eggs are waiting to hatch, when substrate is new, between pupal cell formation and emergence, and during hibernation, care can be hands-free for weeks or months with no ill effects. A little bag of dog food, which a St. Bernard might gobble up in a single meal, can last an entire lifetime for twenty or more eastern Hercules beetles. Relatively little space is required. Pet sitters do not need to be called in when the owner is on a long vacation. In listing reasons as to why *D. tityus* can make better pets than other animals, it is ironic to point out, "Their feces do not stink."

*DYNASTES TITYUS*

Nearly every possible problem that might occur is listed within these pages, but these are not meant to discourage. This way, if something does go wrong, it can be easier to identify the problem and solution. As long as some attention is paid to the care of this wonderful beetle it is not difficult to raise. It may be possible to rear Dynastinae without checking for substrate pests, offering the correct food, preventing excessive ventilation, etc., but skipping the advice and suggestions will likely result in dead grubs.

The following pages are filled with a wealth of information and photographs of *Dynastes tityus*, and it is hoped that this book may one day

*DYNASTES TITYUS* MALE

*DYNASTES TITYUS* HANGS
ON TIGHTLY WITH CLAWS

help *D. tityus* to be as commonly kept as a pet in the U.S. as *Allomyrina dichotoma* (Kabuto-mushi) and other beetles are kept in Japan. Mothers there can buy a live *A. dichotoma* from vending machines for their children to play with. (*A. dichotoma* adults only live about sixty days.) Also, every department store carries food for the larvae and adults.

What follows in the body of this text is information on egg care, larval care, adult care, food, cages, etc. All of the information is taken from experience by the author. It does not guarantee success with rhinoceros beetles, but will make all the difference. Instructions must be followed with caution and the author cannot be there to make sure readers do not cut themselves with a razor blade or burn their house down while baking leaves in the oven.

This chapter is the fourth expanded adaptation of *The Complete Guide to Rearing Grant's Rhinoceros Beetle* (1999), which is no longer in print. *Dynastes tityus* is the species I wanted to write about the first time, but the lack of livestock made it impractical. (Though *D. granti's* range is much smaller, it emerges in mass quantities). I began rearing *D. tityus* in 1995, but it took many years to get the stock established because I began with a single wild female. (They are extremely difficult to find in my state). An expanded section on keeping other species of U.S. rhinoceros beetles from the second edition of the Grant's guide (2001) and a short list of some of the exotics commonly reared in other countries from the *D. tityus* guide (2008) are included. Rearing information has been expanded and new species have been added due to the growing interest of hobbyists in all of the Dynastinae.

ABOUT THE EASTERN HERCULES
*Dynastes tityus* specimens measure in at 1.4″ to 2.6″ (35-66mm) from the tip of the thoracic horn to the end of the abdomen. The wingspan on a large individual can also be expansive at nearly half a foot across. The underside is shiny black and covered in hair (setae). Males have a thick ridge of setae running the ventral surface of the thoracic horn and a tuft of setae over the top of the head that resembles bangs.

The eastern Hercules beetle ties with its close relative, *D. granti*, for the most massive U.S. species. It only measures shorter because the horn is used in measurements and its horn structure is different. The cephalic horn extends further than the thoracic horn even on large specimens, which is the most notable physical different between it and *D. granti*. Large males have a ridge on the dorsal surface of the cephalic horn, not the hook of *D. granti*. Males possess two side horns, which can be notable on large specimens. These side horns are much smaller or do not exist at all on *D. granti*. The base color of *D. tityus* can be tan, army green, gray, or even bright yellow. Base coloration varies somewhat by individual, but is primarily dependent on collection location. *Dynastes granti* are usually only light gray. The beautiful spotting on this creature ranges from no spots to many spots and the spotting can be peppered, form large irregular splotches or stripes, or look like coffee stains. *Dynastes granti* usually have only black or gray spots. Beyond coloration and horn structure the big difference between these species is the long lifespan of adult *D. tityus* (9-12 months for captive-bred) and short lifespan of *D. granti* (2-4 months wild or captive-bred). Despite various differences, *Dynastes tityus* and *Dynastes granti* have hybridized in captivity.

One uncommon aspect of this beetle (and a few relatives, including *D. granti*) is that the entire animal changes to a dark brown in high humidity and returns to normal coloration when dry. This species is designed for physiological color change. The surface of the elytra and pronotum has two layers separated by a microscopic layer of air between. The outer layer is clear, while the inner layer is pigmented. In high humidity, the air is replaced with water, obscuring the color of the bottom layer. The exoskeletons of older beetles react more quickly to changes in humidity.

It is very simple to determine the sex of *D. tityus*. Males have a horn on both the head and pronotum, while females only possess a tiny tubercle on the head. Even the smallest of males has a noticeable horn on the pronotum. Pupae sex determination is just as easy, although predicting the sex of the larvae is a bit more difficult. Larvae with small head capsules are usually females, and larvae with larger head capsules, usually males. A close look at the third to last segment on the underside of male larvae reveals a tiny dark mark surrounded by white. No such mark is visible on female larvae. The tiny mark can be seen as early as 1st instar, but is most readily observed on fully-grown 3rd instar larvae.

The eastern Hercules beetle occurs across much of the continental United States, from New Jersey south to Florida and west to Texas. Despite its expansive range, *D. tityus* is much more difficult to collect than *D. granti*, which is reflected in much scarcer availability and higher pricing for dead specimens.

## COLLECTING

Eastern Hercules beetles, as with most Dynastinae, only fly during the evening, which is an event worth seeing and hearing. Adult beetles are most commonly collected as they land under gas station, parking lot, and tennis court lights.

Adults only fly during the last few months of their lives. The best time to look is between 10 p.m. and 2 a.m. Adults can be found as early as late June and as late as September, but the primary collecting period is during the months of July and August.

Black light traps can be employed, but the density of this species is generally too low to make black lights worthwhile. It's possible to drive down a stretch of highway in a good area and check dozens of different lights in a few hours, while a black light may not attract a single beetle the whole night.

Adult beetles are occasionally found in groups on a log or specific tree during the day. Groups of three to a dozen adults occur and are most commonly reported on ash. These groups are believed to be the result of a congregating pheromone. If a few are encountered, it's worthwhile to check back daily. However, whether collected or not, the following year they won't be found in the same spot. This is a great collection method but happening across such a spot is not common.

Lastly, larvae and adults can be found in tree hole habitats. These habitats are usually difficult to find and even more difficult to excavate. Look for hollow trees, often mostly or partly dead, that are at least a few feet in diameter and have a large

*DYNASTES TITYUS*, MAJOR MALE

*DYNASTES TITYUS*, MINOR MALE

hole where leaf litter can fall in and accumulate. A suitable hole will be a few inches to many feet above the ground, as there shouldn't be access for earthworms that can decimate the habitat. Tree hole habitats are the perfect nurseries for grubs. Often two stages of larvae are encountered, since this species takes two years in nature. Also, adult beetles can be found in pupal cells waiting for the next summer. I have collected various stages of larvae and a hibernating adult male from the same tree hole habitat, five years apart, both times in the month of August.

## Starting Out

It may be difficult to collect *Dynastes tityus* even if it is native to your state. Live adult eastern Hercules beetles are available from a small number of vendors in the U.S. Wild-caught adults are offered in summer while captive-bred animals tend to be offered in the fall or winter. Grubs may be available from hobbyists and some dealers year round. *Dynastes tityus* is harmless to agriculture and forestry, but permits may be needed for specimens brought in from out of state.

If wild adults are received it is important to have an egg-laying cage immediately ready in order to collect as many ova as possible. Since the age of wild-caught adults is unknown, they may live only a few hours or as long as four months. Also, females have laid some or all of their eggs in the wild before capture. Wild females may begin laying ova the first day after capture, if given proper egg-laying substrate. Wild-caught adults should be examined for mites and cleaned thoroughly. Captive-bred adults usually take a few months before laying ova and can take half a year if they are kept cool after emergence. Newly arrived grubs should be immediately placed in rearing containers.

Adult beetles feed on sugary liquids, but not all foods are equal. They accept opened fruits like banana, cantaloupe, watermelon, apple, pear, and pineapple, but are unable to get through the skin on their own. The adult mouthparts are like paint brushes and are very different from the

*DYNASTES TITYUS* FEEDING ON FRUIT JELLY.
MALE HAS FIGHT MARKS ON ITS PRONOTUM.

large, powerful jaws of the larvae. In the wild, there is not much fruit around and adults are normally seen feeding on the sap of wounded trees. Fruit solids that pass the jaws can lodge in the digestive system and cause premature death. A better food than fruit, which increases the life expectancy of the adults, is watered down (1:1) real maple syrup placed in a little dish with paper towels. The paper towels absorb the liquid and prevent the water-syrup mixture from spilling into the substrate. A small jug of maple syrup will last a long time. It is worth the extra time and energy to feed the adults 100% real maple syrup. One part brown sugar to four parts water is a useful and less expensive alternative. Beetle jellies made to feed beetles can be useful but recent formulations include protein and other additives that can encourage severe mite infestations and have no proven benefit to the beetles. Many types of fruit also encourage mite outbreaks.

Handling pet *D. tityus* does not shorten their lives unless they are accidentally smashed or seriously abused. Enjoying their antics up-close is the reason most people keep them. Many other animals are stressed out from being handled but this is usually not a problem for *D. tityus*. Excessive handling can cause specimens in winter diapause to come out of hibernation early. Females that are laying eggs may produce fewer young if played with too often, because they do not have the time to prepare the substrate for egg laying. Adults should be kept in damp substrate between handling or they can dry up.

CAGES AND HOUSING

The container of choice for egg laying and larvae rearing is an ordinary 10-gallon (about 40 liters) aquarium with a piece of glass cut to cover the entire top of the tank. Inexpensive lids can be produced by using a razor blade to cut apart damaged tanks that have been inadvertently broken. A long side piece only needs one cut to fit perfectly, while the bottom piece is ready to go. (It is a good idea to fold clear packing tape or duct tape over the edges of the glass for safety's sake.)

An important part of preparing the tank is to cut exposed silicone sealant out of all corners, but do not cut the silicone between the glass pieces, or the tank may fall apart. Adults are very agile and can use the ridge of excess silicone in the corners to climb out and easily pop off most lids—they are able to lift many times their own weight. Their strength is remarkable. Remember, too, that larvae chew up exposed silicone, which might possibly get caught in their digestive tracts and cause death. (This would be rare, as larvae commonly chew up, but seldom ingest, foreign materials including silicone, plastics, and Styrofoam. Better safe than sorry, however.)

Once the cage and lid are prepared, fill with substrate 4 to 6 inches (10-15cm) and throw in the larvae or adults. Leave four or so inches of space to give adults plenty of room to move around, to keep larvae and adults away from the lid, and to make digging for ova and larvae possible without dumping the entire container. Deeper substrate is unnecessary. Shallow substrate discourages egg laying and can allow the substrate to dry out easily.

*Dynastes tityus* grubs rarely cannibalize healthy siblings under decent conditions, but overcrowding and starvation can lead to steep losses. Larvae can be reared separately to remove

any possibility of cannibalism. Grubs should be kept together until the first molt, or growth can be stunted. If kept together in a small container beyond early 2nd instar, stunting can also occur. Each grub can be placed in a 16 oz. deli cup with five to ten pinholes in the lid (pinholes should be made with thin pins, not thumbtacks, to prevent dark-winged fungus gnats from laying eggs in the container). The substrate should fill the container and will need to be replaced a few times in late 3rd instar as it is consumed. When larvae are fully-grown they can be placed back together to encourage synced emergence of the adults.

If small containers are used for rearing grubs, ¼ gallon (1 liter) or less, it is important to remember that the process of dog food or substrate decomposing may use up all the available oxygen and suffocate the larvae. When there is a lack of oxygen the larvae climb to the surface, pass out, and become quite flaccid. For a few days or more the "passed-out" larvae stay the normal whitish color, but if the problem is still unnoticed

*DYNASTES TITYUS* WITH STRIPES

*Dynastes tityus* Pair

they suffocate, die, and turn black. While being entirely motionless, larvae can live for days with little or no oxygen. A few hours of exposure to fresh air and they are back to normal. This problem is seldom encountered without overfeeding. When using a larger container such as a 10-gallon tank, the problem doesn't occur.

Large containers holding more than 10-gallons are happily accepted by the beetles, but are undesirable for the hobbyist. Anything that holds over ten gallons of substrate is quite heavy and a big cage full of dirt is very strenuous to move. Large containers are also awkward to manipulate and checking on the health of the eggs or larvae, or the amount of food remaining, is much more difficult. Additionally, making enough substrate to fill a huge container can be quite a chore. Lastly, it's more difficult to treat a large amount of substrate if it becomes infested with nematodes or earthworms.

Because the substrate needs to be kept constantly damp, the type of lid used is very important. The use of screen lids would make it too difficult to keep moisture levels in range. Constant additions of water to dry substrate cause alternating too high and too low moisture levels. Plastic wrap should be used to cover screen lids, or water may need to be added regularly. (Remember, also, that adult beetles can destroy a screen lid.) Solid glass or plastic lids (with few to no air holes) allow for a constant moisture level. Be very cautious if adding water to the substrate in cages with glass or plastic lids because the water barely escapes. If the substrate becomes too wet and stagnant with the continuous addition of water, it will lead to anaerobic conditions, which will suffocate and kill eggs and larvae.

The choice of cages is somewhat limitless and can include trashcans, plastic shoeboxes, mason jars, deli cups, and any other plastic or glass containers. Wood, cardboard, or Styrofoam containers would be a big mistake, since these materials present little barrier against escape. The reason plastic containers are not as favorable as glass is that they are hard to see through—even if clear—and if given time, adults and larvae sometimes scrape or chew their way out. Nothing noticeable may happen at first, and then a year later the larvae have crawled out of a hole in the bottom or lid and are found dried up in a corner of the room. What is important is not how thick the plastic is, but how hard it is. A good rule of thumb: if even the tiniest bit of plastic can be scraped off with a fingernail, do not use. Plastic shoeboxes and trashcans have few problems with escape and are economical alternatives to a glass tank.

It is advisable to keep more than one rearing cage or hatching container at the same time, because most problems are unlikely to occur in every container. Determining what went wrong is easier when only one cage has had disease, food shortage, overcrowding, bad substrate, or other problems. It is a good idea to remember the saying, "Don't keep all your eggs in one basket."

SUBSTRATE

The best substrate for keeping *D. tityus* larvae and for egg laying is a mixture of rotten wood, compost manure, and crushed dead hardwood leaves in a 1:1:1 ratio. All three components are inexpensive and each adds to the quality of food for the grubs. Once these ingredients are prepared as follows, mix them together and fill rearing container about 4 inches (102mm) from the top.

Dead leaves are easily collected on the forest floor of any wooded area. Watch out for gardens, yards, etc., that might use pesticide. After collecting leaves, either allow them to dry for one to two weeks, or dry them in the oven in a shallow tray at 250° F for two hours. Only after drying, leaves can be easily crushed in the hands into a flaky powder and added to the substrate or hatching container. Cooking has the added benefit of killing mites, wireworms, earthworms, and other small organisms normally present in collected leaves. Uncrushed leaves do not deter larval feeding, but they make the substrate difficult

to compact and can prevent females from laying eggs or larvae from pupating. Grubs are capable of chewing into whole leaves but feeding is greatly enhanced if the leaves are finely ground. Leaves included in the substrate mixture speed up growth and increase the size of young larvae.

Compost manure can be purchased at garden shops and department stores for use in gardening or mushroom growing. Purchase a mix that is well composted and contains less than 10% sand or no sand at all. Compost should have a slight "mushroom" smell. Low quality compost may contain large clumps of clay and manure that is not fully decayed. Mushroom compost or dehydrated manure are alternatives, but be careful and make certain the medium is not clay-like, anaerobic, or in the early stages of decay (stinky).

Rotten wood can be hunted for and found in tiny wooded areas, forests, or yards. Rotten branches fall off trees all the time—if the wood is crushable with bare hands, it is perfect. Of course, huge rotten logs in a forest supply a lot more food to work with and less time searching. Collected wood should be heated in the oven to kill harmful stowaways. Rotten wood can be "made" by putting logs or branches in a trash can—cover with a layer of dirt or compost and keep very moist. Making rotten wood is inexpensive and easy, but it takes about two years for most of the wood to become edible. Non-rotted wood (especially green wood!) should be heat-treated first to speed up decomposition. Hardwood is preferred but softwood (pine) may suffice if there is no other option. Larvae do not do nearly as well if fed only softwood and it must be very rotten and soft. Beyond low food value, a major problem with pines is that the combustion temperature of softwood is much lower than for hardwood, or even for leaves. Without careful attention, heat-treating dry softwood can cause a fire.

Other substrates can be used: peat, rotten wood alone, compost alone, potting soil, etc., but often yield a much higher or complete larval, and sometimes egg, mortality rate. Besides, lower quality substrates, if they do not kill the larvae, often produce tiny adults that can be much smaller than some midgets found in the wild, which are only around 1 ½ inches (35mm) long.

Depending on the types used, it is possible to have good success with just compost or just rotten wood, but it is a haphazard method. Trial and error is the unfortunate way to see if substrate will work. Also, every piece of wood and every bag of compost are somewhat different. Sometimes wood or compost is just bad for no visible reason and must be replaced. Eggs may not survive or grubs may not grow, despite feeding, if the substrate is bad. Mixing together the different components makes up for most deficiencies in the parts and prevents mass die-offs due to bad substrate.

EGG LAYING AND CARE

The female lays—on average—one egg every other day, but may produce a few in one night or none for days. The adult female deposits 30-60 ova, which were already contained in her body before she emerged from her pupal cell. Each is laid singly as she takes special care in compacting nearby substrate to create a surrounding chamber twice the size of the newly laid egg. If the substrate is not compactable and damp, she does not lay any ova. Egg laying substrate does not need to be able to support larvae, but those must be placed in edible substrate upon hatching. Females can oviposit in many compactable substrates including sand, peat moss, potting soil, and dirt. Sand is not recommended since it provides no nourishment for the larvae, scratches up the exoskeleton of the adult, and is more likely to collapse on the eggs. Whatever type of substrate is used, it is advisable to count eggs so that the substrate can be changed if what was chosen does not work. The female may refuse to lay eggs or aspects of the substrate may kill eggs. (If all the eggs fail to develop they may simply be infertile.)

There are a number of things that can be tried if females are active but eggs are still not being laid. One, add more water, as a very damp substrate is conducive for egg laying. Two, add a few handfuls of finely ground rotten leaves or moldy sawdust. (Used *Lucanus* substrate works as well.) Three, check the substrate very closely for tiny nematodes or other pests, and sterilize if present. (Discard if severely infested.) Four, add a handful of larval frass, if available. Five, start over—discard and replace all substrate.

The ova are white, somewhat spherical, and 1/8 of an inch (3-4mm) across. Eggs are like tiny white grapes and bounce if dropped onto a hard surface. Like grapes, the eggs also squish under enough pressure. When ova are first laid they are smaller, more delicate, and cylinder-shaped. Over the next week they expand into a larger, near-perfect sphere as they absorb surrounding moisture. A small percentage of the ova laid may be yellowish or have brown markings. As long as these discolored ova are not infected or damaged, their successful hatching is just as likely as with normal, white-colored eggs.

*DYNASTES TITYUS* EGGS (1 DAY AND 3 WEEKS OLD)

Predators and disease occurring in fresh substrate can destroy the eggs. Untreated wood and leaves often contain wireworms, which eat healthy eggs. Entomophagus fungus is not completely destroyed by heat-treating so substrate must be replaced and the container destroyed or disinfected with bleach. Dead, infertile, and smashed eggs will usually be fed upon immediately by springtails and nematodes, if present, but these miniature animals usually don't kill healthy eggs. Parasitic and free-living mites do not attach to healthy ova, so this is the easiest stage to rid a culture of mites. Simply remove ova and place in a clean container with fresh substrate.

There is an egg-eating brown mite found on most wild adult *D. granti*. (The same mite is probably found on some wild *D. tityus*.) These mites move fast and are somewhat large (.75mm). Usually, the mites hang out in the crack between the thorax and abdomen on the underside of the beetle. Although these mites appear to have no effect on larvae or adults, they feed on and kill eggs. 1-2 mites can be found on each infested egg. The adult mite expands incredibly after feeding, to 2mm+ across, and appears mostly white. (At a glance it looks almost like a freshly laid *Dynastes* egg except that it moves.) It is important to inspect wild adults to remove and destroy as many mites as possible before placing them in the cage.

Eggs do not possess a hard protective shell. If substrate is pushed by a human hand or an adult female beetle trying to pack substrate to lay other eggs, ova can be smashed. Sometimes eggs become strangely shaped when they survive smashed substrate before they started to expand. Never pushing down on the substrate, and removing eggs once each week or so, are good practices to follow.

To check if females are laying, or to remove eggs, tip the container at a forty-five degree angle and lightly dig in the substrate towards the bottom of the container. Females often compact the entire lower two to three inches of the substrate. The ova are deposited in the middle of small clumps of compacted dirt. When digging, if there are no compacted areas that are difficult to dig through, eggs will almost never be found. A finger, spoon, or other object can be used to pop up the compacted clumps of dirt. Next, when the clumps are gently squeezed in the hand they fall apart and the bright white ova fall out and can be easily picked up and placed into a hatching container.

Setting up and observing hatching containers allows the highest number of ova to survive. Eggs should be counted, removed, and placed in hatching containers every week or two. Any small clear container with a wide mouth does well as a hatching container. Place ova in the bottom of the container about ½ inch (12.7mm) apart and cover with a thin layer of crushed leaves such as oak, maple, and beech, and then cover at least 2 inches (51mm) above that with substrate mixture. The crushed leaf flakes help prevent die-off (which is often 10-20% of the ova). Substrate can be filled to the top and then the container can be inverted so that the eggs are on top. The ova are still protected, have less pressure on them, and newly hatched larvae dig down, away from the other eggs. Since the hatching period of this species takes around a month, it is nice to be able to keep an eye on the ova—just look through the bottom of the hatching container.

There are important things to watch for in the hatching container: massive ova die-off, hatching, starving larvae, and older larvae. If the eggs are not counted, mortality numbers won't be known. Normal die-off of ova from wild females is less than 25% over the hatching period, a few here and a few there. If a high percentage of ova die in a week or two, replace the substrate immediately. A week before hatching, the tiny spiracles and the tips of the mandibles of the developing larvae begin to be visible through the translucent shells of the ova. Ova may hatch fine in poor substrate, but still the larvae starve. Properly fed larvae double their size in the first two to three days and the gut (abdomen) turns blackish-blue. These growing grubs eventually need to be removed from the hatching container to prevent them from crawling around and accidentally smashing unhatched eggs. The ability to see and react to the above situations is what affords the eggs in a hatching container a much better survival rate.

## RAISING THE LARVAE

Upon hatching, larvae are vulnerable and white. Within hours the head and legs have hardened to red brown and after a few days the abdomen becomes bluish-black as it fills with food. Some larvae will move little after hatching and die, but greater than 5% mortality during this period is high. After the first day, the larval stage of *D. tityus* is far less vulnerable. Once they've begun to feed, grubs should be moved to a rearing cage.

After four weeks or more, depending on feeding, the grown hatchlings (1st instar) have their first molt and become 2nd instar. Eight or more weeks later, the larvae go through their second and final larval molt to become 3rd instar. For a day after each of these molts the larvae are again

*DYNASTES TITYUS* GRUB

quite vulnerable and the normally hard brown heads are white and soft. To protect themselves, prior to molting they construct molting cells by compacting the substrate around themselves with their mandibles and body. After each molt a few days are spent in this cell while the exoskeleton hardens and the head changes from white back to brown.

These white, thin-skinned monsters can take a lot of excess moisture or dryness for weeks. The larger grubs can also, just barely, survive months without food or weeks without water. Full-grown third instar larvae are at their toughest, being over one hundred times the mass of hatchlings and larger than a person's thumb.

A percentage of larvae will hatch with deformities common to scarabs. One common deformity is defective abdominal segmentation. The same deformity has been reported in millipedes, cockroaches, and pseudoscorpions, and is common for many beetle larvae. It does not seem to affect growth and is not visible on the adult. Another common deformity is displayed as undersized or unevenly sized larval legs. (This can be severe in some *Megasoma*.) This deformity likewise is not visible in the adult. A less common deformity involves curvature or inflation of the mandibles. This deformity often severely retards growth but can result in healthy adults eventually (though in stag beetles and jewel scarabs it's a death sentence).

Grubs often end up with black spots commonly called "black spot disease." The spots are, however, a symptom resulting from various ills. The black markings are formed by a buildup of melanin and are akin to a scar or scab. Causes include bacterial infections, bites from certain nematodes and mites, malnutrition, and damage caused by other larvae or the keeper. If numerous spots are seen, the first step it to check and replace the substrate. Larvae that have been poorly kept and fed often end up with growing damage spots, so improvements in substrate can be too late. However, most rhinoceros beetles and flower beetles can recover from black spots and

RHINOCEROS BEETLE LARVA
WITH JAW DEFORMITY

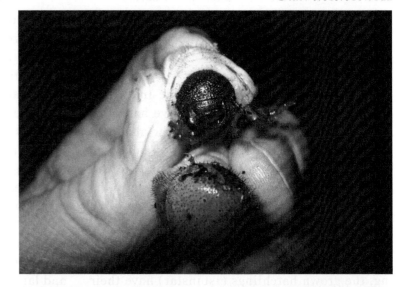

STAG BEETLE LARVA
WITH JAW DEFORMITY

RHINOCEROS BEETLE LARVA
WITH SEGMENT DEFORMITY

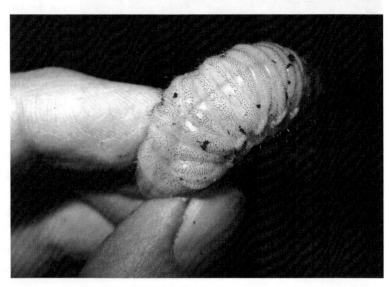

*DYNASTES TITYUS* GRUBS

become strong, healthy adults. Unfortunately, even just one or two black spots on stag, jewel scarab, and darkling larvae are usually a death sentence.

Most small creatures found in untreated substrate materials are not capable of directly killing the thick-skinned *Dynastes* grubs. Earthworms, millipedes, most mites, click beetle larvae, and other accidental roommates bother the grubs only by eating some of the larvae's food. Commensal mites ride on the larvae but do not hurt the grubs or leave any marks. Some species of mites, however, do bother the larvae. Parasitic species not only ride on the larvae, but also leave tiny black or brown spots on the grubs' skin where they have fed. Parasitic mites are rare and can be removed manually. Grain mites don't bite larvae but extreme outbreaks can clog and cover spiracles, resulting in suffocation. Nematodes are harmless in small numbers but can damage larvae in extreme cases. Most molds and fungi do not damage the grubs, but rather are a source

of food. Entomophagus fungus is deadly but extremely rare.

Grain mites are the most common pests, as various substrate materials can lead to outbreaks, the mites can jump from infested containers, and they can even find their way in from outdoors. There are two complimentary ways to reduce grain mite populations. The first is to change substrate or bake the present substrate to kill mites. The substrate mix should be heated to 200° F. Substrate cooked in a shallow pan (¼ inch or 7mm) may destroy the mites in just five to ten minutes, while substrate placed in deeper pans may require as long as three hours to become fully heated. Don't keep larvae in substrate while heat disinfecting! Second, remove larvae and keep in a dry room in a ventilated empty container. Dirt-living mites eventually dry up and fall off since they do not possess the level of protective wax that insect exoskeletons have to conserve moisture. Additionally, the mites dry out because their surface area is much greater in comparison to their mass. It is more important to reduce massive numbers of mites than to eradicate them, so it is better to be safe and not overzealous in drying out the larvae. Without moisture, *Dynastes* larvae can begin to shrink and dry up in as little as two days, but may be very healthy even after a week or two. When both methods are used together, it is possible to completely eradicate all mites. Keep an eye out for reinfestation.

Entomophagus fungus (not the mold/fungus found on rotten wood, dog food, dead leaves, etc.) can kill every single larvae if left unnoticed for more than a few moths. If any dead larvae are found on which are growing external hyphae or which feel completely hard all over (and can be broken in half like a dry pretzel), it is necessary to immediately replace the substrate as well as disinfect the rearing cage with a bleach and water mixture. Do not confuse fungus with a blocked up digestive tract where the abdomen alone is hard (caused by eating the wrong thing—plastic?). Fungal disease in the larvae should be watched for but is quite uncommon. Keep in mind that dead larvae are sometimes consumed by fungus, but that doesn't mean it's an entomophagus fungus that caused the death. Note: milky spore disease bacteria, *Bacillus popilliae,* used by homeowners and garden shops to kill Japanese beetle larvae, *Popillia japonica,* will also kill *Dynastes* larvae.

Food and genetics are major factors in determining adult size, but food is foremost. No matter the potential, a larva that is fed poorly will only be 35-40mm or smaller. Well-fed male offspring of a 35mm wild male will always be over 45mm. Larvae that are fed well and live in the same substrate mix will become males that generally range from nearly 2 to 2½ inches (45-60mm). Minor captive-reared males, which were fed high quality food as larvae, can produce a higher percentage of smaller offspring.

Beetle culturists normally hope to rear the biggest, healthiest, and most impressive adults possible. The most important time period for

rearing large adults is between hatching and the second molt. Larvae fed well at this time often still become large adults even if fed less food or lower quality food afterwards. Larvae fed poorly during this time do not become large adults even if fed incredibly well later on.

Reliance on wood and leaves alone makes it very difficult to rear large adults in captivity. The most successful method for raising large adults of the eastern Hercules beetle is to bury dry dog food pieces in the substrate as a supplement to their regular diet. It is important not to overfeed, but the amount is variable depending on the age, size, and appetite of the animal. Use of dog food (or equivalent, such as ferret food, cat food, and fish food) is a tip the author has shared with a number of friends and has worked well for many species of beetles. Most, if not all, very large captive-reared rhinoceros and flower beetle specimens have been produced using this method. Some species are impossible to raise without this food. Manufactured substrate fortified with a dog food equivalent has become common in the Asian hobby in recent years (Lai, 2008).

Various supplements have been experimented with, including soy and whey protein isolates, powdered milk, flour (as described for substrate fermentation in the stag beetle chapter), sugar (explained in the jewel scarab and stag beetle chapters), and yeast. Protein isolates work nearly as well as dog food with a few species, including *Dynastes tityus*, but have no positive effect on growth for many other beetles and are much more expensive. Powdered milk is nearly as restricted in its usefulness and is what destroyed my *Phileurus truncatus* culture after seven generations (creating oversized, deformed adults). I've also experimented with yeast supplementation on 120 *Dynastes tityus* larvae (95 starting at L1, 25 starting at L3). Each larva was kept separate. Negative results included a 10% higher die-off than previous generations and overall adult size was reduced. Six adult specimens had unusual deformities. A number of adults appeared fine, but as they aged lost the

*DYNASTES TITYUS*, YEAST-FED BEGINNING AT L3, NORMAL COLORATION

*DYNASTES TITYUS*, YEAST-FED BEGINNING AT L1, GRAY COLORATION

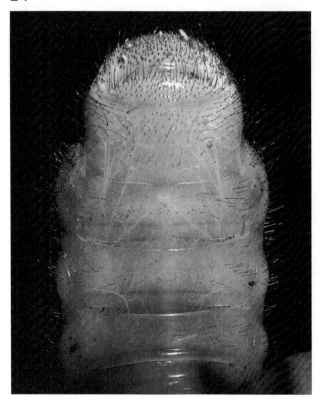

*DYNASTES TITYUS* MALE LARVA

ability to withdraw the flying wings. Positive results were increased speed of development from third instar to pupa and better-synced emergence. Neutral results were that larvae fed from first instar were abnormally gray, while larvae fed yeast in third instar were the normal yellow of this culture stock. Further experimentation to confirm results was not considered due to the negative results and since a 120-count sample size and familiarity with the specific stock was adequate. Similar results were seen in a small group of *Osmoderma*: sped-up development, but sickly adults.

The usual feeding method is to bury a pinch of supplement or a piece of dog food in the substrate near the larva. (Spray supplement with water if substrate is not quite damp.) Cover with substrate. Don't worry about white mold—the larvae like to eat many molds as much as the food. There is a natural progression in the decomposition cycle during which different molds follow one another, so after a few weeks any uneaten dog

food is no longer edible. However, food should be consumed entirely within a few days. Overfeeding (except brown sugar water) will lead to grain mite population explosions and population increases of other pests already present in the substrate. If a supplement is mixed thoroughly into the substrate, fungus is likely to consume it before the larva, excess can't be removed, and pest problems can be accelerated.

Larvae grow at different rates. The use of poor substrate (with no additional feeding) will exaggerate the disparity in size and molting times. Some larvae may still be 2nd instar a year after their siblings are 3rd instar. On the other hand, if larvae are fed according to the methods outlined in this book, 90% of the grubs will molt within a few weeks of each other. Despite the different growth rates, larvae of the same brood that are a few months apart become adults around the same time. Some of the slowest growing may wait till the following year to develop.

There are two common methods used to estimate adult size from the 3rd instar larvae: head size and weight. Neither method is an exact science, but weight is the less precise of the two. Not only is weight variable between larvae, but it also is variable for a single larva at different times. A 3rd instar weighing over sixty grams should be a large male. Head size—measured with vernier calipers from one side to the other—is always the same for any single larva. If all the larvae have 9mm or smaller heads, minor males with tiny horns along with small 35mm females are produced. If larvae head size ranges from 9mm to 11.5mm, then anything under 9.5mm should be a large female. Grubs with 11-11.5mm head capsules should produce major adult males from 2 to 2½ inches (50-67mm) long.

After the larvae have molted twice, they need much more room and food. At this time, make sure that no more than twenty 3rd instar are kept in a 10-gallon (forty-liter) tank. About half a gallon (two liters) should be provided per larva. *Dynastes tityus* larvae can be kept in greater concentrations, but consume substrate quickly,

DRY EXOSKELETON OF *DYNASTES TITYUS* L3 LARVA
SHOWS THICKNESS AND ABILITY TO HOLD WEIGHT

need constant feeding, and could kill each other when overcrowded or food is absent for too long. Make certain that there is still food left, as the frass looks very similar to the substrate (except that frass is usually pellet shaped). There may be no food left despite casual appearances. Although the top of the substrate may be littered with wood, chunks of wood at the surface which are less than four inches (10 cm) across are usually inedible since larvae are unable to get enough leverage to bite off pieces. Some Dynastinae, like the European *Oryctes nasicornis,* have overly cannibalistic larvae at third instar, which hunt down and kill each other. However, *D. tityus* larvae only kill each other when severely crowded or severely underfed. Third instar larvae are usually kept together, which makes them easier to feed and more likely to pupate at nearly the same time.

When the original substrate has been mostly consumed the larvae are easy to feed. Dog food and dry leaves can be buried in the old substrate. Rotten logs or large chunks of decomposed wood can be thrown on the substrate and larvae will burrow up and feed at the underside.

Sometimes the white grubs may be seen constantly crawling around on the surface. There are four common reasons for this behavior: bad substrate, damage, lack of food, and overcrowding. At times, for no apparent reason, the substrate collected may be bad quality and the larvae are trying to escape in hopes of finding something good to eat. Larvae damaged by mold disease, injured by other larvae, or having blocked up intestines do not always climb to the top, but are often brought there by the digging activities of other larvae. As mentioned earlier, substrate looks similar to frass, and starving larvae crawl up top in search of food. When overcrowded, larvae are much more likely to come to the surface, sustain damage, become diseased, and run out of food.

Mature *D. tityus* larvae eventually start to turn yellow and shrink thirty or more percent. Do not worry—they are getting ready to pupate. If larvae run around on the surface all the time at this stage it is due to the fact that the substrate is too dry, too shallow, or too lumpy to make pupal cells. Twelve to twenty-four months after the eggs are laid the 3rd instar larvae use their mandibles and body to compact the surrounding substrate into a rather large egg-shaped cell. There are no secretions used in the initial forming of the pupal cells, so it is important that the substrate is easily compactable. It may be necessary to put in new substrate or just compost.

PUPATION
The time when larvae transform to pupae and then to adults is crucial. In order to protect themselves during these changes, the 3rd instar larvae form pupal cells in the surrounding dirt with their bodies and jaws. The only secretion that even slightly hardens the pupal cells is a black gooey substance produced from the anus a few days before molting and is spread by the wriggling movements of the larvae. The pupal cells are one-sided (there is no defined outside wall) and can only be removed from the substrate inside a large clump of dirt. About seven days before pupating, the larvae lose the use of their legs and mandibles. Larvae only form a new pupal cell if the pupal cell is broken before this point.

Two key visible changes that come before the impending molt involve color and surface texture. Grubs change from white to yellow before they form the pupal cell. The yellow coloration varies and sometimes occurs many months in advance of cell formation. Next, the outside skin of the abdomen begins to wrinkle. If the abdomen becomes notably wrinkled it is important to make sure the substrate is adequate for pupal cell formation. Too large of particles or too much dryness may prevent cell creation. The cells are often built before the wrinkling is very noticeable as long as the substrate is usable.

*DYNASTES TITYUS* PUPA

Substrate that is not compactable prevents pupal cell formation. Sometimes the frass, which is in the form of flattened pellets, is very hard and similar in consistency to a handful of gravel. If substrate is made up of large pieces of leaves or wood (though it can be ground up by the activities of feeding larva) it might be necessary to grind these substances to near powder if the larvae are ready to pupate. Compactable substrate can be squeezed in the hand, and released to form a clump, while substrate that is not compactable will just fall back into a pile when released. If the substrate isn't usable for forming pupal cells the grub will waste a lot of energy and may eventually settle down to pupate in a formless cell on the surface. Excessive energy used will decrease the ultimate adult size and unformed cells can result in dents or extreme deformities.

The substrate depth in the cage should be greater than 4 inches (102mm) so that the pupal cells are built correctly and large males can become perfect adults. (3"-tall 16 oz. deli cups work well for individual larvae.) In deep substrate, the larvae can easily form cells which are slightly inclined or at a forty-five degree angle. The direction of the pupal cell is important because the males' horns blow up like balloons when transforming to the pupa and can be severely deformed if there is anything in the way, including the wall of the pupal cell. Males position themselves so their heads are at the highest level of the cell. In shallow substrate, the pupal cells are made horizontally and only small males with tiny horns and females tend to form correctly. Females usually form horizontal cells.

If a pupal cell is crushed for any reason and the larval appendages are immobile or the larva has transformed to a pupa, it is necessary to make a "fake" pupal cell. A fake pupal cell can be made of many materials including plaster of Paris, floral foam, clay, and plastic. However, use of moist substrate mix allows for the best airflow and moisture levels. The pupal cell should be inclined to vertical, as tall as the larvae, and twice as wide. Also, the walls should be as smooth as possible and the bottom rounded. Place the pupa or prepupa head upward in the cell and place a lid on the container. The lid should have minimal ventilation (ten or so pinholes) to prevent drying while providing limited airflow. If made well, a fake pupal cell can work nearly as well as the real thing. Unfortunately, fake pupal cells are often usable only once or twice because the pupae release a lot of liquid when molting to adult. Larvae that are still active and newly emerged adults can tear a fake cell apart.

At room temperature (75° F / 23° C) the grub becomes a pupa eighteen days after pupal cell formation. The larva slowly changes to a light orange-brown and then molts to become a mummy-like pupa. Large pupae tend to take a few days longer.

Since the pupa and prepupa are defenseless, there are two creatures that easily kill them at this stage: earthworms and wireworms (Elateridae larvae). Both of these can be introduced with untreated rotten wood and leaves. Wireworms are carnivorous and quickly chew through the pupal cell into the *D. tityus* flesh. A few earthworms in the substrate are unlikely to cause a problem but a large number, which usually is not noticeable until too late, crush the pupal cells. Molting in a crushed pupal cell causes massive deformities and death. Whereas wireworms can kill a few pupae, earthworms can wipe out the entire population. To prevent these murderous creatures, either cook the substrate before use or replace substrate when the problem is noticed. Replacing substrate is not necessary until the larvae turn yellow in preparation for pupating. If the cage is placed in an area from 90° to 95° F for a few days, most types of temperate earthworms will die. These slightly higher temperatures do not bother the grubs at all. Additionally, nematodes, springtails, or a small number of mites will eat the dead or dying, but do not kill pupae.

Keep in mind, while pupae can be safely handled, they are extremely fragile. They must be gently rolled or cupped since pulling would immediately tear a piece off. If even a small portion of a foot is ripped off, the pupa will die. A tiny puncture that has no effect on a larva or beetle will kill a pupa. Handle only when necessary (for example, if earthworms are discovered in the substrate).

KEEPING THE ADULTS

First the eyes, then the head, pronotum, and legs of the pupa change to a dark brown color. (If the abdomen turns dark, the pupa has died.) Then, the skin of the pupa cracks and the adult comes forth and stretches its huge wings inside the tiny pupal cell. The new elytra are stark white and can be deformed at this time if the pupal cell is not smooth and rounded. After a few hours, the outer wings turn a dark brown. The adult is now completely mobile but still a bit soft. If it falls or is dropped onto a hard surface the exoskeleton cracks open and normal mold then finishes off the ruptured adult. (If a damaged adult is kept in dry conditions mold may be prevented. A damaged adult can still mate but a female will never

lay eggs without moist substrate.) A new adult stays in its pupal cell for a few weeks until its exoskeleton has hardened and changed to the greenish to yellow adult coloration. The beetle will not even notice minor damage, such as a broken horn or missing leg. Now it could be thrown against a wall with little or no damage. The adult begins to eat, mate, and lay eggs at this point, but does not fly for another week or two. In nature adults can stay in the cool pupal cells for nearly a year.

Wild-caught and captive-bred adults have been raised under different conditions and so their care is slightly different. Eggs inside of captive-bred females are present but may not be fully matured so a cool period can be helpful. Refrigeration isn't necessary, but adults without this period will live shorter lives and may lay fewer ova. Other than this aspect, wild-caught and captive-bred adult care is the same.

Unfortunately the warmest possible setting for even the tiny "college" refrigerators is only 40° F (4° C) and such cold temperatures may be harmful to *D. tityus* over a long period. The adults should be kept at 45°-55° F. (A cool period is not required, and 65°-70° F is adequate.) Adults can be refrigerated at any time but it should be done within a few weeks of molting to adult. In two months to a year the males and females can be removed and placed in egg-laying cages. It will still be a few weeks before the adults begin to mate and lay eggs. Captive-bred adults can be hibernated at 40°-55° F for up to a year. The hibernating adults can still be very active, but will not begin to feed, fly, or reproduce until ready to emerge from diapause. Offer food to hibernating adults once a week to determine when diapause is over. Hibernating adults do not feed for incredibly long periods, but they will starve to death if not fed after diapause is completed. Hibernation is temperature dependent, but separate stocks moved to room temperature can come out of diapause months apart. Captive-bred adult eastern Hercules beetles normally live nine to twelve months as adults—three times as long as the related *D. granti*, which doesn't have a significant natural diapause.

Buying a special refrigeration unit would be incredibly expensive but a serious enthusiast can purchase a tiny refrigerator and separate thermostat for less than a couple hundred dollars. Attaching the thermostat and probe is pretty easy, even for the novice. (Today, small wine coolers can be purchased at a low price and don't require a different thermostat.) There are two primary reasons for wanting to use refrigeration. First, if only a few grubs are reared it's common for them to be all male or female. It's realistic to keep the adults till the next summer in hopes that others are acquired or emerge at that time for mating. All the *D. tityus* pictured in this book come from three females (many generations back) that were hibernated more than a year in order to wait for a male. The second reason is to greatly prolong the life of specimens used for occasional displays.

*DYNASTES TITYUS* MATING PAIR

If possible to obtain, captive-bred eastern Hercules beetles are a better choice, for a number of reasons. The most important is they will live far longer than the few months common for wild adults. The age of the beetles is known.

Captive-bred beetles are accustomed to rearing conditions and can be easier to grow and to grow larger. The number of eggs already laid is not in question. The hatch rate from eggs laid by captive-bred adults is high—over 90%.

Males use their incredible horns to toss rivals out of reach of the female, but this action is more often seen when fighting over food. Sometimes the elytra of a male or female will have a puncture wound from these horns. When active males are kept together, they will have notable scratch patterns on the pronotum from other male's horns. Females end up with notable scratch patterns on the elytra from the males' claws. Fighting is almost always harmless, but one big male I raised (67mm) crushed two females and stabbed countless others before the damage was noticed and he was removed. Bigger is not always better.

Very clumsy, yet very strong, describes the flight of the eastern Hercules. The giant wingspan of the translucent, tan flying wings is impressive. Flights can last over long distances and end with a thud. If "any landing that can be walked away from is a good landing," then these critters are expert at landing. Despite flying full speed into concrete, trees, buildings, and other objects, the beetle is undisturbed and walks happily away. In captivity, a few hours after sunset (beetles know what time it is despite lighting conditions), when rhinos are running around their cage, they can be gently tossed in the air and often take off flying. The loud buzzing sounds like a bumblebee might if it had a half-foot wingspan.

There is no lengthy process involved with getting adults to mate—just put them in the same cage. The male crawls onto the back of the female in the same way that male turtles do. Males may ride on the females' backs for hours or even days but copulation is generally finished in twenty minutes. Wild-caught females have already been fertilized when caught, but captive-bred females need to mate. Females cannot hold live sperm forever, therefore ova laid long after mating can be infertile. One mating lasts up to ninety days, but some infertile eggs may be noticed after sixty days.

## SUMMARY

Eastern Hercules beetles make wonderful pets that are easy to care for. It is hoped the reader will enjoy studying this chapter over and over again and learn to better appreciate and keep *D. tityus* and its relatives. It is very difficult to get bored of a pet that is so amazing and enjoyable to watch, and which is rarely an adult longer than a year. Many of the tips, including substrate composition, use of dog food, hatching containers, and refrigeration, can be helpful in the breeding of other beetle species. The information provided will allow for successful rearing, but production of large adults can be as much an art as a science. This information and your enthusiasm will allow you to keep *D. tityus* year after year. Happy beetle keeping!

## OTHER U.S. RHINOCEROS BEETLES

### *Dynastes granti*
GRANT'S RHINOCEROS BEETLE
Size: 35-76mm, with a record specimen measuring in at a whopping 3.4 inches (85mm). Found: Grant's rhinoceros beetle is found in the United States in Arizona, western New Mexico, and southern Utah. In some areas of Arizona *D. granti* is very common, with 70+ specimens caught in one evening unremarkable. In other areas finding a few adults in a season is a good catch. Every year in the fall, tons of collectors flock to Payson, Arizona, to catch adult *D. granti* for the live and dead stock trades. Grant's rhinoceros fly in mass to the lights of gas stations a few hours after the sun goes down and collectors grab them as they land. Despite the numbers caught (and more notably, the incredible number run over by cars) in Payson over the last 25 years, it still remains a great collecting spot, probably due to the fact that adults start laying eggs before their first flight. Adults can be found

as early as late July and as late as the end of October, but the primary collecting period is August and September.

*DYNASTES GRANTI* 75MM F2 (1999), FROM 76MM F1 (1997), FROM 67MM WILD-CAUGHT MALE (1995)

Grant's rhinoceros beetle was named after a fort named after Ulysses S. Grant. *Dynastes granti* is longer than *D. tityus* but is not more massive. The thoracic horn extends much further than the cephalic horn. The thoracic horn has two tiny denticles at the base and a slight split into two points at the apex of large individuals. (*D. tityus* thoracic horns do not split, no matter how big the individual.) The cephalic horn (except on small specimens) is much shorter and slightly hooked. The bluish-gray background color generally only varies in shades. The body color transforms to almost black in high humidity. Rearing requirements are similar to the eastern Hercules, but average times are very different. The eggs can take more than 4 months (!) to hatch. (3 months is average.) 2nd instar is reached in another four weeks and 3rd instar after another eight weeks. Full-grown larvae wait an additional twelve to fifteen months before forming pupal cells. The grubs of *D. granti* appear identical to those of *D. tityus*. Pupation and emergences time periods are about the same. What distinguishes *D. granti* is the longer larval period and much shorter adult lifespan. Adults (which are always wild-caught in the U.S.) should be examined for mites and cleaned thoroughly, because they are commonly infested with egg-eating mites.

*DYNASTES GRANTI*

*MEGASOMA PUNCTULATUS*, 47MM MALE
(CAPTIVE SPECIMENS LIKE THIS ONE CAN GREATLY EXCEED WILD-CAUGHT SPECIMENS.)

*Megasoma punctulatus*

Size: 20-38mm. Found: Arizona. *Megasoma punctulatus* was once considered the rarest of the U.S. *Megasoma,* but is now being caught in decent numbers. Nevertheless, finding two or more females in a season is still quite a challenge for the collector. It's not strange to find a dozen males and no female. The grubs resemble other Dynatinae, but are quite hairy and have smaller head capsules in relation to body size. All *Megasoma* larvae look this way. Larvae do not try to bite and do not cannibalize, but they can accidentally smash pupal cells. The rearing requirements of this species are also very similar to those of the eastern Hercules beetle. Wild females lay 10-15 eggs, while captive-reared can produce up to 30. Ova hatch in three weeks or so. 1st and 2nd instars normally last three or more months each. The time spent in 3rd instar is usually twelve or more months. Pupation and emergence each require about a month. The life cycle normally takes two years, although the entire cycle can be reduced to one year with supplemental feeding, quality substrate, and temperature kept above 72° F. Captive-bred adults live six to eight weeks, while wild adults usually live a week or two.

*Megasoma vogti*

Size: 35-50mm. Found: Southern tip of Texas. *Megasoma vogti* is the largest of the U.S. *Megasoma* species, and can grow to nearly the mass of our *Dynastes* since the overall short length is due to the small horn. Like a number of tropical members of this genus, the exoskeleton is covered in thick, whitish hairs. Adults eat the normal fares of maple syrup and beetle jelly. The grubs are fed and kept in the same manner as *Dynastes* larvae. *Megasoma* larvae are slower growing and more docile than most Dynastinae larvae. This species has been reared in captivity, but livestock is nearly impossible to acquire. The few *M. vogti* reared in captivity have taken two years from egg to beetle.

*MEGASOMA PUNCTULATUS* MALE PUPA

*MEGASOMA VOGTI* MALE

*MEGASOMA VOGTI* MALE

*PHILEURUS TRUNCATUS*

*PHILEURUS TRUNCATUS* L3

*Orzabus lingroides*

Size: 22-26mm. Found: Southwestern United States, including Arizona. This odd rhinoceros beetle possesses very different gender adaptations than most Dynastinae. The male doesn't have any horns, but has a small bump on the pronotum which the female lacks. However, the notable difference between the two is the shape of the front legs. The female's front legs are ordinary. The male's front legs are flattened, widened, and armed with a large interior spine. Adults feed on most sugary liquids and live 2-3 months. Females lay eggs in substrate composed of two-thirds shredded decaying leaves and a third compost. Larvae do not grow quickly, but the life cycle requires only a year.

*Phileurus truncatus*

TRICERATOPS BEETLE

Size: 35-44mm. Found: Most of the United States, except the far northwest. The Triceratops beetle, and close relatives in the Tribe Phileurini, are certainly the strangest of the rhinoceros beetles. Unlike other Dynastinae, *Phileurus* adults are carnivorous and long-lived. Beetles of this species regularly live two to three years. Adults temporarily accept banana slices (many obligatory carnivores including ground beetles and praying mantids 'accept' banana slices for a period) but eventually need to be fed grubs, earthworms, or other small prey. Larvae resemble other rhinoceros beetle larvae, but oddly vibrate like an air pump or electric razor (without noise). In nature the beetles recognize their larvae by this stridulation and will feed on competing detritivores inside tree hole habitats. In captivity beetles should not be kept in the larvae's rearing container, as it's difficult to keep them fed well enough to prevent predation on their grubs over many months. The time spent from egg to adulthood is only four to six months. Care and feeding for the immature stages are similar to other rhinoceros beetles, but grubs prefer a high-leaf content and should not be fed supplements. Dog food will improve the size of adults but the elytra often don't grow correspondingly big enough to form perfectly. Adults murder each other if elytra are imperfect. The technique used to collect eggs is a little different from that used with eastern Hercules beetles. The same substrate can be used, but there should be an inch or two of dead leaves on the surface and some live earthworms should be added to the substrate. The live worms provide food and induce egg laying. Both wild-caught and captive-reared adults appear to "know" the season and only lay eggs in mid- to late summer. Females deposit 20 to 70 eggs each year for as long as they live.

*Phileurus illatus*

Size: 20-27mm. Found: Arizona. Unlike other *Phileurus*, *P. illatus* adults can be sexed easily using the horn structure. The male has two noticeable horns on the head and the female has only tiny bumps. Adults are carnivorous (the one pictured killed a three-inch stag beetle whose shell was still a little soft) and can live at least a year and a half. This species does not appear to possess the ability to discern between its offspring and food. Eggs must be removed immediately. Females lay 20-30 eggs each summer for as long as they live, usually two years.

*PHILEURUS VALGUS*

*STRATEGUS ANTAEUS* PAIR

*STRATEGUS ANTAEUS* GRUBS

*STRATEGUS ALOEUS*

*XYLORYCTES THESTALUS*

*Phileurus valgus*

Size: 17-24mm. Found: Texas to Florida, and north to Virginia. The three tiny horns on the head of this beetle are only tiny bumps. Adults love to eat large numbers of earthworms during their two-year life. The female can produce at least 40 grubs. Females only lay eggs in mid- to late summer. Adults appear to recognize larvae of their own species and must be starved for a long period before they cannibalize their grubs. Only four months is required for the life cycle. Newly emerged adults are prone to eating nearby pupae, which is odd since they form cells near each other.

*Strategus aloeus*

LARGE OX BEETLE

Size: 30-52mm. Found: Southwest. The large ox beetle is not only native to the southwestern United States, but also to Central America and northern South America. The grubs grow and molt quickly and can attain 3rd instar within two months of hatching. Larvae are less tolerant of severe overcrowding than the other U.S. species and may kill each other in later stages if food and space are limited. The life cycle requires 10-12 months, with over two months spent in the pupa stage. Like most rhinoceros beetles, the adults enjoy feeding on real maple syrup. Females

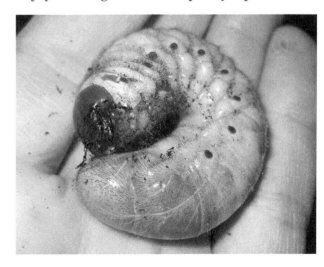

*STRATEGUS ALOEUS* L3

generally avoid highly compactable substrate when laying eggs. Substrate that is three parts leaves, two parts rotten wood, and one part compost, works well for egg laying. Additionally, an inch or two of larger dead leaf pieces should be placed on top of the substrate. It can be difficult to get more than twenty eggs from a female. Most adults live three to five months, but about a third live longer than six months (rarely a year).

*Strategus antaeus*
OX BEETLE
Size: 28-42mm. Found: Ranges widely across the eastern and central United States. Ox beetle males have three horns on the pronotum but minor males have three bumps. In nature and captivity only about 10% of the males grow to be majors. Large males are arguably the prettiest of the U.S. Dynastinae. Major males have long, thin, elegant horns. The entire body is dark reddish-brown and incredibly shiny. Larvae do not survive to adulthood if kept on rotten wood, leaf, and compost mixes like other rhinos. Adults and larvae spend their entire lives in lawns and fields. Sand substrate (90% sand and 10% soil) should be used to raise these creatures. The larvae feed on dead leaves and dog food buried in the sand. It seldom, if ever, takes more than a year for the eggs to progress through to the adult stage. The adults regularly live five to eight months. Females are quite particular about where they lay their eggs. The cage used for egg laying should be at least a two and a half gallon aquarium and include three important components.

1. Four plus inches of fine sand for the adults to tunnel and oviposit.
2. A few handfuls of large, dead leaf flakes on the surface.
3. Live grass (not needed to rear or feed larvae). A chunk of lawn can be dug up from the yard or grass seeds spread on the substrate and watered for a few weeks.

One female will lay about twenty eggs. At times she surrounds the new ova with dead grass, but she nearly always lays them in the middle of the sand. Do not disturb the eggs, as they are easily damaged.

*Xyloryctes thestalus*
Size: 25-36mm. Found: Southwest. *Xyloryctes thestalus* adults are pickier eaters than other rhinoceros beetles. However, they will feed on melon slices, especially watermelon. This species is extremely common in areas of the southwest and can be caught by the bucket-full. Despite reproducing readily in nature, it is very difficult to culture in captivity. Females are more difficult to get eggs from than any other species listed here. It took me fifteen years and I may be the only person who has ever been successful. They will lay in substrate with finely, freshly ground leaves and wood with white mold. *Xyloryctes jamaicensis* looks very similar but is slightly smaller and the striations on the elytra are usually more pronounced. This beetle is found throughout the eastern and central United States. Although very similar, *X. jamaicensis* females lay eggs more readily. Adults live three to four months. The life cycle for *Xyloryctes* in captivity is about ten months. There is a variation of the eastern species that may not be the same animal. This species or subspecies looks like the above two except the elytra are smooth.

TROPICAL RHINOCEROS BEETLES

*Allomyrina dichotoma*
SAMURAI HELMET BEETLE
Size: 35-85mm. Although found in many tropical Asian countries it is best known as the Japanese rhinoceros beetle or samurai helmet beetle. This species is commonly reared in Taiwan and Japan but the Taiwanese version has a narrow horn on the pronotum. The two should not be crossed since resultant offspring are sometimes infertile. This species is very easy to rear. It does

*Allomyrina dichotoma*

best with a high proportion of rotten wood as substrate. Wood content is most important during early first instar and has no effect afterwards. 30-50 eggs from one female is average. Development takes about ten months. Grubs are normally reared together, but cannibalize as soon as they begin to run low on food. Larvae are almost impossible to distinguish from those of *Dynastes tityus*. The much smaller 25-40mm *Allomyrina pfeifferi* is similar in development. The main differences are that larvae are less aggressive and adults squeak like mad. This may be the noisiest beetle on Earth.

### *Augosoma centaurus*

Size: 40-90mm. (In older books this species is listed as *Dynastes centaurus*). This is arguably the most spectacular African rhinoceros beetle, though there are a number of large to massive species in the genus *Oryctes*, gigantic monsters that resemble U.S. *Xyloryctes*. Larvae are gregarious and do not bite, which seems to be a common characteristic of other hairy larvae. Grubs are easy to discern from other rhinoceros beetles as the abdomen sticks out far past the head when the larvae curl up. The normal life cycle is two years. Rearing larvae to adulthood is rather easy, but getting females to produce even a dozen eggs is not so easy. (The pictured male pupa is third generation.)

### *Chalcosoma atlas*
ATLAS BEETLE

Size: 40-115mm. The Atlas beetles from our local zoos are usually imported from Malaysia, but this species has a wide range across tropical Asia. Minor males have a triangular scoop near the front of the cephalic horn while large males

TAIWANESE *ALLOMYRINA DICHOTOMA* F5

*ALLOMYRINA PFEIFFERI* PUPA

*ALLOMYRINA PFEIFFERI* MALE

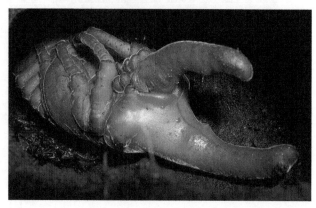

*AUGOSOMA CENTAURUS* PUPA

*Augosoma centaurus* F2 Major Male

*Augosoma centaurus* Pair

*CHALCOSOMA ATLAS* SMALL PAIR FEEDING ON BROWN SUGAR WATER

*CHALCOSOMA ATLAS* MAJOR MALE FEEDING ON GRAPEFRUIT

with long horns don't have a similar structure. The elytra appear dark metallic green due to structural coloration. Photographs from certain angles make them look red-brown like a *Strategus*. This species has very aggressive larvae that bite humans and each other. They have large heads and are not very hairy. When grubs are looking for pupation sites, they tend to eat holes in the lid if they've been kept in plastic containers. Despite the massive size that can be reached, the life cycle takes only one year.

## *Dynastes hercules*
### HERCULES BEETLE

This is the king of the rhinoceros beetles, as it can reach nearly seven inches in total length, much of that the horn. There are a number of different subspecies, which can be difficult to distinguish, and are based almost entirely on variations in the horn development of major males. (Various subspecies and *Dynastes hyllus* successfully cross in captivity.) It's easily reared though it is difficult to rear major males with impressive horn formation without close attention. The grubs are cannibalistic and eat incredible amounts of food. Grubs are very aggressive and can even bite themselves when handled. Grubs should be placed in individual containers at 2nd instar. Time from hatching to adult is normally 14-24 months. Adults live 4-10 months.

## *Eupatorus gracilicornis*
### FIVE-HORN BEETLE

Found: Tropical Asia, including India and Thailand. Graceful horns and contrasting colors make this one of the most beautiful rhinoceros species. The beetle is shiny black with tan to orange elytra after the exoskeleton has finished hardening. (The elytra in the photo are white because the male is still spreading his wings.) Larvae are smooth, have large heads, are very aggressive, and very much resemble *Chalcosoma* larvae. They are successfully reared together if given about a gallon of space per larva. The time required for the full life cycle is just under a year.

CHALCOSOMA MOELLENKAMPI PAIR

CHALCOSOMA ATLAS PUPAE

DYNASTES HERCULES NEWLY MOLTED

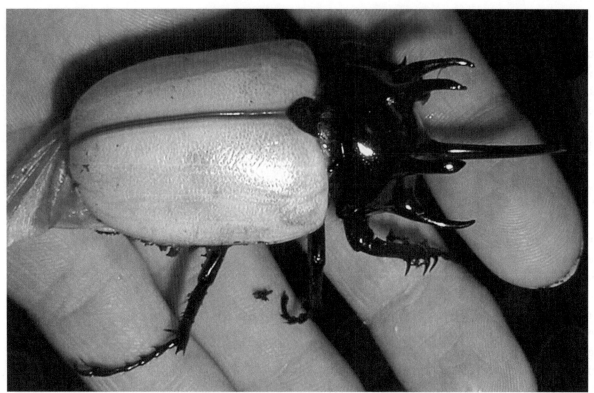

*EUPATORUS GRACILICORNIS*, FRESHLY ECLOSED

*EUPATORUS GRACILICORNIS* MALE PUPAE

*GOLOFA EACUS* SMALL PAIR

## *Golofa eacus*

Size: 25-60mm. Found: Bolivia, Columbia, Ecuador, Peru, and Venezuela. This New World genus includes species with umbrella-like and long thin horns, and *G. eacus* is one of the prettiest. Development takes only about ten months and females lay 30-50 eggs. Larvae are hardy and can be reared together without cannibalism.

## *Megasoma mars*

Size: 60-120mm. Found: Amazon Basin. Although the grubs seem to grow quickly at first when fed correctly, they seldom, if ever, take less than 33 months to mature. Three years is also the normal life cycle of the related *M. actaeon* and *M. elephus*, while the small *Megasoma* species normally take only two years. Like their smaller cousins, despite the longer developmental time, the beetles only live about two months. Grubs of this genus are not very aggressive and seem to prefer hanging out together. Reports of cannibalism are the result of dead larvae due to bad conditions and poor substrate, as they do not attack each other. It's rare to get more than a few dozen eggs from a female and captive-raised females sometimes eclose with no eggs inside them. Of course this can only be discovered through dissection. Males of *M. mars*,

*GOLOFA EACUS* PUPA

*GOLOFA EACUS* MAJOR MALE

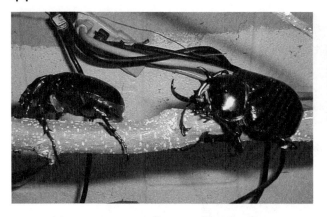

MEGASOMA MARS CAPTIVE-REARED PAIR

MEGASOMA MARS

*M. actaeon*, and *M. elephus* can be grown to a length of nearly five inches. The horn makes up a small amount of the length and these are the most massive of the world's rhinoceros beetles. Despite competing claims, a full-grown 3rd instar of the large *Megasoma* species dwarfs the weight of any insect in the world. (*M. actaeon* male 3rd instar can exceed 200 grams.)

*Xylotrupes gideon*
FIGHTING BEETLE
Size: Varies by subspecies, but rarely more than 70mm. Found: This wide-ranging species occurs throughout tropical Asia, including India and Australia. This is the famous fighting beetle of

*XYLOTRUPES GIDEON*. ALLOMETRY DOES NOT CARRY OVER TO CAPTIVITY. THESE MALES WITH NICE HORNS (SIBLINGS RAISED BY DIFFERENT BREEDERS) ARE REPRESENTATIVE, NOT UNIQUE.

Thailand. Grubs are docile and rarely cannibalize. The time from egg to adult ranges from seven months to a year. Females lay 30-60 eggs. Larvae are fuzzy and are the easiest of all rhinos to rear. They appreciate quality substrate but can be reared on rotten pine needles or strictly dead hardwood leaves. Adults normally live four to five months. Beetles squeak loudly in defense as they contract the abdomen and expel air through the spiracles.

*XYLOTRUPES GIDEON* MALE,
PRONOTUM DAMAGED FROM FIGHTING

# 2
# FLOWER BEETLES

## INTRODUCTION

Incredibly beautiful, the low cost and maintenance as well as easy caging make flower beetles great pets. This family includes many of the largest and most brightly colored beetles in the world. Few other animal groups compare to the variety and brilliance of color and pattern they display. Larvae feed primarily on old decaying leaves, which have no economic value and are easily found for free in most areas. (The hobbyist can get paid to rake up and take away someone's leaves.) Deli-cups and plastic shoeboxes make inexpensive cages and require little room. Most reach adulthood in six months under optimum conditions. Low maintenance requirements make it easy for the hobbyist to take a month-long vacation without hiring a pet sitter.

If considered strictly by the number of species that have been successfully captive-bred, flower beetles are the most successful pet beetles. This is primarily because there are so many species of moderate to large size and most of them are easy to rear by the beginner.

## CLASSIFICATION

Over time, with increased knowledge, many large heterogeneous taxonomic groups have been split up while others have been recombined. A number of former subfamilies of the Scarabaeidae were elevated to families such as the Lucanidae, Trogidae and Passalidae. Some authors and taxonomists placed the Cetoniinae, (Valginae) and (Trichiinae) in their own family, the Cetoniidae.

Krikken's 1984 work moved the Trichiini and Valgini to their present status as tribes of the Cetoniinae. Beyond structural similarities they have a number of common characteristics that set them apart, including less convex elytra that remain closed during flight, two-sided pupal cells, and relatively feeble mandibles. Outlined below is the current taxonomic scheme for the beetles in this chapter.

ORDER COLEOPTERA
FAMILY SCARABAEIDAE
SUBFAMILY CETONIINAE
(FLOWER SCARABS)
Tribe Cetoniini (*Cetonia, Euphoria, Pachnoda, Potosia*)
Tribe Cremastochilini
Tribe Diplognathini (*Conradtia, Diplognatha*)
Tribe Goliathini (*Eudicella, Goliathus, Mecynorhina*)
Tribe Gymnetini (*Gymnetis, Cotinis*)
Tribe Trichiini (*Inca, Osmoderma, Trigonopeltastes*)
Tribe Valgini (*Valgus*)

Only the Cetoniini, Diplognathini, Goliathini, Gymnetini, and Trichiini tribes of the Cetoniinae subfamily are commonly reared by enthusiasts. Valgini and Cremastochilini are listed only for their novelty and familiarity. Though there's only one European *Valgus* and four North American species (one of which is the adventive European

45

*GOLIATHUS ALBOSIGNATUS* MALE F12

*MECYNORHINA POLYPHEMUS*

*Valgus hemipterus*), the beetles are commonly encountered on flowers in many areas and pictured in numerous books. *Valgus* grubs eat rotten wood and have been reared in captivity. *Microvalgus* from Australia are the world's smallest flower beetles at 3mm. Cremastochilini are famous little beetles because they live in ant nests, eat ant larvae, and produce a substance attractive to ants. The grubs live in the soil at the outskirts of the nest, feeding on refuse. Similar behavior has been documented for some European *Potosia* species.

Many of the Old World flower scarabs stretch the definition of the word species. Some historical taxonomists had fun describing and naming every color form as a new "species"—many of these color variations were from the same population and some of these new "species" may well have been siblings. Subgenus, subspecies, and color variety are concurrent methods used to describe the differences, but are used inconsistently and are unreliable in captive-breeding/crossing assessment. Certain species of *Potosia* and *Goliathus* are awarded species designations solely on color, while others listed as subspecies have very different colors, shapes, and sizes. In captivity many color forms and horn structures breed true (or within a specific set of variations) and yet still cross readily to produce viable hybrids. Horn structure and color varies across *Eudicella* species, but the examination of large numbers of specimens from different locations calls into question the species and subspecies designations. In many insect groups, male genitalia diagnostics have proven to mirror the ability to breed in the lab, but this method seems to have been overlooked on the diagnostics of large scarabs like *Eudicella* and *Goliathus*. Furthermore, the propensity for new phylogenetic studies to ignore morphology will likely bring an array of new names and recombinations such as the recently proposed lumping of varied African genera into *Mecynorhina*. Many flower scarab scientific names are constant across literature and specimen lists, but a few, notably *Dicronorhina*, can

*STEPHANORRHINA GUTTATA*

be found spelled half a dozen ways. Many hours of research have been invested in obtaining accurate systematic and identification information, but this book is about breeding beetles.

### FLOWER SCARAB BACKGROUND

The greatest diversity of flower beetles is found in the tropics, though there are beautiful species found in the native lands of nearly any hobbyist. Monstrous orange-and-white velvet *Mecynorhina* and the horned, hologram-colored *Eudicella* hail from tropical Africa. Bright metallic *Jumnos* and heavily armed *Dicranocephalus* live in the tropics of Southeast Asia. Velvety green *Cotinis* and black-and-yellow *Gymnetis* are native to all but the northernmost U.S., while hologram-green *Euphoria* range north into Canada. Central and South America host the large and beautiful *Inca* and *Ischnoscelis*. The cold climate of Northern Europe boasts metallic green *Cetonia*, while southern Europe hosts various species and subspecies of *Potosia* in nearly every metallic color scheme imaginable.

*POTOSIA SPECIOSA JOUSSELINI*

*JUMNOS RUCKERI*

*MEGALORHINA HARRISI*

*TRIGONOPELTASTES DELTA* MALE

The common name for this group (flower beetles) results from the vast number of conspicuous but small species found feeding on flower pollen or nectar. Many are primary or specific pollinators for a number of plant species. They are the only pollinators in some desert and seasonal habitats incapable of supporting general pollinators that require food more than a few weeks of the year. The beetles fly from flower to flower during daylight hours and are often warningly colored. Many of the small, wide-ranging species, including members of the genera *Euphoria, Trichius,* and *Trichiotinus*, mimic bees in color, shape, and sound to discourage predators. Several large species are also warningly colored in black and yellow, while others are green, in exquisite shades and structures—metallic, velvety, hologram—that may help them disappear in the foliage. Not every flower beetle visits flowers, and the thought of a massive four-inch *Goliathus* landing delicately on a flower does seem a bit far-fetched. Then again, according to Morón (1984), *G. orientalis* feeds on pollen and nectar in the tops of flowering trees.

There are several reasons flower beetles have long been popular pets in Europe. Caging and feeding are less expensive for flower beetles than for birds, fish, reptiles, cats, dogs, or other pets. Cage cleaning is seldom required and doesn't include unpleasant smells. Care requirements are minimal when caging is thoughtfully designed. They are often easier to keep than other beetles and less likely to succumb to the terrors of earthworms, mites, and wireworms. Unlike many large beetles that take two or more years to reach maturity (and subsequently only live a few weeks to a few months), most flower beetles can be reared to adults in six months and live four to ten months after emergence. More than just easy to keep, their coloration is dynamic. They are energetic, fun to watch, and a joy to handle.

Flower beetles are day active, which makes them easily observed pets and great display specimens. Unlike most beetles, they usually bury themselves at night. Adults are attracted to the brightest spot in the terrarium during the day. Minimal room lighting is plenty for breeding purposes, but increased light and heat make them more active and excited. However, it is important to avoid incandescent lighting directly on the cage lid, especially with screens. They will be very energetic for a few days, then die because the internal organs have become mummified. They'll snap in half like astronaut ice cream.

Unlike other beetles, the elytra don't open up, which allows them to fly faster and more expertly than other scarabs. The flying wings are black with a purple and blue sheen, and thread out the sides of the elytra. The beetles are a joy to watch in flight—especially the gigantic ones. Other large beetles usually fly during specific hours in the evening and are relatively clumsy. Outdoors the Cetoniinae are impossible to catch if the collector's approach is detected. They take off in a fraction of a second and dart between objects. Even with abundant artificial lighting in a room, beetles will detect even the smallest amount of polarized light leaking around a closed shade and head straight for the natural light. They fly best in larger areas, but an adult *Cotinis* with a wingspan of two inches can stay aloft in a 10-gallon (40 liter) aquarium up to a minute, bouncing up and down against the screen lid.

## COLLECTING

Larvae and beetles are readily collected through various methods. Species of *Cotinis, Euphoria,*

*Trichius*, and *Trigonopeltastes* fly during the day and can be collected on plants and flowers. The same species usually fly to lights at dusk though it's usually only near the end of the season. Black light traps are used to collect various *Euphoria*. Fermenting sugar bait traps attract most species. Various mixes of fruit, yeast, beer, and molasses can be tried. The fluid can be aged for a few days and placed in a vented container in the bottom of a funnel trap or painted on a tree and checked a few hours later. *Euphoria inda* are very commonly found just below the hardwood mulch of landscaped flowerbed islands and in compost piles. In compost piles *E. inda* are often accompanied by the large-jawed predatory *Trox* grubs which eat them.

## LIFE CYCLE AND CULTURE METHODS

Like other beetles, flower scarabs exhibit four life stages. First, the egg is laid. One to three weeks later it hatches into a hungry larval feeding machine. The larva molts twice to become a larger grub each time. The mature L3 grub builds a pupal cell, changes shape, and loses mobility. It then molts into a pupa, the third stage. At last, the mummy-like pupa transforms into a magnificent adult. The adult begins the cycle over again through mating and egg laying. Each stage has specific requirements but only the larva and adult stages feed.

All stages can be kept at room temperature (70°-75° F) and do just as well from 65°-85° F. Grubs grow faster at 85° F than 70° F, but food quality is the significant factor controlling speed of growth. With less than optimal food, temperatures at the higher end of the range will lead to tiny, sickly adults. Tropical and subtropical larvae may withstand much lower temperatures for short periods. Pupae and adults should not be exposed to temperatures lower than 65° F. The pupa stage goes faster at high temperatures, but a major change midstream is dangerous.

It is usually easier to get eggs from wild-caught females than it is from captive-bred ones for several reasons. First, wild females are healthy, whereas captive-reared females may be small or nutrient-deficient due to improper nutrition during the larval stage. Sickly and deformed captive females usually die within a few weeks of eclosion. Lack of eggs is often not the culprit, because dissected females commonly have an abdominal cavity full of eggs. Second, wild females have eaten natural foods as adults that may aid in longevity or help stimulate egg laying. Third, wild females have undergone any necessary natural dormancy period required for eggs to develop. Fourth, wild females have already started laying eggs and will be likely to continue to do so in captivity.

For most flower beetle enthusiasts the most difficult aspect of culturing is getting the females to lay eggs. Beautiful species like *Potosia speciosa jousselini* were once common in the European hobby, but seem to have disappeared from culture because they stopped laying eggs. It's not always possible to know why eggs aren't laid. "Inbreeding" is often used as an excuse for all problems caused by a lack of husbandry information or unfavorable minor variations in substrate materials. The excuse isn't plausible, as nearly every stock lost by one hobbyist continues to breed for others. (Keep in mind silkworm moths, goldfish, pigeons, chickens, dogs, cows, and many others have been "inbred" for thousands of generations and they've only become easier to keep.) Seasonal cues and adult food may influence egg laying but acceptable substrate is the number one factor. Close attention paid to the substrate used for egg laying has allowed hobbyists to keep species for dozens of generations. The following list details components of substrate used to successfully collect eggs from numerous species.

## COMPONENTS OF SUBSTRATE FOR EGG LAYING

50% or more of the mat should be rotten hardwood leaves. Leaves should have been on the ground at least six months and should be crushed to the size of instant potato flakes. Leaves cannot be ground too finely. Mixed leaves containing a large amount of beech, elm, or oak are best.

Some pine needles are fine. Part maple is fine, but if leaves are almost entirely maple, tiny, sickly beetles will result.

10% larval frass. This can be refrigerated or kept at room temperature when not in use. If possible, use from the same species or at least the same genus.

20% compost manure, leaf compost, or mushroom compost. Can be purchased cheaply at garden suppliers. Seasonally available from small garden shops, grocery stores, etc. Avoid smelly compost in early stages of decay.

20% crushed decayed wood. Like leaves, wood cannot be crushed too finely. Rotten logs or fallen branches of any size can be used. Hardwood is preferable. Avoid collecting rotten wood without any visible invertebrate life (such as tiny springtails, isopods, millipedes, or beetle grubs) since it could be treated wood.

Components should be carefully heated to 250° F for two hours to destroy unwanted pests. Do not attempt to speed up with higher temperatures. Freezing for 72 hrs is a less preferable option, unless components are from a tropical area. Make sure to cool or warm to room temperature before use.

Old, decaying leaves are a key ingredient to flower beetle egg laying and rearing. Collect the oldest leaves possible. Leaves that fell in the fall should not be collected till midsummer at the earliest because the excess nutrients normally lead to severe mite outbreaks, even if stored a few years. Leaves can be shredded using various yard machines, though most won't break leaves up finely enough without running them through a few times. Grinding and chopping machines can be very expensive, so enthusiasts who keep only a few species or have a lot of extra energy break up leaves by hand. One leaf-shredding device that's not too expensive is essentially a trashcan with a weed whacker in the bottom, along with some adjustable holes. (The smallest setting is used.) An electric leaf vacuum/shredder can be easier and less expensive, but leaves can pass

through three times or more without reducing to a good particle size. A Black & Decker version barely chops the leaves, while a Troy-Bilt does much better. Chopped leaves should be stored in thick trash bags and tied up. Fermentation will usually kill unwanted pests in a few days, but wait two weeks if possible. Makes sure there are no holes or tears in the bag, or dark-winged fungus gnat infestations are likely. If leaves will be stored more than six months, they should be kept dry in a paper or burlap bag.

*INCA CLATHRATA*

An inch of whole rotten leaves placed on the surface of the mat facilitates egg production in a few species, but is usually not needed for most. The Asian *Dicranocephalus* species are a prime example of a genus that benefits from this extra layer. They require large leaf pieces for the construction of individual egg-laying chambers. Females form a compacted mass of folded leaves about the size and shape of the pupal cell and place a single egg inside.

A 10-gallon aquarium with proper substrate depth is an excellent egg-laying cage for all flower beetles. The egg-laying substrate depth should be 4-8 inches, because greater depth is difficult to search through, while lower depth leads to reduced egg production. Pick out two of the largest and most perfect males and place in the cage with two to eight females—depending on size and predatory tendency of the adults. (Suggested numbers of females per ten-gallon tank: 8

*Gymnetis*, 8 *Dicronorhina*, 8 *Euphoria*, 6 *Osmoderma*, 6 *Eudicella*, 3 *Mecynorhina*, 2 *Goliathus*.) If there are more females the number of grubs produced begins to decline from damage or predation. Using a single male (unless multiple breeding cages are used or males are rotated) risks infertility.

As soon as adults are active and feeding regularly it is important to search through the substrate every 7-14 days to look for eggs and larvae. The eggs are white, yellow, or tan. A careful search will reveal a few eggs if laying is taking place (with the exception of *Chlorocala* eggs, which seem to be invisible). If no eggs or grubs are found, add a few handfuls of freshly ground leaves or finely ground rotten wood. Replace entire substrate if no eggs are laid within ten weeks. Females generally refuse to lay eggs in nematode- or earthworm-infested substrate and likely can sense a variety of problems not detectable to the hobbyist. While species like *Potosia cuprea* may delay egg laying for up to a year, they'll lay eggs within weeks of emergence if the substrate is suitable. Many other species will be dead if they are forced to wait longer than ten weeks (after becoming fully active).

The molting hormone produced by the grubs plays an important role in egg laying. Many flower scarab species—as well as certain species of Tenebrionidae and Elateridae—often won't lay eggs if this hormone isn't present. Molting hormone can be purchased from scientific supply houses. Artificially produced molting hormone is mixed with the adult food to induce oviposition. Substrate used by previous larvae (or larval frass) is an inexpensive and more easily acquired alternative. Frass in the substrate mix is nearly as persuasive as feeding hormone to the female beetles. Another version of this method is the addition of L1 grubs to the cage. (The addition of L3 grubs usually has the opposite effect.) Frass or grubs from other species or genera (or even small mealworms) can be used but the closest relation will yield the best results. Without special care taken to provide this stimulus the females may die

without letting go a single egg—despite otherwise perfect substrate.

Flower beetle eggs are oval to spherical in shape and surrounded by a thin, soft shell. Within a few days they expand 20-50% by absorbing surrounding moisture. Nearly all hatch in two to three weeks. Sometimes the eggs are bright white but more often are a shade of gray, yellow, or brown and it can be difficult to find them. Most flower beetles lay eggs singly. However, beetles in the genus *Cotinis* deposit 10-20 eggs in succession in a circular formation with each ovum laid only a few millimeters apart. Eggs are tougher than most scarab ova and are seldom damaged by casual handling or by being pushed aside by the females as they continue to oviposit.

*GYMNETIS CASEYI* L2 AND L3

One female produces from 40-100 eggs in the vast majority of species. However, the large species in the genera *Chelorrhina*, *Goliathus*, *Mecynorhina*, and *Megalorhina* normally produce fewer than 30. (Wild females may be much more productive.) Cannibalism and die-off in captivity affect accuracy, so averages are based primarily on L1 grub counts.

A bi-weekly search is important for removal of small larvae and refreshing substrate. Grubs are normally not removed till late first instar to early second, because the presence of larvae improves the female's egg laying and grubs grow more quickly in the egg-laying cage. Grubs need

*M. HARRISI PEREGRINA*. (LEFT) 62MM, FROM NORTHERN TANZANIA STOCK, AND (RIGHT) 49MM, FROM COMMON CAMEROON STOCK. BOTH ARE NEAR MAXIMUM SIZES OF THEIR RESPECTIVE STOCKS.

to be removed regularly for best production because overcrowding leads to destruction of eggs and larvae and termination of egg laying. A few cups or large handfuls of the substrate are removed with the grubs and replaced with fresh, ground rotten leaves. *Megalorhina* should be collected and removed as eggs. Any grub will eat

eggs and larvae accidentally damaged by overcrowding, but *Megalorhina* grubs actively hunt down eggs and other grubs.

A notable, conspicuous strange behavior of flower beetle larvae is that they "walk" on their backs. The grubs have well-developed legs, but they are used to drag food down from the surface or catch food rather than for locomotion. Most species can move very quickly. The rippling motions of the body rapidly propel the larvae, whether at the surface or in the substrate.

If possible, try to keep at least two dozen grubs of each species, each generation. They should be split into two or more containers. Small populations are quickly decimated by higher than expected die-off. Deformities and runts should be removed and destroyed if there are adults to choose from. Optimum size and color can be selected from large populations. It's possible to keep six or eight grubs and care for them closely with success, but large, staggered cultures are the only reliable way to ensure the culture survives.

Although the larvae of many flower beetle species are found in the ground, they feed on decaying organics, fungi, or other invertebrates. They do not feed on live plant roots, as is widely believed. If offered only plant roots in captivity they starve to death. Grubs can be reared in nutrient poor substrate including peat moss, potting soil, and sand. Of course supplemental feeding is necessary but the chances of success are lower and the adults small.

The best larval growth is achieved with a substrate similar in composition to the outline for egg laying substrate. Like any recipe the percentages don't have to be exact. Dead leaves are the most important component of the diet, while rotten wood and compost improve the diet and aid in rearing large adults. It is important to crush dead leaves and rotten wood into fine pieces, because larvae have a difficult time biting into large pieces. Whether leaves are ground up by hand or machine, grinding is easiest if the leaves are dried beforehand. (Dry, dusty leaves can be problematic with the keeper's allergies, however.) Grubs are substrate feeders and though they nibble on the edges of whole leaves and wood, they may not get enough to survive. Many flower beetles can be reared on high quality rotten wood or decayed leaves alone.

In the middle of winter rotten leaves may be impossible to get for short periods. A temporary substrate can be made from items available at the local pet shop and garden shop. This temporary mix can support some species but is not recommended for long periods.

    2 cups compost manure or mushroom
        compost (damp)
    2 cups corn cob bedding (dry)
    2 cups coconut fiber (constituted/pre-
        mixed)
    ½ cup water
    2 tablespoons brown sugar.

Dissolve sugar in water. Mix solid components thoroughly. Add liquid evenly. Place in thick plastic bag and allow it to sit 2-30 days before use.

Shredded aspen bedding or hardwood sawdust can be mixed in at 10-20%. Fungi rapidly colonize finely ground, damp wood flakes, but take months or years to completely break down the wood. The way it's added is important. If grubs are placed in a container of damp wood flakes they will all starve to death. If grub density is so high that the flakes end up on the surface, they will be inedible. It could take ten years for the wood to break down enough to be eaten. However, L3 grubs can be fed almost entirely on wood flakes buried in damp substrate. Fungal spores and nutrients in used substrate or compost allow fungus to grow quickly and at least part of the wood can be edible in a few weeks. Fungus growth is not always visible. The best growth looks like very fine white threads and forms clumps of substrate in one to two weeks. In some cages fungus grows better and pieces can be transplanted into substrate of cages where it's not growing well. New wood should be added once a month, sooner if consumed. Too much or too little moisture slows down fungus growth. Substrate pests eat fungus but aren't noticeably accelerated by wood flakes.

The addition of a kibbled food, such as dried dog food, ferret food, cat food, fish food pellets, etc., greatly speeds up the growth of larvae and is the method used to rear most, if not all, of the largest documented captive beetles. Leaf and wood substrate is still very important. The container should not be much wider than the grub's length so that food doesn't go unnoticed, and to make substrate changes easier. White mold grows on dog food in the first few days and is also eaten, but subsequent green, brown and black molds are inedible and the food should be removed. Moist kibbled dog food may work better since it's less prone to mold and remains edible longer. Certain seeds and nuts also work well. They must be smashed or cracked so the grubs can access the meat because their jaws cannot open seeds. With correct use of supplemental foods, the largest flower beetles like *Mecynorhina* and *Goliathus* can be reared to adulthood in six months. Consistent feeding and close attention is required to produce maximum size specimens.

Note: Supplemental foods should never be offered in quantities greater than what larvae completely consume in 48 hours. Dog food is good for a dog, but not if the dog is buried in a pile of rotting dog food—this is also true for beetle grubs. Overfeeding is difficult to monitor because excess food mixes with substrate and looks like dirt. Complete replacement with clean substrate should occur once a month during the L3 stage. Noticeable mites, springtails, nematodes, or other small animals are a late-stage indicator of overfeeding and substrate should be promptly replaced.

## Substrate Pests

*Grain mites:* Caused by overfeeding supplemental food, some composts, and use of leaves that haven't been on the ground at least six months. Large outbreaks should be treated with complete substrate replacement and can be followed by use of only old rotten wood and well-decayed leaves. Tiny grain mites form a crust on the grub's body surfaces and are a sign of spoiled substrate. They do not feed directly on the grub but cling around the spiracles and may stress or suffocate grubs in extreme cases. Large infestations give the cage a sickening-sweet smell like applesauce mixed with wet dog food. In captivity, the mites encountered are very tiny and white, but slightly larger orange or brown "mite crusts" are found on various wild larvae (and their offspring if not treated). Cooking substrate after a large infestation is only a temporary fix because mites jump cages (it is not easy to safely remove every mite from the grubs) and repopulate to become even worse. Grain mites are everywhere and some are inevitable. The key is to prevent large outbreaks while still feeding grubs optimally.

*Nematodes:* Even in huge numbers these tiny roundworms are often unnoticed. They can be the most damaging pests. They occur normally in rotting leaves, wood, and soil. Soil nematodes destroy the substrate's food value when they reach large numbers. They reproduce quickly on rotten leaves and supplemental foods, but take a very long time to reach plague proportions on wood alone. If many are visible and the substrate has a pasty consistency, the substrate should be discarded. In large numbers when the food is exhausted they can directly damage eggs and pupae. Even when substrate is changed, grubs that lived through large infestations often die as pupae. If some nematodes are noticed and the substrate appears normal, substrate can be cooked and reused.

*Dark-winged fungus gnats:* These small flies (Order Diptera, Family Sciaridae) can infest most types of substrate but are primarily problematic with flower beetles since they can reproduce in plague proportions on rotting leaves. They live outdoors worldwide and find their way to substrate indoors because they fit through window screen. Sometimes whole garbage bags of leaves turn into maggot frass. Other times the flies are just annoying, since they like to fly in human eyes and noses. Sealed containers with thin pin holes (small thumb tack holes are too large) are needed to prevent infestations.

*Earthworms:* One or two are no problem, but a large number destroys the substrate to starve grubs. More aggressive flower beetle grubs eat earthworms, but use as a food only leads to trouble.

*Springtails:* Large numbers can be a sign of substrate problems. If mites are a constant issue, springtails can be added purposefully. Larger types (close to 2mm) compete with mites but don't cling to or stress grubs. Extremely tiny species don't effectively compete with mites. Keep in mind springtails are a lesser evil, not a sign of great husbandry.

*Terrestrial isopods and small millipedes:* These don't harm grubs or affect substrate unless there are thousands of them. They are not good at competing with mites. If there are any holes in the pupal cells, these crawl inside and eat holes in the pupae.

Cannibalism is an issue with many flower beetle grubs. The larger species in the genera *Goliathus, Mecynorhina, Megalorhina,* and a few others can damage or kill each other despite plenty of food. Still, with the exception of *Megalorhina,* if larvae are well fed and provided plenty of space they don't always harm each other. (Plastic containers are too inexpensive to justify the risk of damage, cell destruction, and smaller adult size, but when you have 500 larvae, placing each one in a container that needs feeding may be out of the question.) Medium-sized beetles including *Amaurodes, Cheirolasia, Pachnoda,* and *Eudicella* species are seldom cannibalistic under optimum conditions, but quickly eat each other when starved or overcrowded. These should not be kept in densities greater than l larva per ½ liter (one-eighth gallon). They can be reared separately for best survival. Other medium to small flower beetles including those of the genera *Cotinis, Euphoria, Gymnetis, Osmoderma, Potosia, Rhomborrhina,* and *Dicronorhina* do not bite each other even when severely overcrowded, but can decimate food rapidly and interrupt pupal cell formation.

## CAGING

Most species: 12 to 20 in a 1.5-gallon (six-liter) plastic shoebox. The lid snaps on loosely and provides plenty of ventilation. These containers are very inexpensive and available at any department or dollar store. (They are not, though, fungus gnat-proof.)

Large species (*Mecynorhina, Megalorhina*): 1 per 16oz. to 24oz. container. If not on a supplemental feeding and substrate replacement regimen, larger containers produce larger beetles. Most containers this size are airtight, so it is important to put pinholes in the lid. If the substrate dries noticeably in less than a few months, there are too many holes. Disposable containers or deli-cups are available at grocery stores, Chinese restaurants, etc.

The moisture level of the substrate is very important and their needs change as larvae mature. Dry substrate is bad for small grubs, as they prefer very damp surroundings. Moderate dryness doesn't bother mature larvae, but low moisture can prolong the time needed to reach adulthood. If the substrate stays overly wet for long, late L3 larvae or pupae can rot, turn black, and die. The substrate should be moist, but not leave behind water if left on a piece of paper for a few seconds and then removed. Rearing containers with a solid glass or plastic cover dry slowly and usually do not need periodic misting. Grubs are pretty tough animals and can survive overly dry or wet substrates for months. Warning: Substrate should never be dry enough to repel water.

"Soil cocoon" formation is one of the outstanding features of the flower scarabs. The unique pupal cells are more like Lepidoptera cocoons than the simply constructed cells of other beetles. They have an outside wall and can be removed from the substrate. Pupal cells can be formed even under completely dry conditions as larvae glue materials together to create a somewhat hard and thin-walled pupal cell. Conditions that are excessively dry will prevent cell formation. The wall is only 1-2mm thick but can look a lot thicker depending on what is glued to the outside. Under dry conditions the walls become nearly rock hard, but they are flimsy under wet conditions. If the substrate is too damp and

THE ULTIMATE GUIDE TO BREEDING BEETLES

loose, the cell may collapse while it is being constructed.

A week or so before pupation the grub runs around eating substrate. It usually knows exactly how big its cell needs to be. Grubs with small heads can make large cells and grubs with large heads can make small cells, so it is difficult to tell how big the adult will be before this time. A well-kept grub looks strangely deformed a few days before it makes the cell because it ingests enough to make a large cell. If a grub looks exceptionally squat and dumpy, do not disturb it. At last it chooses a spot and constructs its cell. The unfortunate aspect of this type of pupal cell is the larva can create only one. If the substrate is very moist it is important not to dig in the substrate. If a larva is disturbed during construction or the pupal cell is crushed, a handmade or used

MECYNORHINA LARVA ENGORGED
PRIOR TO FORMING PUPAL CELL

pupal cell must be substituted or there is no chance of survival. The "soil cocoon" is unique because the inside is barely larger than the pupa it contains and its exact curvature is needed for molting and wing development. Additionally the flower beetle pupa is specialized for this type of cell. There are projections along the abdomen and pronotum to keep it in the proper position. A fake cell is worth a try, but without the original cell the larva or pupa almost always dies. Cells are formed (and should always be stored) horizontal.

INSIDE A PUPAL CELL (HORNS ARE FOLDED)

Larvae collect materials from around the cage to incorporate in the exterior cell wall. Large particles are brought nearby, while fine sand may be ingested. Sand can be added to the substrate prior to pupal cell formation (if not already present in raw materials). Many species form weaker cells without sand and a few can't form stable cells without it (notably *Cheirolasia*, *Cotinis*, and *Goliathus*). Even species that don't need sand to make a good cell will make their cells right next to, or in, a handful of sand buried in the substrate. Large sand particles about 1mm across appear to be the most useful. However the addition of more than a small handful of 1mm particles should be avoided because some, like *Dicronorhina* and *Eudicella*, get very excited about this size particle and collect too much. The adult beetle emerges deformed because the pupal cell is partly filled with a pile of extra sand.

Flower scarab horns are different from other scarabs because they aren't in the normal position on the pupa. They are adapted to the tight fitting pupal cell. Horns are folded backwards against the head and pronotum and gradually move into normal position over a two-week period following emergence. Be patient—if forced into final position the horn will usually break and fall off a few days later.

The massive changes taking place inside a pupal cell are normally unseen. Only a few species regularly build pupal cells against the sides of the container (*M. polyphemus* and *E. trilineata*), where the changes from larva to pupa then adult are easy to see. It is possible to determine if a larva has pupated without breaking the pupal cell. When the cell is lightly shaken the pupa rattles, while the adult and larva will not. The progress of a pupa can also be observed by making a small hole in the pupal cell. However, a hole decreases the chance of survival and if the larva is still active when the hole is made it will escape and eventually die. Adults generally emerge around two months after the pupal cell is built.

Although the tough walls of a pupal cell shield the pupa from the dangers of earthworms, wireworms (Elateridae larvae), desiccation, etc., they cannot protect the pupa from extremely high moisture levels, because the cell walls become weak or collapse. Conversely, conditions must be pretty dry to kill a pupa sealed in its pupal cell. Pupal cells with manmade or natural holes need to be placed in a closed container with an inch of moist substrate in order to prevent desiccation.

A percentage of animals die in the pupal cell—entire batches of pupae can even die. Certain flower beetles are more prone to this problem, including most *Eudicella*, *Euphoria*, *Goliathus*, and *Mecynorhina* (except *M. torquata*). Too little ventilation is sometimes blamed and increased ventilation may improve survival if the substrate was very wet. However, high die off (30-100%) is often the result of poor food quality and lapses in care during the larval period. They can't always fully recover from problems suffered as far back as early L1. Incorrect moisture, barely chopped leaves, and excessive nematodes or earthworms are primary culprits. It is frustrating because when the problem occurs it's often months too late. Although die-offs can occur with very large (seemingly very healthy) pupae, it can then usually be traced to excess nematodes or simple neglect.

As long as the larvae are fed properly, the entire cycle of even the largest flower beetles from egg to adulthood is ten months or less. If larvae are incorrectly fed or kept below room temperature, the cycle can take much longer. If fed poorly at the beginning, proper feeding later on is still helpful, but adults can still be small or deformed. *Euphoria* species, including *E. rufina* from the southwestern U.S. and *E. inda* found across the east and central U.S., are able to complete the entire life cycle in less than three months. Species from temperate climates that take two years to complete their life cycle in the wild can do so in less than a year at room temperature. It's amazing that giant flower beetles like *Goliathus albosignatus* can grow from egg to adult in six months, while many tiny beetles from other subfamilies must spend two to five years to complete a single life cycle.

A very beautiful species from Asia, *Jumnos ruckeri* is one of the more difficult to rear. It is metallic green with white to orange spots, and grows to 43mm. The larvae grow very easily but it's difficult to get them to make pupal cells. Every few months after maturity, one will make a cell, which makes timing the adults a nightmare. A long period (three months) of rather dry substrate followed by excessive moistening (as moist as rhinoceros beetle substrate) brings about pupal cell formation. However, after pupation the cells have to be promptly and carefully removed from the overly wet substrate or the pupae die from the excessive moisture. Other species that refuse to pupate may also be induced to form pupal cells in this same fashion. This method of inducing pupation only works with mature larvae. Trying to induce an L3 larva that is improperly fed or still growing will not work.

A few weeks to a few months following pupation, the pupa molts to adulthood. Pupal cells are constructed, and should be stored, in a horizontal position. Although the pupal cell is barely larger than the adult beetle the large flying wings expand and harden perfectly inside. If removed from the cell within twenty-four hours of molting to adult, the flying wings expand but usually never fit back under the elytra. Adults emerge on their own when mature, but if the pupal cell is dry and hard as a rock, they will be trapped inside to die. If removed early from the pupal cells the new exoskeleton will still be soft and must be treated gently. If premature adults are put in with mature adults, they are often killed accidentally with their abdomens ripped open. Premature, soft adults crack if dropped. Keep them alone on damp substrate until their armor hardens completely.

All flower beetle adults will feed on slices of fruit, including banana, peach, apple, pear, and grapes. Fruit should be sliced so the beetles can get to the food. Beetle jellies also work, but like fruit they can invite mite problems. Water and brown sugar in a small paper-towel filled dish is an alternative food with fewer pest problems. In the absence of other food, adult *Eudicella* and *Osmoderma* will eat moist dog food. *Eudicella* females are infamous for chewing up their own L1 grubs. Coleopterists commonly sprinkle fish food flakes on the fruit to provide protein in the hopes of aiding egg laying or reducing predation. Adults of some genera, including *Osmoderma*, can mate and lay eggs if never fed, but their lives are greatly shortened.

The primary consideration in the adults' cage is damp substrate. Just ½″ is fine if breeding isn't desired. The beetles can survive some extreme dryness, but die after a few days if they lose too much water weight. In addition, large chunks of wood or branches should be placed on the surface, since the beetles are prone to getting stuck on their backs. They usually don't lose tarsi on logs or sticks, as some other scarabs are prone to get caught.

Sex determination in some flower beetle species is nearly impossible. *Cotinis*, *Gymnetis*, and *Potosia* contain species in which adult males and females are nearly identical, though males may be slightly smaller or exhibit subtle differences in the abdominal sternites and pygidium. These species can be sexed as L3 larvae (with males placed in one rearing cage and females in another, prior to pupal cell formation). Males have a small black dot in the middle of the underside of what looks like the largest terminal segment. L1 and L2 can be sexed the same way, but it's easier to see on late L3 grubs without magnification. Adult *Pachnoda*, *Euphoria*, *Cetonia*, and *Chlorocala* males look the same from above, but have a noticeable longitudinal indent across the abdominal sternites. The hollow resembles the indentation on the underside of many male turtles. Most large species exhibit very clear sexual dimorphism. Male *Dicranocephalus*, *Eudicella*, and *Mecynorhina* all look very different from their female counterparts. Males have horns, often enlarged and spike-covered fore legs, and can be colored differently—in addition to the concave underside of the abdomen. Tiny males can have incredibly small horns, but females have a completely flat or rounded front of the head.

The male's horns are used to fight over food and mates. Many species have short horns or elongate heads, while some have huge, intricate horns like *Megalorhina harrisi* and *Eudicella gralli*. Many have a complex of horns on the head, but with the exception of the genus *Theodosia*, flower beetles do not have opposable horns. Non-opposable weapons are not as powerful as those of the Lucanidae or Dynastinae, which can grab, throw, and puncture the opponent.

The elongate, spiny front arms of males are also used in battles and to hold tightly onto the female. Males fight over females and can be seen sitting on the females a good portion of the day. If the males are not seen sitting on or guarding the females, mating may not be taking place.

Flower scarabs are a group every beetle enthusiast should try. The energetic personalities and incredible coloration of flower beetles catch the attention of beetle hobbyists. The immense variety of presentations (metallic, velvety, satiny, and holographic) places these incredible beetles among the most beautiful insects

*COTINIS NITIDA*

*EUPHORIA INDA*

in the world. Even the largest species take a relatively short time to become adults (while many of the large rhinoceros and stag beetles take years to reach adulthood).

## FLOWER BEETLES IN THE U.S.

### *Cotinis nitida*
GREEN JUNE BEETLE

Found: Eastern, central, and southern U.S. Size: 20-24mm. Adults are found on certain shrubs during the day, in groups of three to a dozen. In midsummer they can be baited in numbers with ferment traps and sometimes they come to lights. It's easy to get females to lay 60-80 eggs. Rearing the grubs is simple and rapid—three months from egg to pupal cell—if the substrate surface is kept slightly dry and wild bird food (cracked corn with other seeds) is scattered on top. The cage should have no lid or should be full screen. If fed only leaves and wood, survival and size are minimal, and the cycle will take one or two years. L3 grubs require a very sandy, somewhat dry substrate for pupal cell formation (at least 50% fine particle sand). Overcrowding and minimal disturbances cause larvae to flee cells and can cause 100% mortality. Never dig up cells from the substrate prior to pupation. They need one month to pupate and another to transform to adult. Both sexes have horns on the head, but the male's abdominal sternites are slightly concave. Adults live

about three months. *Cotinis texana* is very similar and requires identical husbandry; it is found in the southwestern U.S. *Cotinis texana* averages larger in size, and the femurs are green where *C. nitida*'s femurs are mostly yellow.

### *Euphoria* spp.

These are generally small beetles with a maximum adult size from 7 to 19mm. Found: North, South and Central America. Two of the most commonly encountered and widespread species across the U.S. are *E. inda* (Bumble flower beetle—to 16mm) and *E. fulgida* (Bottle green flower beetle—to 19mm). Adults can be seen flying

*COTINIS TEXANA*

*EUPHORIA* SPECIES FROM ARIZONA

*EUPHORIA FASCIFERA* FROM ARIZONA

*OSMODERMA EREMICOLA* MALE

in the daytime, but are more easily taken at lights. Grubs are common in compost and manure piles. *Euphoria* grow rapidly in captivity with a complete turnaround time often less than three months. In the wild adults may hibernate the remainder of the year, though many species likely go through two generations a summer. At room temperature, adults are immediately active and live one to two months. The various species readily lay around three dozen eggs in pulverized, well-rotted leaf mulch on compost. The rapid growth means larvae must be constantly supplied with quality leaf mulch (finely ground, aged, moldy oak and beech mix). Unlike other genera where growth slows down greatly with minimal and substandard food, *Euphoria* either go fast or die in late L3 or pupation. They're easy, but demand constant care, which can make continuous culturing difficult. Larvae consume a lot of food and grow to three times the size of the adult.

flower beetle from the United States. It's not only the most incredible looking but it's big, long-lived, and easy to keep. Adulthood is reached after six or twelve months depending on food and temperature. Females lay multiple eggs in one spot but not in the circular formations of *Cotinis*. Some of the other *Gymnetis* (*G. holosericea* and *G. pantherina*) have sexually dimorphic sternite coloration, but the gender of this species is difficult to distinguish. The sternite coloration does vary, but has nothing to do with gender. Females are usually larger than males reared in the same cage. Beetles are long-lived at four to eight months, rarely longer.

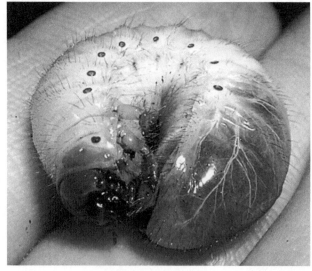

*OSMODERMA* L3

*GYMNETIS CASEYI*

*Gymnetis (flavomarginata) caseyi*
HARLEQUIN FLOWER SCARAB
Found: Southwestern United States into northern Mexico. Size: 20-25mm. This is the ultimate

*OSMODERMA* PUPAL CELL

*CHEIROLASIA BURKEI*

*Osmoderma eremicola*
HERMIT BEETLE
Size: *Osmoderma eremicola* reaches up to 32mm, while *O. scabra* grows to a maximum of 25mm. Members of this genus are commonly kept by hobbyists in the United States (*O. eremicola* and *O. scabra*) and Europe (*O. eremita*) since they're among the largest native beetles and they're easy to find. They are naturally gregarious and usually found in groups from a few to a dozen, even though both "eremicola" and "eremita" mean hermit. The elytra of *O. eremicola* and *O. eremita* are smooth and glossy, while *O. scabra*'s elytra appear finely wrinkled with a purplish black luster. Males have a ridged head, and a deeply sculptured, larger pronotum than females. If adults are hunted at lights, they will seem to be extremely rare. On the other hand, grubs are easily collected by the hundreds since they can be found in any

and every tree hole in many eastern hardwood forests. Grubs prefer to eat mostly rotten wood.

OTHER FLOWER BEETLES

*Cheirolasia burkei*
CLOWN FLOWER BEETLE
Found: Southern Africa. Size: 20-34mm. This small beetle is handsomely colored and has decent horns, but the front legs of the male are what set it apart from everything else. The legs are long and the tarsi have thick ventral setae that look like fuzzy mittens. Females aren't special looking, but even tiny ones can lay 40-80 eggs. Grubs grow well on the usual flower beetle substrate. They are reared in groups successfully, but will cannibalize if extremely overcrowded or without food. It takes less than six months from egg to

*DICRONORHINA DERBYANA OBERTHURI*

pupal cell formation, but another four months are spent inside the cell. Pupal cell formation requires a sandy substrate.

### *Dicronorhina derbyana layardi*
WHITE-STRIPED BULLDOG BEETLE
Size: 28-48mm. Found: Southern Africa. In a display filled with flower beetles, this is the beetle people notice. White stripes cross a base color of hologram green with red highlights, and in some animals the red highlights take over the green. It's one of the easiest to get eggs from. The large grubs take more overcrowding and less attention

*DICRONORHINA DERBYANA LAYARDI*

*DICRONORHINA MICANS*

*DICRONORHINA DERBYANA CONRADSI* MALE

*DICRONORHINA DERBYANA CONRADSI* FEMALE

than almost any other species. This genus contains the only flower beetles with a decent chance (40% instead of 1%) of surviving a fake pupal cell. Maturity is reached in about ten months. Adults live 3-5 months. Coloration in this genus is highly variable, so species are primarily determined by horn structure and angles of the male's head. *Dicronorhina d. derbyana* from southeastern Africa looks different because the central white bands on the elytra are anywhere from

*EUDICELLA SCHULTZEORUM*

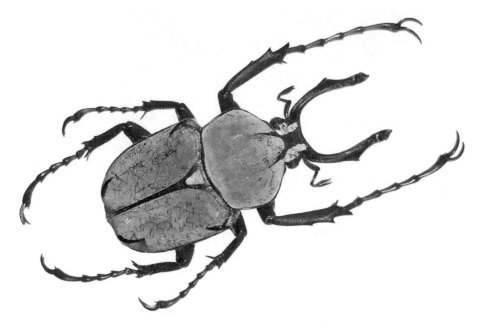

*DICRANOCEPHALUS* FROM TAIWAN

*MECYNORHINA* HYBRID

non-existent to 30% complete. (They are 80-100% complete on *layardi*.) Another subspecies, *D. d. oberthuri* is similar, but the front sides of the male's face are more pointed, and the abdominal sternites are marked in white. (There are sparse to no white marks on *D. derbyana*.) The cultured stock is green from above but blue viewed from the side. There's a purple form found in Kenya and Tanzania with the stripes of *D. d. layardi* that is often labeled *D. o. conradsi*. (It would technically be *D. d. o. conradsi*—with the present state of taxonomic hierarchy a sub-sub-species may not be as absurd as it sounds.)

## *Eudicella* spp.
### BUFFALO BEETLES
Found: From the Ivory Coast to Ethiopia and south to Namibia. Size: Individuals of all species vary greatly in size, but *E. ducalis* is the largest, growing to 55mm. Other species (or varieties or subspecies or forms) grow to maximums between 38mm and 50mm. The African buffalo beetles in the genus *Eudicella* have been popular pets for decades. Many of the *E. smithi* (Jade-headed buffalo beetle) and *E. gralli* stocks are close to thirty years old. *E. smithi* and *E. trilineata* (Ruby-headed buffalo beetle) are the easiest to get eggs from, while *E. gralli, E. schultzeorum, E. euthalia*, and others usually require closer attention. (*E. trilineata* is also known as *E. woermanni trilineata interruptefaciata*.) There are

*EUDICELLA GRALLI HUBINI*

numerous species, subspecies, and color forms in the genus, and fertile hybrids have been produced among many of them, so there is some question as which is really a species, subspecies, or race. Depending on the taxonomist, there are sixteen or more species and numerous subspecies, but even many "valid" species readily cross in captivity to produce fertile hybrids. One female lays 25-60 eggs. Maturity is reached in four to eight months and adults live two to four months.

## *Mecynorhina oberthuri*
### TANZANIAN TRIDENT BEETLE
Found: Tanzania. Size: This is the smallest *Mecynorhina* at 40-65mm. *Mecynorhina* are the second largest flower beetles after *Goliathus*. This species has been called "the Jewel of Tanzania" in the trade, but though it's a pretty beetle, the reference was the high price of specimens (which has dropped a lot in recent years). The elytra are orange or yellow, or black with yellow to orange spots. While successfully reared by a number of coleopterists, most find their entire stock dies in the pupal cell. If cells are dug up shortly after pupation and placed on top of the substrate, losses seem to be slightly reduced.

*EUDICELLA EUTHALIA*

*EUDICELLA SMITHI* FEEDING
ON FRUIT JELLY.

*EUDICELLA GRALLI ELGONENSIS*

*EUDICELLA TRILINEATA*

*Mecynorhina (Chelorrhina) polyphemus*
POLYPHEMUS BEETLE
Found: Central and West Africa. Size: 35-75mm. The Polyphemus Scarab was the only common, successfully reared, giant flower scarab until *Mecynorhina torquata* showed up in the late '90s. Grubs are more accepting of neglect than most flower beetles, and females have laid eggs in various substrates, though seldom more than thirty. Adult males are beautiful velvet green, while females are glossy, hologram green with red highlights. Males live two to three months and females can live five. Egg to adult averages nine months. *Mecynorhina (Chelorrhina) savagei* major adults are easily reared with close attention and supplements, but neglected grubs change into extremely small adults or die. They are far less forgiving than *M. polyphemus*. Females are notoriously stingy about laying eggs, and twenty from one female is exceptional. *Mecynorhina savagei* grubs are quite different from *M. polyphemus*, having a smoother, darker head capsule, a much lower head capsule to body size ratio, and flaccid larval behavior. Usually grubs from the same genus, or even related genera, are impossible to tell apart, but *M. savagei* grubs look very different from the other *Mecynorhina*.

*MECYNORHINA POLYPHEMUS* L2

*MECYNORHINA TORQUATA UGANDENSIS*

*Mecynorhina torquata*
EMERALD TRIDENT BEETLE
Found: West and Central Africa. Size: 42-90mm. This is the most widespread *Mecynorhina*, but least variable in coloration. It's easier to culture than most small flower beetles, but it's not always easy to raise males past the 60mm range. The life cycle normally takes ten months, though lower levels of care can add an additional year. Fifteen to thirty eggs per female are normal, but it's easy to get every female to lay that many.

*Mecynorhina torquata ugandensis*
UGANDAN TRIDENT BEETLE
Found: Uganda and eastern Zaire. Size: 40-85mm. This population was originally described as a species, but later moved to subspecies status. Although found in a small area, it comes in an amazing variety of patterns and colors, including black, green, brown, indigo, white, and orange. Varieties that are green like *M. torquata* are easy to tell apart because the rear and hind tibias are orange. As in *M. oberthuri*, color varieties other than green once were very expensive dead specimens. This subspecies sometimes experiences high failure rates in the pupal cell, unlike the nominate, but grubs are larger and it's easier to rear lengthier males. Much of what's around today are crosses with normal *M. torquata*, since hybrids aren't prone to cell death.

*MECYNORHINA SAVAGEI* MAJOR MALE

*MECYNORHINA TORQUATA* PAIR
(FEMALES OFTEN RESEMBLE MALES, BUT
LACK THE IMPRESSIVE HEAD AND FRONT
LEG ARMATURE.)

*MECYNORHINA POLYPHEMUS* PAIR
(FEMALES LESS COMMONLY DISPLAY A
DIFFERENT COLOR PATTERN OR SURFACE
TEXTURE.)

*MECYNORHINA POLYPHEMUS* CLAWS

*MECYNORHINA TORQUATA* CLAWS

*MEGALORHINA HARRISI* CLAWS

*MEGALORHINA* WINGS OUTSRETCHED

*Megalorhina harrisi*
MAMMOTH TUSK BEETLE
Found: Central third of Africa. Size: 28-62mm. The genus name means *giant horn* and males of most races have the largest horn of any flower scarab. There is only one species in the genus. "Subspecies" have listed color forms that occur across subspecies, but by varying percentages of the populations. (For example, the color forms "haroldi" and "quadrimaculata," so one can have a *M. harrisi procera "haroldi"* or *M. harrisi harrisi "haroldi"* or *M. harrisi procera "haroldi procera"* and so on. . . . It sounds crazy, but is based on actual natural variation.) Allard lists six color forms and five subspecies. However, a commonly kept stock from Cameroon has the size, horn structure, and protibia spines of *M. h. eximia*, but has spines in front of the eyes, so it doesn't key as any of the five listed subspecies.

A strange aspect of this beetle is that specimens from some races grow to twice the maximum size of nearly identical looking populations from other areas. Still, even the runt populations grow to 50mm with decent feeding and are still among the biggest flower scarabs. Females produce 30-40 eggs, but they can disappear quickly after hatching. Grubs are extremely predacious and cannibalistic but surprisingly easy to rear on a rotten leaf-only diet. This is the only genus other than *Goliathus* in which larvae are equipped with retractable talons at the end of the larval legs, though these are not as specialized. They

MECYNORHINA TORQUATA HYBRIDS,
RED MALE AND ORANGE FEMALE

POTOSIA AERUGINOSA

grow rapidly and make pupal cells in four to five months with decent care. However, they remain a grub inside the pupal cell for 4-6 additional months. The grub remains very active inside until the last month. If a ½ cm hole is made to check progress, the grub seals it back up. It can perform very extensive repairs, but is almost never able to remake a whole cell. (The single documented cell reformation ended with a dead larva anyway.) The pupal cell is strange because larvae often build it on the surface of the substrate.

MEGALORHINA HARRISI MALE (HORN NOT YET AT NORMAL POSITION) AND FEMALES

*POTOSIA* LOVE CHAIN

*GOLIATHUS GOLIATUS*, CAPTIVE-BORN 1997

*Potosia aeruginosa*
GREEN TINFOIL BEETLE
Found: Southern and eastern Europe. Size: 20-27mm. This is a hobbyist favorite due to the spectacular metallic body and the ease of captive care. Females produce 20-40 eggs with little prompting. Adults are rather long-lived at 4-10 months. *Potosia affinis* is a related species naturalized in the U.S. that looks very similar. Range information doesn't seem to be available, but specimens have been collected in Oklahoma and California.

*Rhomborhina splendida*
This attractive, active species is found commonly in Taiwan in midsummer. Most adults are solid green hologram (yellow to orange highlights), but one out of every few dozen wild adults are ruby red (without any green). Females commonly lay 100 eggs. The grubs are abnormally hairy and lethargic. Under good conditions the life cycle takes less than a year.

*Goliathus* species

Members of this genus are the absolute kings of the flower beetles and the number one dream beetle for many enthusiasts. They are impressive, but also have specific rearing requirements. Goliath scarabs have more than size in common with the giant they're named after. Like the real Goliath from the Bible story, it doesn't take something big to kill them. Only a few breeders have ever grown them from egg to egg, and this chapter details how it has been done. (All live *Goliathus* pictured in this book are captive-reared.) Captive hybrids have even been produced.

Numerous coleopterists tried to rear grubs on rotten wood and leaves between 1976 and 1997, but most larvae died and the few to survive grew so slowly it was believed they needed five years or more to reach adulthood. A simple discovery of feeding dog food pellets was key to formulating a procedure for normal development of goliath grubs in captivity. I had been using dog food to feed elaterid larvae and improve the size of rhinoceros beetles and suggested its use to T. Suzuki, who first tried it on *Goliathus goliatus* with surprisingly good results. This simple tool made it easy for anyone to grow grubs, but without good husbandry practices they could still be mite-covered, small, and sickly. Pupation can be another hurdle.

While each enthusiast may have his or her preferred food, the correct feeding procedure is the essential factor. Soft kibbled foods can be easier to use because they start out soft and mold more slowly, but dry kibbled foods become soft after a short time in damp substrate. As long as the food is designed for a predator like a cat, dog, or ferret, whether fish-shaped, or gravy flavored, the only significant issue is procedure. (Herbivore foods like rabbit and gerbil pellets are of no value.) Wild bird seed that's primarily cracked corn (cracked corn alone is fine, but not preferable) is also useful for *Goliathus* and can be used every other or every third feeding.

*Frequency and volume of feeding:* Grubs should be fed a small piece of food, about ½ the

*GOLIATHUS ALBOSIGNATUS* F12 Pair

diameter of the head capsule, every 2-4 days. Feed a higher volume if consumed rapidly, but be sure it's not just being smashed into the substrate. Unless the grub refuses to eat (short periods at premolt and prepupation) it is very important not to miss feedings.

*Substrate composition:* Though a small portion of the diet, good substrate is important. Any mix that the hobbyist finds works well with other flower beetle grubs is good—generally, 50% ground rotten leaves and the rest compost and soft rotten wood.

*Ventilation:* Equal to the area of the grub's head capsule. Cloth or microscreen should be glued over the holes.

*Humidity:* Damp, but not sopping.

*Removal of uneaten food:* Search through and remove any leftover particles two days after feeding. Reduce feeding quantity if noticeable leftovers occur regularly. The goal is to feed as much as the grub can eat without leftovers.

*Substrate replacement:* Substrate should be replaced once every six weeks. (Once a week, if there are pest issues.)

*Cage size:* Small cages, no more than twenty times the mass of the grubs, are important so that food is easily located by the grub. Uneaten food is easier to remove and it's easier to replace a smaller amount of substrate.

*Temperature:* 72°-80° F. Short periods (a day or two) below 60° F won't bother the grubs, but if the rearing environment is constantly much below 70° F grubs can enter a strange, lethargic state. If this occurs they can continue to "live" for years but will not recover.

*GOLIATHUS* TARSI, SHOWING CLAWS

All six tarsi of the grub end in a retractable talon resembling the toe of a bird of prey. If pushed with a finger from back to front they open up and grab on (independent of the grub's movement). The raptorial forelegs are unique and look very different from the blunt tipped tarsi of species often considered their closest relatives, like *Fornasinius* and *Mecynorhina* (not including other genera recently made subgenera or moved to *Mecynorhina*). As mentioned, *Megalorhina* possesses clawed, raptorial legs, but they do not retract and are not as highly adapted as *Goliathus*. Oddly, *Megalorhina* are much more likely to eat their siblings than are *Goliathus*.

Larvae do actively hunt. Other beetle grubs can be fed to *Goliathus* larvae. The results aren't easy to control and there are zero supported reports of breeding success using primarily live food. A single L3 *Goliathus* can eat dozens of grubs in a few weeks and there's a lot of waste. Grubs are incredibly more expensive and time consuming to rear than obtaining a bag of dog food. *Goliathus* also eat crickets—the substrate must fill the entire container and the cricket is placed in a grub tunnel. Live foods used every so often to supplement the described feeding regimen may be slightly helpful but keep in mind successful use of live food as a singular diet has never been documented because it doesn't work in captivity.

A single popular reference states that grubs are found in rotten trunks of a variety of trees, but the larvae's predatory adaptations, high energy level, and the need for sand to build a good pupal cell imply a terrestrial habitat. It's likely grubs could be found under rotten logs. They would almost certainly die inside a log (with the exception of treehole habitats directly below large bird or mammal nests).

Even if grubs are reared perfectly, they cannot become beetles without a good environment for pupation. If they run around the surface constantly, they have not been given an acceptable environment to pupate. If a deep, worn path is seen around the upper edges of a mature grub's container, it is trying to escape to find a good place to build a pupal cell. Due to substrate pressure (depth) requirements and a thin cell wall, they probably dig down a foot or two for pupation in nature. If the attempt to make a pupal cell fails, they'll move around for months and eventually settle down on the surface and die trying

CAPTIVE-BRED *GOLIATHUS ORIENTALIS* (FEMALE IN MIDDLE)

*GOLIATHUS ORIENTALIS* HYBRID. NOTE RED UNDER WHITE.

*GOLIATHUS ALBOSIGNATUS* F8 PUPA

*GOLIATHUS ALBOSIGNATUS* F12, JUST MOLTED

to transform without a cell or simply expiring. Often they'll turn black while still a grub. Of course there should never be other grubs of any type in the same cage if pupation might be near.

As 3rd instar grubs seem to be approaching full-size, three things should be done. First, add a few handfuls of fine sand (most aquarium or sandbox sand is suitable) and make sure the substrate consistency is similar to soil. Substrate with too many large chunks, wood pieces, and frass pellets can prevent formation of thin-walled cells. (Other than our native *Cotinis* and *Goliathus*, most flower beetles have thick cell walls and make sturdy pupal cells with large particles.) Second, make sure the substrate is packed tightly to the lid (though not too tight, as there should be some play for the grub to travel and leave tunnels). Last, make sure the lid is extremely secure, because L3 are very strong and active. Escapees that have been out more than a few hours usually don't make a pupal cell and eventually die. Commonly available disposable containers for food (the most popular brand is Gladware) are usually secure enough without added reinforcement. Something heavy can be placed on top, or the containers can be kept in a large tub as an added precaution.

The acquisition of grubs older than early L2 should be avoided. It is very unlikely they were kept under adequate conditions and by late L2 it is usually impossible to reverse damage from poor husbandry. *Goliathus* can be "killed" years before they actually die. Even when the damage can be healed, improperly fed L3 will take a year or two to pupate no matter what care is later given. They lose any sense of timing and siblings can build pupal cells well over a year apart. In contrast, when fed consistently from a young age, all but the uncommon straggler form pupal cells within a month of each other.

*Goliathus* adults are long-lived, though half the time is normally spent in dormancy. They usually transform to adults approximately three months after pupal cell formation, but remain in the cell for an extra three months. They can be removed when they mature, but they'll dig to the bottom of the dirt and refuse to eat or mate until the three months are over.

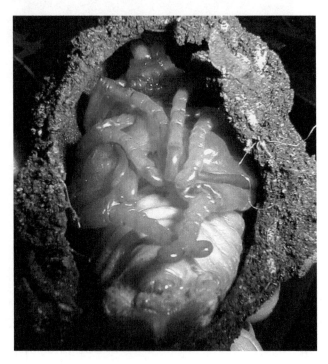

*GOLIATHUS ORIENTALIS* PUPA

It's best to rear a few dozen grubs per generation to prevent loss of the culture. A quarter or more often die in the pupal cells. Even when healthy adults emerge they may mature a few months apart and the female can lay dozens of eggs in the bottom of the cage right next to lethargic males. They show no interest in her because they are three months behind. It's not uncommon for females to live more than six months, but older females lay few to no eggs. The one redeeming aspect of rearing *Goliathus* is when you can get a female to maturity and mated, it's easy to get her to lay eggs. A 10-gallon with 4-8" of substrate for egg laying (as described earlier) is best, but most substrates are accepted. Females have even dropped eggs in ½" of substrate!

*Goliathus albosignatus*
Found: Southeast Africa. This is the smallest of the Goliath beetles, with a maximum size of 70mm. Adults have been observed drinking Acacia

sap in the wild. The stock presently kept in captivity has been kept for a dozen generations, whereas *Goliathus goliatus* was lost after seven generations. With heavy feeding and temperatures around 75° F, the entire life cycle is easily completed in six months, though most keepers rear specimens in just under a year.

GOLIATHUS CACICUS MALE

### Goliathus cacicus
Found: Western Africa, in the same range as *Goliathus regius*. A rare wild hybrid of the two is well known and named "Atlas." Size: Adults grow to 100mm. *Goliathus cacicus* is the most colorful Goliath and appears to be covered in half satiny gold and half satiny silver. The male's horns have a wider angle than the other species. Females look similar to the male with more black or are almost entirely black. Full-size specimens have been reared in captivity following the prescribed methodology.

### Goliathus goliatus
Found: Across central Africa. It's range ends in the south where *G. orientalis* begins, and in the west where *G. regius* is found. *Goliathus orientalis* and *G. regius* are sometimes listed as subspecies of *G. goliatus*, as color is the only way to tell specimens apart (and the color varies).

This beautiful species is the largest, along with *G. regius*, at a maximum of 110mm. Beetles congregate on a specific tree (*Veronia conferta*), which may be more about finding mates (like *Dynastes tityus* congregations on ash trees) than feeding. Although geographical varieties range from 5% to 80% white (the remainder red-brown to black), males from the same stock generally look the same. On the other hand, females, even siblings, can have quite variable white markings.

### Goliathus orientalis
Found: Zaire and Tanzania. Size: 40-100mm. Usually *G. orientalis* subspecies are known for having a lot more white markings, yet some are very dark. This species has been reared through a few generations.

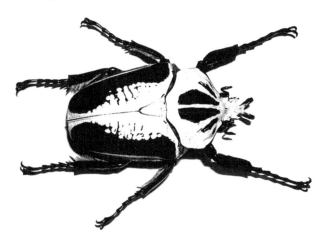

GOLIATHUS REGIUS MALE

### Goliathus regius
Size: 40-110mm. Found: Across western Africa, including Nigeria and the Ivory Coast. The color is variable, but normally the elytra have a characteristic (large and white) central marking bordered by broad black margins.

# 3

# DUNG BEETLES

## INTRODUCTION

The majority of U.S. beetle enthusiasts are familiar with the rainbow scarab, but haven't attempted to rear this beetle. Live specimens are not commonly encountered and husbandry is not well known. The rainbow scarab is a common species in most states but rarely seen unless it's hunted for. Methods for attracting and trapping dung beetles are included in this chapter.

This chapter is written in hopes of inspiring others to keep and rear the spectacular *Phanaeus vindex* (rainbow scarab) and other dung beetles, primarily larger members of the scarab subfamily Scarabaeinae. While hobbyists presently keep a variety of beetles in the family Scarabaeidae (mostly from the subfamilies Cetoniinae and Dynastinae), the dung beetle hobby is distinctly lacking. Practical husbandry details provided here offer another possibility for keepers who wish to raise beetles but are limited where few beetles are found in their region—colorful, horned dung beetles can be collected almost anywhere.

There is more than one reason dung beetles are the first thing on any scarabologist's mind, yet have gone largely unnoticed by insect hobbyists. The idea of handling dung does not appeal to everyone. Depending on the type of dung it may take a little getting used to, but deer and rabbit dung are rather innocuous and most of us handle dog dung with regularity. When a person moves past the dung aversion, these beetles prove very interesting. If one gets to the point of

eyeing fresh animal droppings with uncontrolled excitement or employing one's own dung, it may be going too far. If your personal lunch menu is planned with the idea of growing the largest beetles with the best horns, one's sanity may come into question. The second reason dung beetles aren't popular is related to the first. Only a few species are drawn to lights (instead, they're drawn to dung, which is avoided by most humans), so many beetle hobbyists are unaware of the great variety and beauty of native dung beetles.

The adults of this group are curious, active, and comical captives. Dung beetles are arguably the most amusing and personable of insects, so much so that their behaviors have been observed and documented since humans have been drawing. The beetles can be long-lived in captivity, but like other scarabs most live only a few months outside of hibernation. They don't have sharp claws, and can't pinch or bite, though they are strong and can be painful to keep in a closed fist. Though we have some very nice species here in the states, there are some gigantic, long-lived species from Africa and Asia that would make amazing pets were they available.

Most people first learn of dung beetles when they are taught about ancient Egypt. The dung beetle was highly revered for thousands of years and can be seen depicted in statues, paintings, hieroglyphs, funerary art, and jewelry. Heart scarabs were carved into stones and placed on the chest of the dead for protection. The scarab was

AFRICAN *HELIOCOPRIS* ARE THE LARGEST OF THE SCARABAEINAE

*PHANAEUS DIFFORMIS* BLUE FORM FEMALE (© STEVEN BARNEY)

a symbol of eternal life, likely inspired by the life cycle and emergence of adult beetles from the earth. The mummy-like pupa stage was the likely inspiration for the practice of mummification. The sacred scarab is the most famous beetle in the world, and is probably the most famous insect of all time. The oldest known reference is from around 3100 B. C. under the reign of Menes.

The species most often referred to as the sacred scarab is *Scarabaeus sacer*, but there are twenty-seven similar Nearctic and at least fifty Afrotropical *Scarabaeus* species differentiated primarily by spines, striae, tubercles, punctures, and setae. In the late 1980s and early '90s this beetle (or a closely related *Scarabaeus* species) could be found in U.S. pet shops from time to time. They were long-lived for dung beetles (surviving about two years), and would provide hours of enjoyment as they rolled dog food pellets continuously around the cage.

The instructions outlined in this text are based on experiences rearing *Phanaeus vindex* and a handful of other North American species. The methods outlined here have proven successful and repeatable with the listed species and are likely useful for many species. There are, however, countless variations among the great variety of dung beetles around the world. Some species, like *Liatongus monstrosus* and *Onthophagus rufescens*, use the refuse of leafcutter ants to fill their brood

chambers, which may be impossible to substitute in captivity. Many common species will make do with a variety of resources, but other species are specialists that require dung of a specific freshness from a specific species of animal to induce nest building and egg laying. You might imagine an animal that eats feces wouldn't be so picky, but most are careful connoisseurs of freshness and won't build nests with crap that's too old. Vertebrates from African and Asian elephants, to giraffes, dogs, tigers, iguanas, tortoises, and snakes have their own dung beetle species, often groups of species, that may be difficult to breed without the proper dung.

Dung beetles are rare on exhibit and are almost never seen in smaller exhibits. Thankfully, a few large insect zoos, including the Audubon Insectarium in New Orleans, Louisiana, feature dung beetles in public displays. Their display is in the shape of a large dung beetle rolling a ball—a glass terrarium is in the center of the ball, displaying the beetles. Zack Lemann, Visitor Programs Manager at the Audubon Insectarium, said: "The dung beetle exhibit is cleverly located next to our restrooms. (*Yes we think it's funny, too.*) Prior to opening, our understanding of this group of scarabs was minimal. There was enough concern about being able to have live dung beetles year round that we insisted on having a diorama made as well so that we could offer a

SIZE COMPARISON OF VARIOUS DUNG BEETLES

'snapshot' of a rolling ball of soil and poop with a couple of beetles hard at work for our visitors to see. We are able to show live dung beetles to our guests at the Audubon Insectarium all year long and have not used the diorama once since we opened." There is a permanent *Phanaeus difformis* exhibit at the Fort Worth Zoo in Texas.

BACKGROUND ON THE RAINBOW SCARAB
The genus name *Phanaeus* is a Greek term for the sun god meaning, "bringing light." The specific name *vindex* comes from a Latin legal term for someone who assumes debts and has come to mean "avenger" or "protector." This may or may not be a reference to the beetle's great efforts to rid the world of smelly dung. In 1819 the descriptor couldn't have known this species name would correspond to a very common household cleaner today (in Latin *v* is pronounced *w*). The common name is quite suitable to describe the kaleidoscope of metallic colors covering the exoskeleton.

This beetle is an absolutely stunning creature sought after by dead specimen collectors for its great beauty. As a live specimen this species is not only beautiful, but active and fascinating. The brood ball it creates is a work of art. Toiling

*PHANAEUS VINDEX* GOLD FORM

inside the brood ball, the homely grub looks like the Quasimodo of the scarab world, with its strangely humped back, a feature only common to scarabs confined to small brood chambers during growth. Nevertheless, in nature and captivity the homely larva is usually unseen (and even temporary removal from the brood chamber often results in death).

*Phanaeus vindex* (14-23mm) has the widest range of any *Phanaeus* in the United States. It is most common across the southeastern third of the country, but is found from Arizona east to Florida and ranges north into Vermont and Michigan. This species is common across several regions and ecosystems. It may be the easiest *Phanaeus* to breed in captivity since it accepts a variety of soil and dung types found throughout its native habitats.

ORDER COLEOPTERA
SUPERFAMILY SCARABAEOIDEA
FAMILY SCARABAEIDAE
SUBFAMILY SCARABAEINAE
(DUNG BEETLES)
GENUS *Phanaeus*
SPECIES *vindex*

*Phanaeus vindex* is our most well-known and widespread species, though various members of the genus *Phanaeus* are commonly called "rainbow scarabs" or "rainbow dung beetles." This genus is only found in the New World. There are seven extant species of *Phanaeus* native to the United States. They are *P. adonis*, *P. amithaon*, *P. difformis*, *P. igneus*, *P. quadridens*, *P. triangularis*, and *P. vindex*. None of these species vary greatly from one another in habit or form. They all feed on and form brood balls out of dung. They are day active (diurnal) tunnelers, often with brilliant metallic coloration. Males are capable of growing large, curved horns. Females may have small horns but are usually easy to discern from small males.

*PHANAEUS VINDEX* PAIR

The spectacular metallic colors of *Phanaeus* species are usually the same for members of the same species, but green, blue, black, and red forms are not uncommon. A typically green species can have the rare red or blue form, while a typically blue species can have the rare green or red form. Even a typically black species can throw colorful aberrant forms. The color variations are often found only in certain geographic populations, ranging from very rare to quite common. Uncommon color forms are genetic, so they can be isolated in captivity in a generation or two. The *P. vindex* form with blue elytra was awarded the subspecific name *P. v. cyanellus* in the early 1900s, but is not considered valid because it is not isolated from the general population.

*COPROPHANAEUS BONARIENSIS*

*Phanaeus* are well known for male dimorphism, with two primary male forms that can be generated depending on threshold development of the grub. Males either have a long or short horn and associated pronotum armature (or a short or no horn). The enhanced weaponry for fighting can be turned off if the grub doesn't have enough nutrients, so that the overall size of the beetle may not be greatly diminished. In dimorphism the larger males employ their weaponry in head-on fights over females, while small males are thought to rely on stealth. One aspect of small males, obvious in captivity but missing from scientific reports, is that undersized males develop more rapidly and may have first crack at the females. Specimens are commonly referred to as minor or major males, though the exact point of differentiation is not cut and dry and can become very blurred in captive specimens.

Recently male trimorphism has been documented in wild specimens for three of fifteen *Phanaeus* species studied. In trimorphism there are three distinct threshold development levels for a species (usually long, short, and no horn). Of five U.S. species studied, only *P. triangularis* employs trimorphism, while *P. difformis, P. igneus, P. quadridens*, and *P. vindex* males only display dimorphism (Rowland and Emlen 2009).

Allometry is the name for disproportionate horn growth and is a common thread in many Scarabaeoidea characters, notably the jaws of large stags and the horns of large rhinoceros beetles. Even in captivity where the food and environment seem to be consistent, results vary, and the exact functionality of allometry is difficult to prove. It may be little more than a function of survival. If needed resources are diverted away from horn growth, the underfed larvae are more likely to survive otherwise inadequate nutrition.

Beyond the U.S. *Phanaeus* there are about four dozen tropical species from Mexico south through Central and South America. They include the monstrous and very colorful *Phanaeus imperator*. At one time, the genus *Phanaeus* had nearly 100 members, including even larger species like *P. ensifer, P. lancifer,* and *P. bonariensis*, but these monster species were later moved to *Megaphanaeus,* later returned to *Phanaeus*, and now are usually listed as *Coprophanaeus* (the dung of subgeneric classification not to be mentioned). There were about forty species relegated to *Coprophanaeus*, including a single U.S. native in south Texas. *Coprophanaeus* have two small, more-pronounced appendages at the front of the clypeus, are more accustomed to carrion, and females of horned species are often as endowed as the males. The prefix *copro* is Greek for "dung," which is the most unlikely choice for renaming carrion feeders from a dung-feeding genus. (Perhaps *copro* referred to the unnecessary generic split.)

In the U.S., *Phanaeus* only occurs as far west as Arizona, though there is a fossil head of an extinct species, *P. labreae*, from California. It was found in asphalt deposits and is probably from the Pleistocene. Fossil brood balls, which may be from *Phanaeus* and are also from the Pleistocene, have been found in Jalisco, Mexico. Two of the oldest known scarabs are *Geotrupoides* and *Proteroscarabaeus* from the early Cretaceous and *Aphodiites* from the early Jurassic.

MORE BACKGROUND ON SCARABS

### SUPERFAMILY SCARABAEOIDEA
### FAMILY SCARABAEIDAE
SUBFAMILY SCARABAEINAE (DUNG BEETLES)
SUBFAMILY APHODIINAE (SMALL DUNG BEETLES)

### FAMILY GEOTRUPIDAE
SUBFAMILY GEOTRUPINAE
(EARTH BORING DUNG BEETLES)
SUBFAMILY BOLBOCERATINAE
(FANCY DUNG BEETLES)

Dung feeding scarabs are found in more than one group of the Scarabaeoidea. Though not touched on here, there are also various species of "dung beetles" represented by many different families of beetles, even water scavenger beetles (Hydrophilidae). The classic dung beetles, including the sacred scarab, are beetles from the subfamily Scarabaeinae. This subfamily contains the majority of species that specialize in large dung, and can be up to 65mm in length. The majority of these beetles feed and raise their young on animal dung and create a brood ball for each egg. There are species in this subfamily that specialize in other foods, such as rotting mushrooms

(tiny species) and rancid meat (some very large species). Many species display incredible sexual dimorphism but even within the dimorphic species there is a lot of variation (so large females can have bigger horns than small males).

*TWO COMMON NEARCTIC SCARABAEUS (LEFT) S. LATICOLLIS, ATLAS MOUNTAINS (RIGHT) S. SEMIPUNCTATUS, FRANCE*

The basic shape of a dung beetle is a very rounded body with a broad and flattened head that is used like a knife and shovel for working with manure and shaping dung balls. The wide clypeus is often attributed to digging, but many other scarabs dig for a living and do not have such widened, shovel-like faces. If it weren't for the massive clypeus, some species would be difficult to tell from rhinoceros beetles and many other burrowing scarabs. As with most beetles, they have protective front wings called elytra that allow them to bury themselves without damaging the delicate hind wings. Most fly very well—they could go extinct if they had to walk to find dung. Coloration is most commonly dark black, but many have colorful metallic sheens and some, like *Phanaeus*, are outfitted with wild, metallic colors. This subfamily is of course the group of most interest to hobbyists.

Members of the subfamily Aphodiinae are usually known as the small dung beetles. These do not get very big (3-15mm) and are usually more elongate in shape than other dung beetles. Some can be difficult to tell from the Scarabaeinae, but for most the shovel-like head is flared out on both sides rather than the front. They are mostly endocoprids that breed inside the dung pat and do not prepare special chambers for their young like the other groups. Some live in tortoise or ant nests, while other species attack brood balls of Scarabaeinae or eat grass roots. In nearly all species the males and females are difficult to tell apart. Due to a lack of armature, unimpressive size, and the absence of fascinating nidification behavior, members of this group are of almost no interest to the hobbyist.

*Enoplotrupes* Species from Thailand, 39mm

Size Comparison
(Top) *Coprophanaeus lancifer*
(Bottom) *Phanaeus vindex*

Members of the family Geotrupidae (*geos* from the Greek meaning "earth" and *trypetes* from the Greek meaning "borer") are often called earth-boring scarabs. This family was, until recently, the subfamily Geotrupinae of the Scarabaeidae. Like Scarabaeinae most are quite round and males often have horns and pronotum armatures that differ greatly from the female. The

most visible difference is the head is comparatively tiny. The antennae have eleven segments, while normal scarab antennae are eight to ten segments. Geotrupidae beetles can be up to 40mm in length. Members of this group do not move dung very far horizontally, but are known for digging very deep tunnels (3 to 6 feet or 1 to 2 meters) that are packed with dung towards the bottom, where eggs are laid at regular intervals. In Europe there's a strange geotrupid species, *Lethrus apterus*, with huge jaws that specializes in grape leaves. (The giant jaws of this species aren't intimidating as they look like an old man's beard.) Some species in this family have been reared in captivity, including the minotaur beetle, *Typhoeus typhoeus*, which feeds on rabbit pellets. Members of the subfamily Bolboceratinae look a lot like Scarabaeinae and are known as fancy dung beetles. However, they are no longer considered dung beetles and supposedly form brood balls from forest litter rather than dung. Nevertheless, at least in the eastern U.S., they tend to be found in numbers only near farms.

As part of creation's cleaning crew, dung beetles do an important service for large herbivores and man. Nature wouldn't be enjoyable if dung were not removed and festering, flesh-eating flies and rank vegetation completely replaced kindly dung beetles and quality pastureland. By burying the manure, beetles remove breeding material for flies whose maggots eat dung, including the face fly, *Musca autumnalis*, and the blood-sucking horn fly, *Haematobia irritans*. (These flies are known to cause illness and can lead to death in cattle.) Burying the dung also aerates the soil and fertilizes pastureland plants. Dung piles that sit on top of the substrate encourage the growth of rank plants that cattle won't eat. The dung ties up nutrients but will eventually be eaten by termites, millipedes, terrestrial isopods, and other creatures. Nature would not become saddened or cry tears if dung beetle biomass were replaced by termites and small detritivores, but it would be a major problem for humans and grazing animals.

In recent years farmers have become more aware of the value of dung beetles. The various paracoprids and telecoprids are encouraged through purposeful introduction from other pastures by farmers, because the beetles bury dung. Burial not only reduces harmful flies but also greatly reduces the chances of livestock transmitting parasitic helminths. The tiny endocoprids (mostly Aphodiinae) also provide a valuable service removing dung and are far more beloved than flesh-eating flies, but can be intermediate hosts of helminths. Many farmers understand it is important to use pesticides better targeted towards flies. If they aren't careful they'll wipe out the dung beetles and as the flies become accustomed to the pesticides, it will result in a terrible mess for us all (and the loss of these spectacular creatures).

When man replaced buffalo with cows in eastern North America it likely had little effect on native dung beetles, though buffalo dung is a bit drier. (Nevertheless the introduction of various competing generalist European species must have affected native species.) However, when humans moved cows into Australia and California, where there had been no large herbivores with massive dung, the results were disastrous. It didn't take many years for pastureland to become rank, fly-infested, and look like the result of a disaster science fiction movie. Dung

beetle projects were started in Australia and later California. From 1973-1977, 680,000 dung beetles were introduced in California by the federal government (Evans and Hogue 2004). The U.S. government attempted to introduce 15 Old World species from 1972-1987 (Fincher 1996), but only five became established: *Digitonthophagus gazella*, *Euoniticellus intermedius*, *Onthophagus taurus*, *Onthophagus depressus*, and *Onitis alexis*. The first three are well established with multiple state ranges, while *O. depressus* is only established in Florida and *O. alexis* is only found in southern California. Dung beetle introduction reduced a very terrible problem magnificently, but of course as always happens, the ramifications on native species were later pondered as though there had ever been a reasonable alternative.

In addition to our native *Phanaeus* and purposefully introduced Old World Scarabaeinae, the United States is home to hundreds of dung beetle species. Nearly any U.S. beetle enthusiast has dozens of colorful and amazing species not far from his or her backyard, but they've never seen or heard of these beetles because they are not attracted to lights. Many dozens of our native species are metallic green and red or have metallic sheens. Males often have a pair of horns on the head or a pincer-like combination of a single horn on the head opposing one on the pronotum—like the more familiar rhinoceros beetles. We even have fascinating carrion-feeding species including the large, widespread *Deltochilum* and rare *Coprophanaeus*. Our native geotrupids also include a number of impressive and colorful species. Nevertheless, the U.S. must have had even larger and more colorful species just a few thousand years ago.

According to the fossil record early dung beetles shared the planet with dinosaurs. Many forms and families we know and love most were likely at their height later when mega-mammals like mammoths, mastodons, sabertooth cats, *Camelops*, and giant sloths ruled the planet. It may be upsetting for hobbyists to learn the "golden age" of dung beetles has come and gone, and its peak was probably not long ago, during the Pleistocene. Gargantuan beetles that specialized on oversized dung from mega-mammals disappeared along with their food source.

Africa and Asia didn't lose all their large mammals and thus are rich in dung beetles. The most massive of the modern world's dung beetles are *Heliocopris* species, of which the largest specialize in elephant dung. They construct brood balls inside open chambers deep underground like *Phanaeus vindex*, but on a much grander scale. They are likewise meticulously coated in earth. People have mistaken excavated brood balls for ancient cannon balls.

In Thailand, farmers have been encouraged to farm the huge native *Heliocopris bucephalus* dung beetles in recent years. This came about after they noticed a decline in the number of beetles collected to sell as souvenirs to tourists. However, only a small number taken by man make it to the tourist industry—the bulk of collected *Heliocopris* are eaten as food. In some areas of Thailand the pupae are consumed as a delicacy. The Thailand Forestry Service published an instruction manual (authored by L. Kayikanata) on how to successfully farm the dung beetles in screened outdoor pens by simply offering the beetles Thai swamp buffalo dung at prescribed regular intervals. Elephant dung can also be used, but many farmers still keep the buffalo. Despite increasing popularity of farming these magnificent beauties, the threat to the dung beetle population has not lessened since increased pesticide use is wiping them out in some areas.

Recently, Hollywood has unfortunately chosen to portray Egyptian sacred scarabs as flesh-eating, swarming, deadly man-eaters. This has given rise to a whole slew of misconceptions and wonderful questions like "Don't scarabs crawl under your skin?" and "Aren't scarab beetles extinct?" Not only is there no scarab that is even remotely capable of harming, much less overpowering and consuming a human, there are no

*HELIOCOPRIS BUCEPHALUS*

species that move or swarm like the computer animated versions. Real dung beetles only swarm on a steamy fresh pile of dung, and even though it's soft, they take some time to carve it up and roll it away. True Egyptian scarabs just tumble around, comically rolling turds.

## DUNG BEETLE BEHAVIOR

Parental care is the most significant behavior of dung beetles, but the specifics of nest building differ for many species and are unknown for many more. Most go to great lengths to collect and protect the food source that will supply each larva through its development. Unlike many other types of beetles that spend very little time caring for their eggs or young, it is normal for dung beetles to practice extensive parental care with long hours involved in food collection and brood ball construction. Some species, including members of the genus *Copris*, stay on to protect their brood until the offspring reach adulthood or the parent dies. Extensive care leads to a high success rate but in some species the females rarely produce more than half a dozen eggs. Despite the variety of nidification, most species can be divided into members of three main nesting patterns: endocoprids, telecoprids, and paracoprids.

Dwellers (endocoprids) live and breed inside dung. The simple nidification pattern is the lack of nesting behavior. They are generally rather small beetles that don't move or bury the dung. Most are members of the subfamily Aphodiinae. *Ataenius* and *Aphodius* are commonly seen in mass seasonal flights on farmland. *Aphodius* is a large genus of dung-dwellers, though many species encountered in the U.S. were introduced from Europe with cattle. Since endocoprids don't bury the dung, they are more likely to be intermediate hosts of helminths that affect livestock. In captivity this group requires little to no substrate depth or breadth. If anyone wanted to raise them it should be rather easy.

Ball rollers (telecoprids), also called tumblebugs, are the fast food junkies of the dung beetle world. They are highly energetic as they roll dung balls backwards with their hind legs while standing face down on the front legs. They seem uncoordinated and tumble all over the place but eventually get the job done. They prefer "take out," as they gather dung up into balls and roll it away from the source. They do not have to compete for space like tunnelers or dwellers, nor are they limited to the location where the dung was dropped. In addition to opening up more options for burial, the rolling helps to shape the brood ball and the action can smash fly eggs and small larvae if present. Despite these benefits, they end up with a nearly finished ball that has to be buried in one piece, so brood balls have to be buried close to the surface. It's not common, but brood balls are sometimes rolled over to a piece of wood or rock and buried directly below. In captivity ball rollers need as much surface area as possible and minimal depth. Of course the exact size of the cage depends somewhat on the species, as some have been documented to move the dung ball as much as 30 meters from the pat. A round container can only be expected to fool them so far. Some genera that employ this method include *Scarabaeus, Melanocanthon,* and *Canthon.*

Tunnelers (paracoprids) dig tunnels and lay eggs under or near dung piles. They are limited to the area around where the dung was dropped, but do not have to worry about burying the brood ball in one piece. Since they can keep going back until the surface is cleared of usable dung, they are able to build larger brood balls than ball rollers. This also allows them to bury their brood deeper underground and farther away from predators, drought, and freezing. Besides tunnels and chambers for brood ball construction, paracoprids create food chambers or feeding tunnels where they store dung to be eaten in privacy and away from predators. In captivity, tunnelers need deep substrate that is not too loose. They'll bury dung in tunnels in the loose substrate, but won't form brood balls if they can't form a chamber. Some genera that employ this method include *Phanaeus, Copris,* and *Heliocopris. Dichotomius, Onthophagus,* and *Geotrupes* are tunnelers, but pack chambers with dung (often ovoid in shape) rather than forming brood balls inside a hollow outer chamber.

Many species, especially those in the subfamily Scarabaeinae, work together in mated pairs during nest construction. Males help to transport the dung and form the brood balls. The spectacular social coordination of the male and female is usually termed subsocial, as compared to the behavior of advanced ant and bee societies. Much greater social coordination is recorded and observed in nature than in captive conditions, which means social behavior is strongly affected by the environment and the beetles' perception. In addition, when dung beetles are collected they are most often in pairs, but they seem to lose interest in each other when placed in a cage.

The food mass constructed for larval development by the adult beetles can be compacted into a chamber, rolled and buried, or formed inside an open chamber. The type of construction determines whether it is considered a brood ball or brood mass. Compressed balls of dung, sometimes coated in earth, and formed by ball rollers and tunnelers for reproduction are known as brood balls. Brood masses formed by many tunnelers, including most *Onthophagus*, are similar and can look like brood balls, but are simply compacted into an open ended chamber and not molded by the adult beetle before burial (ball rollers) nor after burial inside an open chamber (tunnelers). One larva lives in and feeds on the brood ball or mass until it becomes an adult beetle. The pupal cell is always formed inside the brood ball and usually formed inside the brood mass.

Dung beetles locate food with highly sensitive antennae. Considering the potent smell of most of their foods it would seem the antennae wouldn't need to be so fine-tuned. However, they are searching for specific content and freshness. The only time we've seen a *Deltochilum gibbosum* anywhere near a black light was one night when we had a sealed tub of rotten meat handy for the next day's trapping. None of the humans present could smell the meat, but one beetle flew in and landed next to the container.

Scarabs must locate fresh dung for food and reproduction and a few employ extreme methods. Probably the most common method used by dung beetles can be called perching. They wait on plant branches (the height from the ground may be determined by the scarab species and the type of dung being sought) with their antennae clubs held wide until the scent of dung is detected in the air. In arid regions clouds of dung beetles are said to follow flocks of sheep or goats. There is a small species from Australia that attaches itself to the fur near the rump of kangaroos and wallabies, patiently waiting until dung appears—on emergence the beetle jumps onto the dung and takes a short ride to the ground. This ensures it will be the very first creature on the scene. Some species may even go in after the dung and there are a few rare reports from India of children living in squalid conditions with live Aphodiinae beetles and larvae in the rectum (Bily 1990).

All of the dung beetle species worked with for this book have proven to be vibrotaxic and will move in response to vibrations. This strange and somewhat comical movement is most likely a tactic for predator avoidance. The best way to observe this behavior is to dig an adult out of the substrate and leave it exposed. Next, scratch or tap the side of the container or the substrate. The beetle will move along with the vibrations and will freeze and remain still when the tapping stops. If a few adults are placed together they can be made to dance in unison. If they are dug up in the wild they would move along with the footfalls of herbivores whose movement would likely be more distracting to a predator than a small beetle's. This is similar to the response of many phasmid species that begin feeding and moving during the day when the cage is sprayed, since the spraying approximates rain that would mask their movements. Another possible explanation for vibrotaxic behavior in dung beetles is so they move at the same time as a predator digging to find them. This would make it more difficult for the predator to locate them since their movement would be masked.

CAPTIVE REPRODUCTION OF *PHANAEUS*

Since *Phanaeus vindex* is a paracoprid (tunneler), the depth of the substrate is much more important than the surface area. They are day active like many flower beetles, so they will fare better with a proper day and night cycle in captivity. *Phanaeus* are noticeably more active when exposed to light but do not need extremely bright light and do need dark periods for rest. Whether kept indoors or out, direct sunlight should be avoided or the temperature may rise

*PHANAEUS VINDEX* MAJOR MALE
(© STEVEN BARNEY)

to deadly levels. The beetles are accustomed to high humidity most of the day and though lighting makes them more active a too-close incandescent can readily desiccate their internal organs. It's much more difficult to fly too close to the sun than to a light bulb. Temperatures below 72° F will discourage reproductive behavior and temperatures much above 85° F can lead to excessive activity (generally unproductive) and premature death.

For the container a medium-sized (18-gallon) plastic tote is inexpensive, readily available, and a good size. This is found at your local "megastore." Semi-clear totes allow in plenty of light. The lid that comes with gray totes should be replaced with a piece of thick glass to allow light in.

For observation and easy checks, special caging can be built for the beetles. A wooden box with removable sides and a glass lid is the simplest construction. Hinges and latches can be used to hold it together. (The cheapest and simplest method is to screw the sides together with wood screws. The whole thing is easily disassembled in seconds with an electric screwdriver.) Ball roller caging can be made with round cardboard cement forms as the sides and a sheet of wood for the bottom. For either cage a clear glass or hard plastic lid can be secured by grooves or hardware, but the beetles can't climb well and the weight of the lid should be adequate to thwart any flight escapes.

For substrate the dirt from your yard can be sifted using the screen top from a terrarium (assuming they are the newer style—older style lids have thin, finely-vented window screen that would make the job very difficult). Topsoil can be purchased and mixed with some sand if natural material is unavailable. It is important to next compress the dirt into the container, which can be done by hand. As you compress the dirt, try to roughly match the consistency of soil they might encounter in the wild. Then add another layer of dirt to the top, about an inch, and leave this layer uncompressed. The total depth should be about eight inches (20cm). Do not worry you'll compact

*PHANAEUS VINDEX* MINOR MALE
(© STEVEN BARNEY)

the dirt too much—you could jump up and down on it. *Phanaeus* tunnel under dung in very rocky areas that are too difficult to dig up even with tools. Keep the substrate damp, but don't overwater since there is no drainage.

The next step is to add dung, throw in one or two beetle pairs, and wait. Try to keep a constant supply of food available because they are extremely active and burn through energy quickly. Brood ball construction can stop if the food becomes too old. Once a week a portion of cow dung the size of a baseball should be placed on top of the substrate. Dung from pigs will also work well. Horse manure might also work as adults are sometimes found under horse manure "outdoors" (*in nature* or *in the wild* wouldn't really apply to farms or horse trails). Manure available in bags from garden stores is too decomposed to be of any use.

Usually, the female will construct the brood ball by herself in captivity. The female digs a tunnel, usually right next to the dung, cuts off small pieces, and then drags them into the tunnel backwards, holding each piece with her front legs. When she has collected enough dung, she closes

*PHANAEUS VINDEX* BROOD BALL SHOWING
CAVITY WHERE EGG WAS LAID.
(© STEVEN BARNEY)

*PHANAEUS VINDEX* PUPAL CELL
(© STEVEN BARNEY)

*PHANAEUS VINDEX* PUPA
(© STEVEN BARNEY)

*PHANAEUS VINDEX* EGG (© STEVEN BARNEY)

off the entrance to the tunnel to hide it from pests and predators. She can then go about constructing the ball at the bottom of the tunnel. Males are sometimes found in tunnels, especially in the wild, but in captivity males never seem to carry dung into the tunnels to help with brood ball construction.

*Phanaeus vindex* brood balls are about 40mm, a little bigger than a golf ball. They are almost perfectly spherical except for a small knob on the top. There is an outside layer of dirt, about 4 to 5 millimeters thick, that is compressed around the dung. The whole thing feels very sturdy and the outside is nice and smooth. There is no way a human could confuse a finished brood ball with a clump of dirt. The female lays one egg per ball inside the little knob at the top and she then covers over the egg with a thin dirt cap.

One of the most amazing aspects of *Phanaeus* is the tremendous size of the egg. The eggs of large rhinoceros and flower beetles are pretty big eggs, but those beetles are many times the size of *Phanaeus*. Even gigantic *Megasoma actaeon* eggs are only around 5mm in diameter. In contrast, the eggs which *Phanaeus* females lay are comparatively huge—around 7mm. Unlike other beetles with a pair of ovaries, most dung beetles like

*Phanaeus*, *Onthophagus*, and *Canthon* only have a left ovary. The female not only devotes much time and energy for construction of a single brood ball but also devotes a lot of nutrients to a single egg.

To check for brood balls (if the cage doesn't come apart), use your hand and start piling dirt from one half of the container over the top of the other half. Slowly work down near the bottom in this fashion, then reverse and check the other half. The brood chamber will almost always be found all the way at the bottom of the container. Another way to check is to scoop dirt from the top of the rearing container and dump it into a second container and work your way down to the bottom. Immediately before a brood ball is encountered, there will be a notable empty spot, devoid of dirt. This is the brood chamber and the brood ball sits right in the middle of this empty chamber. Do not dump the whole container out at once, as this will most likely damage any eggs or grubs present. *Phanaeus* grubs are more delicate than dynastid or commonly kept lucanid grubs. They are not made for crawling around and will die if the brood balls are greatly damaged.

Please use caution when checking the container. *Phanaeus* adults are very quick and agile fliers and will be long gone by the time you notice they have flown off. It's a good idea to keep a small container with a lid handy and put the adults inside as they're encountered.

Brood balls should never be sought for until about seven days after feeding or about seven days after most of the dung has been buried. It takes quite a while for the female to construct the ball (seven to eight days). If she is disturbed before she is done, you will find an unfinished ball with no egg inside. The female will have to start all over again, wasting needless energy and time.

Move any balls that are found to a separate container and carefully bury them upright in a layer of moist, preferably heat-treated substrate. Make certain the substrate does not dry out but do not overwater. Brood balls that have been removed from their chambers can dry out pretty quickly. They can't be left exposed in a closed

*PHANAEUS VINDEX* TENERAL FEMALE
(© STEVEN BARNEY)

container and wetted periodically (as with rhinoceros beetle eggs) because they will dry out. The primary reason to remove brood balls from the container is to free up space for more laying, instead of setting up an entirely new cage.

When the grub hatches it will dig directly below the knob on top of the brood ball and into the center to start eating. Grubs are able to patch cracks and small holes in their brood balls. This can be helpful when a brood ball is damaged but makes it rather difficult to watch what is going on inside. Although larvae patch up small holes with little trouble they cannot reconstruct or repair a severely damaged brood ball.

An attempt at constructing an artificial brood ball was made to replace a ball accidentally destroyed while digging. A clear plastic vial (3″ tall and 1½″ in diameter) was used. A compressed layer of dung about an inch deep was placed in the bottom. In the center of this layer a cup-shaped hole, a little larger than the grub, was hollowed out. The grub was placed inside and covered with another layer of dung. The grub lived for quite some time, but died during pupation. Replacement brood balls may work but need more testing.

When they are ready to pupate, the grubs build a second pupal chamber inside of the brood ball. Although these are much more spherical, they are very similar to flower beetle pupal cells and can be removed from the brood ball when they are finished. When the beetle first emerges from the pupa it is brown and soft (teneral) with a metallic shimmer. Coloration only reaches full potential after a few days when the exoskeleton has fully hardened (sclerotized). In captivity the development time from egg to adult is six months to a year. Adult specimens are said to live a long time in various un-researched reports, though more than a year is not common and four months is a reasonable expectation.

TRAPPING AND COLLECTING DUNG BEETLES
The main technique used to collect dung beetles is to use a pitfall trap baited with dung. A hole is dug in the ground and a container placed in the hole so that the top edge of the container is level with the ground. This allows beetles and other insects to walk along the ground toward the bait, where they then fall into the trap. Dung beetle tarsi are not made for climbing and they can't climb out of relatively shallow containers, but they can fly.

Unfortunately, pitfall traps are generally set up with soapy water, vinegar, or antifreeze to catch and kill any insect that falls in. As you can imagine, dead dung beetles aren't very active, aren't much fun to watch, and are terribly difficult to breed. Collectors interested in working with live specimens must devise different pitfall traps. A funnel covering the trap is useful to keep them from flying away. Funnels can be made from

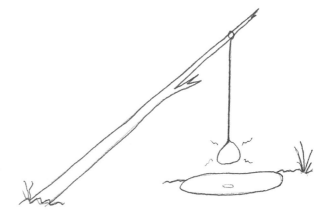

DUNG BEETLE PITFALL TRAP

sheet metal, plastic, or even a paper plate. The diameter of the funnel's bottom hole is important. If it's tiny, large beetles won't fall in, but if it's more than an inch or two, some beetles can fly back out. The angle and smoothness of the material also affects catches. The beetles can't fly straight up, so a narrow pitfall container is a second option, but a narrow container may provide too little surface area or fill up too quickly.

The easiest way to construct a pitfall trap is to cut the top off of a 2-liter soda bottle, invert the top and place it inside the bottle. Place tape around the edge where the top and bottom meet to keep the two together and close up any holes. For a smaller trap, a 16oz. deli cup with a 1½" hole cut in the lid will work, but it isn't as effective for trapping or holding the beetles. It is helpful to poke a number of holes in the bottom of the trap so rainwater can drain. If the ground isn't porous, it won't drain without construction of a drainage channel.

Carefully choose a spot for your trap. The location can be more important than the effectiveness of the trap construction or the drawing power of the bait. Catches will be severely limited if there are only dogs and rodents in the area. Different species of dung beetles often stay in their own microhabitats and a trap placed in a different type of habitat in the same area can catch different species. Some species prefer to fly in open, sunny pastures, while others stay deep in the woods. Pitfall traps must be placed strategically to facilitate trapping the desired species.

When the trap has been built and carefully placed, the next step is the bait. The easiest method is to place the bait in the bottom of the trap, but much of the alluring smell may be hidden and the catch messy. A common method, the Dunging-Pole, suspends the bait over the mouth of the trap. A stick is pushed into the ground at a slant so that the top of the stick is in line with the mouth of the trap. The bait is hung in a cloth bag or old sock and tied to the end of the stick.

A second method is the Two-Hanger Dung Scaffold. Two wire clothes hanger hooks are bent sideways towards each other and joined using pliers or by wrapping with small gauge wire or duct tape. A cup with holes or an old sock full of dung is placed inside the joined hooks and the bottom edge of the hangers comprise the legs. This second method takes a little more forethought, but doesn't fall over easily and works on any ground type. Unless the ground is cement it can be secured with wire foot anchors that are many times easier to push into tough ground than a stick. A 16oz. deli cup trap can be placed below this (not buried in the ground) if the surface is rock.

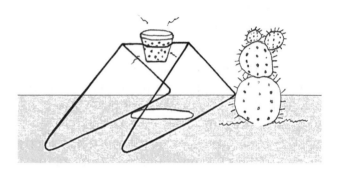

TWO-HANGER DUNG SCAFFOLD TRAP

Michael Barney devised a technique for *Phanaeus* collecting called a "sub-surface trap." A large plastic tub is buried so the top edge is level with the ground. The tub is filled with the soil that was removed for the hole and the area is leveled off so its existence is no longer visible (of course the tub can just be set on top of the ground if there's no risk of it being molested by people or livestock). A pile of dung is placed on the surface of the dirt in the middle of the tub. *Phanaeus* are attracted to the dung and will start to dig tunnels directly beneath the pile. After an hour or so it's time to return and check for tunnels near or under the dung. If any tunnels are spotted, the tub is removed from the hole, along with the soil and any beetles inside. The soil is then sifted to locate the beetles.

Although the sub-surface trap can't be left for a day or more with the expectation of finding beetles, it has some advantages. It is much easier to locate beetles in the tub than by digging below dung in bare soil, since it confines the space they will be found in and allows for sifting of the soil to locate beetles. In most soils shovels are a necessity, as hand digging is too difficult, but shovels often smash or cut *Phanaeus* in half. This technique is also easier than a pitfall trap in that the dung does not need to be suspended over the hole. A much larger amount of bait can be placed on the trap without the hassles of tying mesh bags filled with dung or having the stick that is suspending the dung break.

Another collecting method is light collecting. This method is generally only effective from 10 p.m. to 2 a.m. Beetles can often be found at the bright white lights of gas stations within flying distance of farms. Of course in some rural areas there are no such available lights and you'll have to bring your own. A light rig can be set up in a pasture or near woods. Although light collecting is the best method to use when searching for many types of beetles and various giant silk moths, only nocturnal species of dung beetles are attracted to lights. Some common, larger species that can be collected at lights are *Digitonthophagus gazella, Dichotomius carolinus,* and *Dichotomius colonicus,* the first often in large numbers. Tiny *Ataenius* species sometimes fly to lights in huge numbers in the spring. Some of our prettiest and hardest to find creatures like *Onitis* and fancy dung beetles (Geotrupidae: Bolboceratinae) can be caught in numbers at lights, but only in the right place at the right time.

A light rig usually consists of one or more black lights and a clear mercury vapor bulb (frosted bulbs don't work as well) shone on a white sheet. The brightness (output is a function of wattage) and color (wavelength) of the light affects how many insects are attracted in a given area. Small black light fluorescents can be run on batteries or a car charger, while large bulbs and mercury vapor will require a portable generator. Blue and ultraviolet lights are used because they attract insects better than daylight white. Extremely yellow light usually does not

*PHANAEUS* WITH MITES

attract insects. However, *D. carolinus* appears to be one of the few insects to show up under yellow gas station lights.

Flight-intercept traps are often part of packaged black light traps. These are simply upright pieces of hard plastic below the light that insects fly into. They then fall down through the funnel into the trap. These can be useful for some day-flying dung beetles, as they fly rapidly over large areas. A few types of packaged black light traps are made with 5-gallon buckets, flight intercept vanes, funnel, light, and lid. The flight intercept vanes are usually just 6-12 inches high and appear as an X from above. Bait can be placed in the bottom of a packaged black light trap if the vanes are see-through. (Some traps have opaque vanes but diurnal dung beetles can see during the day.) An inexpensive, larger version can be made with a bucket, funnel, and clear plastic vanes.

Other than using traps, searching is the best way to collect dung beetles. It's important to scout areas for beetle activity before spending the time and energy to set traps. A simple and effective method of scouting for beetles is to search in, under, or near naturally deposited dung. Dung can also be purposefully and strategically placed on the ground in areas dung beetles are thought to occur. Of course, if the desired species is found while scouting, there's no need to build or set traps.

For tunnelers, look for holes under or near the dung. For ball rollers, you will need to either wait for them to fly in or search a wider area around the dung where you will find them rolling it away. It will usually take a ball roller a little while to carve out their desired amount of excrement from the pile, which makes it a bit easier to find them on the dung than rolling in the surrounding area.

Good places to find wild animal dung are around water sources. These are good spots to set traps, since the beetles will generally hang around in areas where they often find dung. Other good places to look are around water troughs in pastures or even around swimming pools. There are some species that are almost always found in gopher burrows.

Another easy way to collect tunnelers, especially in ground that is difficult to dig, is to pour water down a hole that you suspect to be occupied by one or more adults. First, locate a large hole under or near the edge of a dung source. Next, fill it with water. Keep adding water as the level goes down and after a little while, if anyone is home, you may see the water start to move. If the level of the water is kept even with the opening of the hole, the adult should stick its head out of the water. This works well with *Phanaeus* species and *Dichotomius carolinus*.

FOOD AND BAIT

The adult beetles have large jaws, but in most species they barely open and are lined with setae (hairs) that restrict the adults to a liquid diet. This feature is thought to ensure adult beetles find the freshest, wettest food. However, many adult Scarabaeoidea whose larvae don't eat dung are also liquid feeders. (Even predatory adults of Dynastid scarabs in the Phileurini are liquid feeders.) Most dung beetles will feed on the fluids from melon, beetle jellies, or even moistened dry dog food pellets, if dung is not immediately available. The adults feed mostly on the fluids from dung in nature but only require dung in captivity for nest building.

Larval dung beetles have large, slicing jaws that open wide to chop and consume solid food. They can't survive on dead leaves or rotten wood like many scarabs, and have no ability to carve into harder, rotten wood like jewel scarabs and stags. Substitute foods are unlikely to work.

Whatever food or bait is chosen, it's helpful to have something sturdy to manipulate it. Large spoons and tongs should be purchased (and can be found at any dollar store). Of course these should be marked with a biohazard symbol so they don't end up serving your dinner one evening. Dung and rotten meat can contain bacteria or parasites dangerous to humans.

The dung beetle's preference for mammalian dung is well known, with their favorites being herbivore or omnivore dung. *Phanaeus* species are found around cow and horse dung, while some *Canthon* in Louisiana can be seen rolling otter dung. Nevertheless, it is well documented that the dung most attractive to Scarabaeinae (and therefore most used by scarabologists and scarabophiles) are pig and human. Cow dung is not nearly as useful for traps and horse dung is almost worthless. Calf dung from nursing calves is attractive bait. Keep in mind there is likely to be a lot of cow dung in areas with dung beetles that utilize cow dung. They are unlikely to leave the pat they're on if the bait isn't more enticing.

Being one's own near-perfect bait machine, although safe, portable, and free, may be completely out of the question for many would-be beetle hunters. If you are fortunate to find someone locally that keeps potbelly pigs, they probably won't mind parting with a few buckets of waste. Dog dung can be used to rear a few species but is generally worthless as bait.

We suggest you never use airtight containers when transporting dung because there seem to be a number of reports of exploding containers. However, the only published report we've found (Warner, 1991) is the case of a glass jar in a hot car, and the author purposefully omits the name of the actual perpetrator. We can neither confirm nor deny.

*PHANAEUS TRIANGULARIS* MALE (© STEVEN BARNEY)

*P. TRIANGULARIS* FEMALE (© STEVEN BARNEY)

For culture material it can be helpful to freeze dung ahead of time. This can kill many pests that are already in the dung. There are often maggots, smaller dung beetles, and various other creatures crawling around in it. Unless you have a dedicated freezer, this will most likely be difficult for people who may not want manure rubbing up against the frozen beef or ice cream. Cooking would work better to kill pests, but it changes the moisture level and composition of the dung to the point where females are unlikely to use it in nest building. Also, the aroma would be unacceptable in any household.

If possible, talk to the owner of the cattle (or other dung source) to find out if the animals were recently fed any medicines in the form of invertebrate pesticides. These chemicals are usually called "wormers" for horses, but "dewormers" for cattle, dogs, goats, etc. It is strange that any would be called wormers, since it doesn't sound like a good objective. These chemicals are simply poisons that kill intestinal parasites. They are targeted for invertebrates and are dosed low since the host weight is so much greater than the parasite's, and potency is relative to dosage per weight. It is best to wait a few weeks after the

When trying to attract beetles with dung, fresher is better, especially for larger species like *Phanaeus* and *Dichotomius*. This is likely because fresher dung is most likely to have more product available and the number of other creatures infesting the dung is fewer. Although the female eliminates some pests by carefully forming the brood ball, infestations of fast-growing small insects can cause failure of the brood. If only older dung is available for traps, it can be soaked in water, since the moisture will increase the aroma and possibly fool some beetles. Likewise, adding moisture to dung in a culture container can improve nest-building behavior.

*PHANAEUS IMPERATOR*

*PHANAEUS IGNEUS* PAIR, MALE ON RIGHT

animals have been dewormed to collect dung. Some types of dewormers can kill dung beetle grubs, reduce egg laying, or even kill adult beetles. There are some brands of dewormer that are said to be safe for dung beetles. Many farmers familiar with the helpfulness of dung beetles treat the livestock just before the return of warm temperatures so poisons have passed before the beetles emerge.

*Rotten meat:* Carrion is, surprisingly, another good bait used to attract dung beetles. Although this works best for *Deltochilum, Coprophanaeus,* and other carrion-loving beetles, *Phanaeus* have also been drawn to rotten turkey pitfall traps. Ground beef has proven effective for rearing carrion-feeding scarab beetles but it doesn't usually produce much odor. It does not need to be aged for use as food. Chicken and fish are the most commonly used baits. Good bait must be aged until it smells attractive.

There are various ways to allow meat to become aged and smelly, but here we'll outline one. This method to properly age and hold meat requires screen mesh, staples, and a plastic bag. Make a pouch from the screen that will be used to hang the meat over the trap. Fold the piece of mesh in half and staple the sides. Cut a chunk of fresh meat and place it in the mesh pouch and use more staples to seal the top. The pouch is placed in a sandwich bag and hung outside for at least a day. It should be hung at least six feet off of the ground to keep scavengers away. (If there are bears in the area, aging or baiting with meat is not advised.) Flies, then maggots, almost always find their way into the bag, but don't hurt anything. When the smell is bad enough, remove the mesh bag from the sandwich bag and pierce the top of the mesh with a stick or metal coat hanger to hang the meat over the mouth of the trap. You can try any uncooked meat: whole chicken pieces, ground turkey, ground beef. Please use extreme caution when handling raw or rotten meat. (DO NOT lick your fingers after setting a trap.) Keep a large bottle of hand sanitizer handy and use it. Keep in mind the smell of sun-warmed rotting meat is not a favorite of neighbors, so you may have to find a well-ventilated and people-free area for bait fermentation.

A small cooler can be purchased for the express purpose of carrying dung and rotting meat. This should be appropriately labeled with biohazard symbols so that it is not confused for a drink cooler. Careless handling can be dangerous.

In the insect world, dung beetles are far from being alone in their craving for rotten meat. Rove beetles, hide beetles, carrion beetles, and of course flies will be attracted to the bait. Specific species are attracted to carrion at different levels of decay. Carrion beetles, for instance, seem to be more attracted to fresher fare. Hide beetles show up late.

When using dung as bait, you don't have to worry about other animals outsmarting you and stealing your bait. When baiting with meat or fish, depending on where you live, you will have at least a few powerful adversaries to contend with. Red ants are notoriously crafty and it's possible your trap will collect a few thousand more insects than anticipated. A method to keep the ants at bay is to rub petroleum jelly on the edge of the trap, wire coat hanger, or stick used to suspend the meat over the trap. This layer can be very thin but should be a few inches in width to stop the ants from climbing the trap to eat the rotten meat. The most difficult adversaries are large scavengers like raccoons and possums that will dig up, tear apart, or walk off with the entire bait rig. Vultures will come for chicken legs if there's a big enough hole in the funnel. A method that has worked well for scarabophiles is to place the bait in the pitfall, but cover it with a large square of thick, wire mesh that is staked securely in place (Streit 2006). Again, if there are any dangerous animals living in the area such as bears, baiting with meat should be avoided.

*PHANAEUS DIFFORMIS* NORMAL MALE
(© STEVEN BARNEY)

OTHER U.S. DUNG BEETLES

*Phanaeus adonis* was only recently discovered to be living in the US in extreme southern Texas (1995—Cameron Co., TX—C. Cate & M. Quinn). It's a small species, 12-17mm, that's black with a blue sheen.

*Phanaeus amithaon*: Around 15mm. Southern AZ. This is another very rare species in the U.S. simply because its range barely reaches this far north. It's a small, metallic green species with deep striae on the elytra.

*Phanaeus difformis*: 19-22mm. South central and southwest: LA, AR, CO, NM, OK, TX, KS. It is found in sandy, mostly coastal areas. This species has been successfully bred in captivity many times over. *Phanaeus difformis* usually has

*PHANAEUS DIFFORMIS* BLUE FORM FEMALE
(© STEVEN BARNEY)

*ONTHOPHAGUS HECATE*

metallic green elytra but sometimes they are bright metallic blue or deep purple. In areas where blue or purple forms occur, most specimens usually have the regular coloration. The purple form can be found in south Texas near the Gulf of Mexico. The elytra have distinct shallow striae and punctate intervals. It resembles *P. vindex* except for the narrow shape of the crescent.

*Phanaeus igneus* is found in NC, SC, GA, FL, AL, MS, and LA. It is a smaller species that prefers sandy or coastal areas. It is less sexually dimorphic than other species, since the males are rarely equipped with large cephalic horns.

*Phanaeus quadridens*: 16-23mm. Southern AZ, southern NM. This good-sized, handsome species is metallic green overall.

*Phanaeus triangularis*: 14-24mm. The beetle is usually found in its all black form and looks like it's made of shiny, black tar. Red specimens are known. The beetles are found primarily but not exclusively in areas near rivers or streams, generally in floodplains with sandy or loose soil. It is found in several southeastern states including Florida and Texas. South Texas is home to the closely related carrion-feeding *Coprophanaeus pluto*, 18-28mm, which somewhat resembles *P. triangularis*.

*Onitis alexis*: 12-20mm. Nocturnal burrower. This handsome species with a green pronotum and brown elytra is a native of southern Europe and Africa. The beetle has no horns, but the male has a large spine on the inside of each rear femur. This is one of the species released in quantity by government agencies in Australia and the United States. It is attracted to lights in numbers in some areas of southern California, but does not seem to have become established elsewhere. It's the largest species purposefully introduced for dung control.

*Onthophagus hecate*: 6-9mm. This is one of our most common native species, which is attracted to just about anything rotten, including watermelon rinds and the dead smell of an old pitfall

*PHANAEUS QUADRIDENS* FROM *ARIZONA*

*D. GAZELLA* GRUB (© STEVEN BARNEY)

*DIGITONTHOPHAGUS GAZELLA* PAIR (© STEVEN BARNEY)

trap. From the side it looks like a tiny *Xylotrupes*, but the horns are usually flat and wide. (Really large males can have relatively thin horns.) It is black with a very slight purple tinge. This and the smaller, mat-black *O. pennsylvanicus* may be the first species you encounter when baiting. Members of the genus *Onthophagus* usually pack a number of cells off branching tunnels with dung and don't form an outer chamber. "*Onthophagus*" is from the Greek: *onthos* = "animal dung" + *phagos* = "eater." This is a huge genus containing 2,000-2,500 species worldwide, and males exhibit a range of spectacular horn structures. This genus has more members than any other beetle genus in the world, though this may change as species are reorganized, like the following.

*Digitonthophagus (Onthophagus) gazella* (GA-ZELLE SCARAB): 8-13mm. Nocturnal tunneler. Males have short horns that resemble Martian antennae more than a gazelle's horns. In the early 1970s these were purposefully imported from Africa and released in Texas and later California to help deal with cattle dung buildup. This species has spread and can be found throughout

*D. GAZELLA* FEMALE PUPA (© STEVEN BARNEY)

*CANTHON INDIGACEUS* FROM ARIZONA

*CANTHON* SPECIES FROM ARIZONA

most of the southeastern and southwestern United States. They are very easy to breed in captivity and are not at all picky when it comes to dung or substrate types. They are mostly nocturnal but can be found during the day by flipping dung in pastures. They are also easily attracted with black light. This seems to be the most common species in the U.S. if you collect at lights. There are some reports of double-sided, glass terrariums built to allow observation of *D. gazella* nesting. This would be an interesting setup to try, though getting the dimensions just right to encourage nest building against the glass could be difficult.

*Onthophagus taurus* (BULL-HEADED DUNG BEETLE) was purposefully introduced in Texas and California, but may have accidentally been introduced into Florida (also in the 1970s with the same program). The males have a pair of curving horns that resemble a bull's horns, but are quite long. Minor males have short horns. This species is smaller than *D. gazella* and now seems to be found throughout much of the United States, although not in the numbers that *D. gazella* has reached. This species seems to prefer dog dung and has been collected in dog parks with some regularity.

*Canthon chalcites*: 13-20mm. *Canthon chalcites* is one of the many species of ball rollers in the genus *Canthon*. They are day active and can be collected in pitfall traps. For rearing, round containers with glass used as a lid are suggested. A round container will allow them to continually roll without getting stuck. It's possible to have limited success collecting brood balls in rectangular terrariums by piling up dirt in the sides. This helps them to roll without getting stuck in the corners. Also, with these and other ball rollers, overcrowding should be strictly avoided. When females bump into each other several times while rolling, they give up and abandon their brood ball construction. For best results there should just be one male and one female to construct the brood balls.

*Geotrupes blackburnii*: 10-20mm. These paracoprids are black with a glossy sheen and metallic blue undersides. Adults show up in the fall in good numbers and can be attracted with carrion. Although little is documented on captive rearing, this species should be easy to breed with the right

*C. CHALCITES* BROOD BALL (© STEVEN BARNEY)

*CANTHON CHALCITES* ROLLING OTTER DUNG (© STEVEN BARNEY)

*DELTOCHILUM GIBBOSUM* MALE (© STEVEN BARNEY)

*GEOTRUPES BLACKBURNII*                    *DICHOTOMIUS CAROLINUS* FROM SOUTH CAROLINA

setup. Females construct tunnels a few feet deep (around 3 ft or 1 m) in nature, so a trash can filled to six inches from the top with compacted substrate can be used as a habitat. Much shallower caging is likely to result in no reproductive behavior. Fresh dung can be placed on top as needed and adults shouldn't be kept in the cage for more than a month or two as digging will eventually disrupt brood chambers. *Geotrupes splendidus*: 10-18mm. Found from Florida north to Canada and west to Arizona. Adults are usually metallic copper green, but also come in bronze, red, or blue.

*Deltochilum gibbosum* (HUMPBACK DUNG BEETLE): 20-27mm. This nocturnal telecoprid is one of the largest dung beetles in the U.S. The genders are easy to tell apart because females don't have lumps on the elytra. The adults are not attracted to light but are highly attracted to rotting meat. Wild beetles are attracted to a wide variety of bait including human excrement, dead fish, rotting seafood, decomposing melon, and fermenting beer bait. They can be collected most readily using chicken or turkey meat after the bait has set out in the sun for a day or two. They have been known to roll animal hair, fur, and small bird feathers for use in brood balls. In nature they roll brood balls for twenty feet or more before a shallow two-inch burial. The brood ball is approximately the same size as *P. vindex* but is shaped

more like a daffodil (*Narcissus*) bulb and coated with a much thicker layer of earth, often mixed with leaves. The center contains feathers or carrion. The egg is quite large at 9mm. In captivity, specimens can be reared on ground beef. The time from completion of the brood ball to pupation is only about three weeks. Our subspecies is *D. g. gibbosum*, while the Mexican version is *D. g. sublaeve*. There is one other U.S. species in the genus, *Deltochilum scabriusculum*, which is found near the southern tip of Texas.

*Dichotomius carolinus*: 20-30mm. Nocturnal tunneler. These are powerful burrowers capable of digging down, in seconds, through hard clay that few other species could penetrate. *Dichotomius* is one of the only large dung beetles that can be attracted to lights at night. It's possible to have very good success using pitfall traps baited with pig dung. Like *Phanaeus*, they make tunnels that are ten to twelve inches deep to construct their brood chambers. In captivity adults rarely live past three or four months. On several occasions we have observed *D. carolinus* pushing and rolling large pieces dung in front of them, presumably to move it away from competition. *Dichotomius colonicus* is similar in size and appearance, but is found in the southwest— it used to be considered a subspecies of *D. carolinus*. Both have deep grooves lined with setae at the rear of the elytra that are caked with

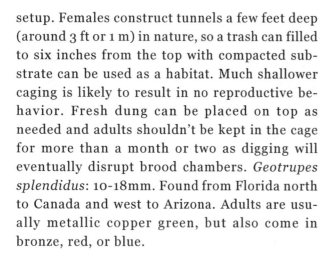

*COPRIS MINUTUS* MAJOR MALE

*COPRIS FRICATOR* MINOR MALE

*EUONITICELLUS INTERMEDIUS* MALE

*EUONITICELLUS INTERMEDIUS* FEMALE

dung in nature. These are the only two members of this genus in the U.S., but there are a number of large tropical species.

*Copris fricator*: 12-17mm. Nocturnal tunneler. Members of this genus often look like small *Oryctes* or *Xyloryctes* rhinoceros beetles, except for the wide clypeus. There are nine *Copris* species in the U.S. They make brood balls, but ones that are not covered in soil like those of *Phanaeus*. Females make as many as seven at once and look after the brood balls while the larvae inside develop into beetles. They keep the surface clean of mold and sometimes die before offspring emerge. It would be interesting to see how long the mother's attention is necessary in captivity.

*Euoniticellus intermedius*: 7-9mm. Diurnal tunneler. This small species would be incredible were it a bit larger. The male has a horn and a powerful oversized prothorax that the female lacks. The body is tan but marked with darker patterns and metallic copper and green highlights. The legs are cream. It can be reared in captivity on a variety of dung, including cow and dog. This African species was a success story of the dung beetle projects. It is found across the U.S. from California to Florida, but only in warmer areas. Introductions in the U.S. appear to have spread, as this dung beetle is found on most any cattle farm in Mexico.

# 4
# JEWEL SCARABS

## INTRODUCTION

The beautiful metallic scarabs from the tribe Rutelini are famous for their amazing colors and resemblance to precious metals. The familiar North American goldsmith beetle, *Cotalpa lanigera*, appears to be dusted in gold. The glorious beetle, *Chrysina gloriosa*, looks like its stripes are painted with liquid silver or gold (and the stripes can appear black at certain angles). A number of species from Central and South America look like living, glowing pieces of metal. *Chrysina chrysargyrea* is a common species from Panama and Costa Rica whose normal form is silver and the rare form is gold. Related species like *Chrysina resplendens* are normally gold but can have aberrant silver or red forms. Only the Rutelini tribe of the family Rutelinae have been of interest to hobbyists.

### FAMILY SCARABAEIDAE
### SUBFAMILY RUTELINAE
### (JEWEL SCARABS)
### TRIBE RUTELINI (*Chrysina, Chrysophora, Cotalpa, Pelidnota*)

Jewel scarabs are often confused with flower scarabs, but differ in many ways. The grubs do not "walk" on their backs. The pupal cells are not earthen cocoons, do not have a defined outside surface, cannot be separated from the substrate, and can be reformed. Adults have hooked, unequal tarsi (claws), and a broadly oval body. (Most Cetoniinae bodies are pentagonal.) The elytra must open and lift up for flight. The adult males of some species, notably the *Chrysophora* and some of the *Chrysina*, have enlarged rear legs for securing a female during mating, directly opposite the elongate front legs found in most flower beetle males. (There is a Central American exception in the genus *Spodochlamys*.) Lastly, many commonly kept flower beetles have horns on the head while Rutelini do not.

*CHRYSINA CAVEI* MALE

Rearing can be difficult due to larval die-off and pupation problems, but attention to the feeding requirements and techniques outlined in this chapter will minimize die-off. Overall husbandry is simple, but mistakes often show up in later development. Some species, like the grapevine beetle, *Pelidnota punctata*, and the glorious beetle, *Chrysina gloriosa*, have been cultured very successfully by numerous hobbyists in the United States. Captive-bred species have been primarily New World natives, though the

108

*CHRYSINA GLORIOSA*

spectacular Central and South American *Chrysina* seem to only be available in Japan. Members of the genus *Fruhstorferia* look like other rutelines, but have long, curved, sickle-shaped jaws. These have been reared in Asia, but there's little information on multiple generation success.

## COLLECTING

Our native *Chrysina*, *Pelidnota*, and *Cotalpa* are most commonly collected at lights. There are usually plenty of gas station light to collect eastern species like *Pelidnota punctata*, which can be collected in numbers. *Cotalpa* is rarely attracted in volume. The western species are usually collected with black light traps because there are few, if any, attractive lights in the right areas. Watching dozens of our most magnificent *Chrysina* fly in hourly in Madera Canyon in Arizona is an experience every beetle enthusiast should seek. Despite some poorly researched books' claims that *Chrysina gloriosa* and *Chrysina beyeri* are endangered, both are very common according to all scientific literature and are not listed by the U.S. Fish and Wildlife Service

as endangered. The beetles begin to lay eggs before their first flight, so it would be nearly impossible to over-collect them. (Habitat destruction, synthetic chemicals, biological control agents, and "natural" pesticides are the real threats to these species.)

Larvae can be collected inside rotten logs and stumps. *Pelidnota punctata* are found in a variety of wood types, while *Chrysina* habitats are limited to a few hardwoods. Keep in mind that a large part of a dead tree is found below ground. One of the best places to find larvae is in buried rotting roots that are at least three inches in diameter and six inches underground.

*CHRYSOPHORA CHRYSOCHLORA* FROM PERU

## LIFE CYCLE AND CULTURE METHODS

Two to three weeks after molting to adulthood, females begin to lay eggs. Properly fed (as larvae) captive-bred females can lay up to 60 eggs, while wild-caught females deposit 10-40, since they had already begun laying before their first flight. Wild-caught females start to lay eggs in less than 24 hours (often in a few hours) if given agreeable substrate. Substrate suitable for egg laying is finely ground, soft, brown decayed wood flakes. In some species, captive-bred females are pickier and it may be necessary to try a few different wood mixes. Compost or shredded rotten leaves can be added if wood alone isn't working. Ova should be collected every four to five days. The egg laying period is only a few

GRUBS HAVE SMOOTH HEADS AND STRAIGHT JAWS,
RESEMBLING STAG BEETLE LARVAE

weeks, so checking for eggs in the substrate used is crucial.

Ova are one to two millimeters in diameter and start out bright white, so they are very easy to see in the substrate. They are less tolerant of handling, female's laying activities, and minimal dryness than flower beetle eggs. As with all scarab ova, they rapidly dehydrate if not kept damp, since the shell is thin and water-permeable. If the initial egg die-off is greater than 10%, change the substrate. Ground, rotten hardwood leaves placed around eggs can improve hatch rate.

Tiny white grubs emerge from the eggs after two to three weeks. They immediately search out and burrow into pieces of wood, so it may seem like they all have disappeared if the wood is not finely ground.

Although larvae will feed on many substances other than decayed wood, it's important not to use more than a small amount of compost, dead leaves, etc. They may seem healthy or even grow

faster for a period, but die in late third instar or during the transformation to adult. 90% decayed hardwood flakes along with 10% compost or ground leaves works well as a larval substrate. Common fungi and molds that grow on rotten wood or other larval food do not pose a threat to the grubs. Larvae feed and grow well on nearly any soft, decayed hardwood but the wood should be dark yellow to brown—not white, light yellow, or black. Decayed wood is the exclusive natural larval food, as most species have been collected inside the wood of rotten tree stumps (where there is nothing else to eat). Exceptions of note include some species in the genus *Paracotalpa*. Those larvae live in sandy soil and feed on rotting roots and decomposing leaves.

Grubs are faced with the same pest problems outlined in the earlier chapters, but are far more sensitive to the presence of pests. Larvae may seem to withstand pest problems, but are likely to fail in late development. Rutelines are very susceptible to one large enemy: wireworms. These are the larvae of click beetles, family Elateridae. Though seldom encountered in numbers, a single, small wireworm can take out a number of jewel scarab grubs or pupae. Eliminate any possible wireworms by heat-treating the wood. Submerging wood in water or freezing the wood is unlikely to kill them. Jewel scarabs are sensitive to most pests, so cooking substrate is the key to survival. (A small piece of oyster mushroom from the grocery store can be buried in the substrate if the hobbyist feels a need to reseed the substrate. Surprisingly, dried mushrooms grow better than fresh, and as an added benefit are less likely to have microworms or nematodes that occur on store-bought fresh mushrooms).

The die-off rate can be extremely high if nematodes or mites are visible in the substrate. A handful of tiny pests often aren't visible. If there are enough to be visible upon close inspection, and levels haven't reached plague proportions, the substrate should be replaced with clean and the problem is solved. However, if there are tons of pests, the grubs may never fully recover

*CHRYSINA GLORIOSA* (ONE TENERAL)

*CHRYSINA CAVEI* PAIR

*CHRYSINA WOODI* EATING BEETLE JELLY

and eventually wither away despite replacement of the substrate.

Supplemental feeding is helpful to growth and to prevent barren females. Kibbled pet foods should be used sparingly, and not before 3rd instar. Supplements should not be ground up and mixed into substrate. A small piece of dog food is buried near the grub once or twice a month. Food should not be crushed, since a grub has no trouble chewing into objects and grinding makes removal of the uneaten portion difficult. Remove leftovers after a few days to prevent attracting pests. A few milliliters of brown sugar (1 part) and water (4 parts) can be added to the substrate a few times a month even at L1. The liquid mixture isn't as nutritious, but damage and death caused by overfeeding are extremely less likely. The sugar mixture can be used to adjust the moisture level but should not be added if the substrate is extremely damp. Supplements visibly improve growth but if the wood chosen is not adequately decayed, the grubs will most likely die or become sickly adults.

Larvae grow quickly, molt twice, and are full-size in three to four months. 12-15 grubs can be kept in a 2-gallon plastic shoebox or 1 per 16oz. container. Grubs seldom pose a threat to each other but can accidentally kill each other at higher densities, particularly during molts. Medium-sized species like *Pelidnota punctata* and *Chrysina lecontei* consume up to a liter per grub. When most of the wood flakes have been converted to frass (which are rectangular pellets in drier conditions or a dark brown paste in wet substrate) replace the top half with new substrate. If they wander around constantly at the surface, the food has been consumed or is low in food value. If grubs wandering the surface are fat and yellow, they may be looking for an acceptable place to make a pupal cell.

Rutelini larvae start to construct pupal cells seven to nine months after hatching. If the environment is not suitable, they may wander around in the substrate for years. Like most beetles (except flower scarabs) the pupal cell is formed as the larva's jaws push against the substrate until a smooth, oval cell is formed. The cell can be removed in a clump of substrate. There isn't a definite outside wall. This type of pupal cell formation is impossible if the substrate is dry. Wet—not waterlogged—substrate is a requirement. Normally, grubs take three to six weeks to pupate following cell formation. However, if the cell is formed too late in the season, grubs can hibernate inside the cell as third instar larvae until the following spring. Disturbances cause larvae to flee their pupal cells and they will wait at least another month (up to a year) before making a new one. Excessive delays in pupation can kill grubs or shrink adults.

*Chrysina* Pupa

Various techniques increase successful pupation. 1. Place a large piece (small log) of solid, but chewable, decayed wood in the rearing container when larvae appear very yellow and ready to pupate. The grubs chew into the wood to make sturdy pupal cells. 2. Add 10% compost as suggested so the substrate is more easily formed. 3. Place each grub in its own container so other wandering grubs don't disturb it. 4. Do not move rearing containers when larvae begin to form pupal cells.

The pupa stage of these animals is the most crucial, and the entire culture can easily be lost at this point. If they weren't fed wood as outlined, prepupa or pupa is usually the time they turn black and die. These changes are much more energy intensive and complex than the simple molts between larval instars. It's often possible to observe transformations because cells are commonly formed against the bottom or corner of the container. A unique aspect of Rutelini pupation is that larval skin is stretched to fill the cell and surround the pupa rather than being crammed into the far end of the cell. It almost looks like a mis-molt in pupation, which can initially startle someone familiar with other beetles.

*CHRYSINA CAVEI*, MALE REAR LEGS AND PYGIDIUM

In nature Rutelini adults feed minimally on the leaves of specific trees or bushes. *Chrysina gloriosa, Pelidnota lugubris,* and *Paracotalpa puncticollis* feed on juniper, *Chrysina beyeri* and *Chrysina cavei* eat oak leaves, and the leaves on which the grapevine beetle feeds is obvious. In captivity, adults generally ignore most fruits but will accept pear slices and some flavors of beetle jelly.

Jewel beetle mating is similar to most beetles, with the male simply climbing on the female's back. Males with huge, exaggerated hind legs in the genera *Chrysina* and *Chrysophora* use them to hold onto and defend their claims to the

females. After mating, males may continue to ride on the females for a few hours to a few days to protect their investment. Males in the genus *Paracotalpa* are overzealous—four or more males may be seen in a tower on top of one female waiting for the unlikely opportunity.

Gender determination in species where males do not have enlarged rear legs is generally still straightforward. In many *Chrysina*, like *C. beyeri*, the bottom edge of the female's elytra is much wider than it is on the male. Females are usually about 20% larger, but size is not always a good indicator. The female's pygidium appears V-shaped and is flat or rear-facing, while the male's is rounded and curved down and forward.

Jewel scarabs have large wings and are strong fliers. Unlike stags and rhinos, they tend to land on plants or other objects rather than crash-land. Many adults fly after dusk and can arrive at streetlights in huge numbers. Some species, like the little bear (*Paracotalpa ursina*), commonly fly around fields during the day. *Pelidnota* and *Chrysina* are rarely seen during the day.

Although jewel scarabs are not the most nimble of flyers, a lid is necessary to keep the adults contained and to maintain humidity. A solid glass lid should be positioned with .125″ gap on one side, or a screen lid can be covered with plastic wrap to provide a little air exchange while preventing the substrate from drying. Ventilation can be increased as long as the surface of the substrate doesn't dry in less than a month.

## CONCLUSION

Hopefully jewel scarabs will become more commonly cultured over time. The metallic silver and gold beetles, the glorious beetle, and others deserve to be reared by enthusiasts throughout the world. Captive breeding may be the only hope for the preservation of some Rutelini species because continued expansion of agriculture and construction in North and South America could easily poison or eliminate the habitat of species with very small geographic ranges. Captive-bred animals

*CHRYSINA BEYERI*

*PELIDNOTA PUNCTATA*

*PARACOTALPA PUNCTICOLLIS*

*PARACOTALPA PUNCTICOLLIS*

*CHRYSINA GLORIOSA*

might reduce pressure from the dead-stock trade, but the ephemeral adults lay eggs before flying, so over-collecting is improbable if the collecting ground hasn't been turned into a shopping mall.

Jewel Beetle List

*Adults are found on specific foods in the wild as listed. Adult lifespan isn't detailed for each jewel scarab because it is the same across various species and genera: approximately six weeks following the molt to adulthood. Species found over longer periods in the wild represent less precise emergence times or seasonal variation over different years, not greater longevity.*

*Chrysina lecontei*

Chrysina beyeri
BEYER'S JEWEL SCARAB
Found: Arizona and adjacent Mexico. Size: 26-35mm. Adult Food: Oak. The purple legs and green body are reminiscent of a pastel Easter egg. Adults commonly have one or two small blue spots on the elytra, while rare ones are covered in blue spots. Beetles fly to lights by the hundreds after dusk, primarily July to early August. Females lay 15-25 eggs.

Chrysina gloriosa
GLORIOUS BEETLE
Found: Arizona, New Mexico, Texas, as well as Chihuahua and Coahuila, Mexico. Size: 22-

30mm. Adult Food: Juniper. This is the most spectacular U.S. ruteline, and is as handsome as a beetle can be. The adult is striped in liquid metallic gold over a hologram green background. The background isn't always green—it's red on a few rare Texas specimens and purple on uncommon Arizona specimens. This species is found in mixed forests because the larvae eat rotten hardwood (mostly sycamore). On a good night, adults are found by the hundreds at lights, though a few dozen at a light trap is a more common. Adults emerge primarily from July to early August.

*Chrysina woodi*

Chrysina lecontei
Found: Arizona, New Mexico, and widely across Mexico. Size: 20-27mm. Adult Food: Pine. The primary body color is forest green, and the legs and underside are dusted in metallic gold. Some specimens are covered in brown splotches to give a neat calico affect. It is very common and has a huge range through Mexico, but in the U.S. it's not as often found in huge numbers at lights as the other three *Chrysina*. On the other hand, grubs collected from rotten stumps (commonly oak), are most often *C. lecontei*. It may be more common but less strongly attracted to lights. Beetles fly to lights from June to August.

Chrysina woodi
TEXAS JEWEL SCARAB
Found: West Texas. Size: 24-33mm. Adult Food: Black walnut, *Juglans nigra*. This beautiful,

monster jewel scarab is easy to find in huge numbers in the wild, but it seems the local area is devoid of live collectors so only dead specimens are easy to acquire. Captive-bred grubs show up now and then, but live adults are never available. Wild adults are collected from June to October. It can be collected in the daytime, sometimes in large numbers, feeding on walnut trees in the Davis Mountains of Jeff Davis County.

*PELIDNOTA LUGUBRIS* ON JUNIPER

*Paracotalpa puncticollis*
Found: New Mexico, Arizona, and California. Size: 12-16mm. In California it is common in the San Jacinto Mountains of Riverside and San Bernardino Counties. In Arizona it can be found throughout the Verde Valley and Globe area. The type specimen is from New Mexico. The pronotum can be green, gold, or copper, with all three forms usually present in any handful of collected beetles. Adults can be found in juniper trees in March and April. As usual for the genus, the adults are very hairy. Eggs are laid in sand mixed with a small amount of soil at a depth of three or so inches. Rotting grass roots and dead

hardwood leaves are buried in the soil for the larvae to feed on.

*Pelidnota lugubris.*
Found: Arizona in Yavapai, Maricopa, Gila, Pinal, Pima, and Santa Cruz Counties. Size: 15-23mm. Not all jewel scarabs are colorful, though *Pelidnota lugubris* are a handsome, almost unreal, jet black. They are usually caught in light traps. Adults eat juniper, while larvae feed on many types of rotten wood. Females lay 20-30 eggs, and larvae are easily kept.

*Pelidnota punctata*
GRAPEVINE BEETLE
Found: Central and eastern U.S. and Canada. Size: 20-25mm. Adult Food: Grape. Normally the males have black legs and a half-black head, while females are solid light bronze. However, in at least one southeastern population the coloration isn't sex determined. Living adults are usually very pretty with metallic highlights, but they darken and lose their beauty after death. The grapevine beetle is a very common species found at lights from late May to August. Females lay 20-40 eggs. Larvae are common in rotten stumps below the soil and rotten logs above.

# 5

# STAG BEETLES

This chapter provides the necessary breeding techniques and special requirements for culturing the elephant stag beetle in captivity. This is the only huge and impressive stag beetle species in the United States. Most U.S. beetle enthusiasts have considered breeding stag beetles too difficult, but rearing the incredible elephant stag beetle, and other stags, is not hard if the proper steps are followed. It is just that *Lucanus elaphus* has specialized rearing requirements and is impossible to breed if those requirements aren't met.

In contrast to the U.S. hobby, breeding stag beetles in Japan has been popular for thirty years or more. There are several big differences. Japan is home to a number of species in numerous genera that are as big as or larger than *L. elaphus*. Accessibility certainly helped their hobby. Many giant stags there, especially *Prosopocoilus* and *Dorcus,* are easy to rear and very common, so requirements could be learned quickly through trial and error. Food for specific larva, mat, adult food, and precise rearing instructions are available at any department store in Japan. Quality mat and logs are processed and treated to provide reproducible rearing results and remove the guesswork. Imagine the state of any pet hobby (birds, cats, tropical fish, etc.) in the United States if hobbyists had to collect and make their own food. Even with all these advantages, though, members of the genus *Lucanus* are among the least common in the Japanese beetle hobby.

Elephant stag beetle livestock was effectively unobtainable a few years ago. However, the serious enthusiast can now find larvae or adults available sporadically from invertebrate shops and beetle hobbyists. In addition, the related *Pseudolucanus capreolus* and *Pseudolucanus mazama* are commonly bred.

The instructions outlined in this text should be carefully followed to increase the probability of success. While there are different ways to reach this goal, the methods outlined here have proven successful and repeatable. Readers under eighteen must consult their parents, and adult readers are expected to use good judgment. The author cannot be there to prevent the hobbyist from chopping off fingers with hedge pruners or burning down the house while cooking wood in the oven.

### ELEPHANT STAG BACKGOUND

*Lucanus elaphus* is by far the longest and most extravagant stag beetle found in North America. The adult male is a strange creature growing to over two and a half inches. He is outfitted with a wide, oversized, armor-plated head built to hold the massive mandibles. The gigantic, curved, multi-point jaws usually comprise close to half his entire body length. They curve downward and then forward in a manner resembling the form of elephant tusks.

A number of books list the maximum length of *L. elaphus* at 60mm, just under 2.4 inches. (Length is measured from the end of the abdomen to the end of the mandibles. Legs are not

A STAG AND RHINO BEETLE, BOTH POPULAR WITH BEETLE ENTHUSIASTS

TWO U.S. STAG BEETLES: *LUCANUS* (LARGE) AND *PLATYCERUS* (SMALL)

included.) Dead specimens from across the eastern U.S. normally range between 45-55mm with 60mm specimens being the exception. I have collected one wild male at 48mm. However, I reared a captive-bred specimen at 63mm and another at 64mm (a third was even larger, but did not eclose successfully, and the damaged wingcases prevented accurate measurement). These large specimens came from two dozen captive-reared males, which suggests a maximum size closer to 70mm (a little over 2.7 inches).

*Lucanus elaphus* is a member of the family Lucanidae, the stag beetles. Previously, stag beetles were listed in the family Scarabaeidae along with the passalids, trox beetles, dung beetles, rhino beetles, etc.

*LUCANUS* PUPA SHOWING MALE GENITALIA

ORDER COLEOPTERA
SUPERFAMILY SCARABAEOIDEA
FAMILY LUCANIDAE
GENUS *Lucanus*
SPECIES *elaphus*

Most other beetle genera in the superfamily Scarabaeoidea are isolated to a specific continent or geographic region. In contrast, the family of stag beetles is an ancient group with numerous genera found worldwide. Most U.S. genera, including *Ceruchus*, *Dorcus*, *Lucanus*, *Platycerus*, and *Pseudolucanus*, have members found across the globe.

The genus *Lucanus* contains upwards of a hundred species, and about a third of these—primarily large tropicals—are commonly available as dead specimens. *Lucanus elaphus* (North America), *Lucanus cervus* (Europe), *Lucanus cantori* (India), and *Lucanus maculifemoratus* (Taiwan, Japan) are a few members of this genus. Common characteristics include a plated head with ridges along the sides and back, heavily serrated, tusk-shaped mandibles, females with slightly pointed elytra, and extravagant male genitalia.

There has been a strong push in the last decade to reverse 150 years of literature and

*PSEUDOLUCANUS* PUPA SHOWING MALE GENITALIA

common usage by suppressing the genus *Pseudolucanus*. Many hobbyists and foreign authors have begun to list *Pseudolucanus* as *Lucanus*, but the change is based on personal preference rather than morphology or solid taxonomy. *Pseudolucanus* males do not have the complex jaws with numerous denticles of *Lucanus*, nor a plated head at any size. *Pseudolucanus* males have extremely short male genitalia (obvious on the male pupae), versus the lengthy, coiled *Lucanus* genitalia. Larvae, at least for U.S. species, are also easy to differentiate by a close look at the head capsule. The difference between *Pseudolucanus* and *Lucanus* is the ratio of the length of the cranial suture to the length from the cranial suture to the clypeus (2.5:4 *Pseudolucanus*, 3:4 *Lucanus*).

There are around three dozen stag beetles native to the United States. Only members of the genus *Pseudolucanus*—*P. capreolus*, *P. mazama*, and *P. placidus*—compare to *L. elaphus* in body size. However, they possess relatively small, simple mandibles, which set them an inch behind in overall length. The large, bulky *Lucanus* and *Pseudolucanus* are hobbyist favorites, while members of the remaining genera elicit little excitement because they are tiny. *Dorcus parallelus* is the next largest and seldom tops out at over an inch. The other thirty or so native Lucanidae—genera *Ceruchus*, *Diphyllostoma*, *Platyceroides*, *Platycerus*, and *Sinodendron*—are in the neighborhood of half an inch.

## COLLECTING

Nearly every book with a section on U.S. beetles contains an illustration of the elephant stag beetle. Even my 1984 dictionary includes a life-size color photo in the beetle section. I stared at that photo thousands of times before my first encounter with *L. elaphus* in late June of 1996. Although I live in the natural range of this species, I had never seen one dead or alive. Books were the only reason I knew this beetle existed.

The elephant stag beetle had always been a primary objective on collecting trips. Still, over many years and trips I never saw or found a body part. (When collecting, you're far more likely run across a body part than a live animal. Adults are seasonal and on the move, but the head, elytra, and legs can stick around for years.)

In fall of 1995 my brother said his friend mentioned finding monster stag beetles inside rotten logs "all the time" where he used to live. He said they looked like the photo of an elephant stag rather than the common red-brown stag. Though a remote chance and only having the name of a town, I decided we'd drive the fourteen hours on our next collecting trip. I chose the end of June because many books state June-July is the time for *L. elaphus*. We stopped at gas stations on the way down to buy gas, food, and to search.

I was not excited when I found my first elephant stag beetle (June 27). I had no idea I had found the animals I had been hoping to find for so long. Six hours from our destination, behind a gas station on the side of a wooded hill, under a small, partly rotten log—five-inch diameter by two foot long—I found six extremely tiny grubs, less than a quarter of an inch long. I knew immediately these were stag beetle grubs, but wasn't impressed. I've run across uncountable numbers of tiny stag grubs while collecting, and they've always been larvae of tiny stags. Like a man who buys a lottery ticket every week for so long that he stops checking the numbers, I tossed the grubs into a deli-cup and continued my quest for neat inverts. How did I immediately know the tiny animals were stag grubs? They look nearly identical to scarab grubs, but Lucanidae larvae have a very different looking rear.

After hours of driving and numerous stops we made it to our destination. The town was disappointing. We saw no promising wooded areas and nowhere to collect. We continued south down the interstate another hour. It was getting late, so we stopped for coffee. In a short walk around the gas station, we found a very large dung beetle (*Dichotomius carolinus*), a male red-brown stag (*Pseudolucanus capreolus*), and a grapevine beetle (*Pelidnota punctata*).

We went back four exits to a private campground and pitched camp. Once settled, we drove up and down the highway exits between camp and our exit, checking gas station lights (far more powerful than the little black light trap we hung up back at camp). Over the next hour we found a male eastern Hercules beetle (*Dynastes tityus*), five male and three female red-brown stag beetles, wheel bugs, fiery searchers, giant silk moths, dobsonflies, huge longhorn beetles (*Prionus* and *Ergates*), and other insects. We set up a black light funnel trap back at camp with a Polyphemus moth as the only interesting catch.

This night, at 11 p.m., I had my second encounter with the elephant stag beetle, and this time I was excited. On the northeast corner of the building, twelve feet off the ground, a magnificent male stag looked down at me. He was just

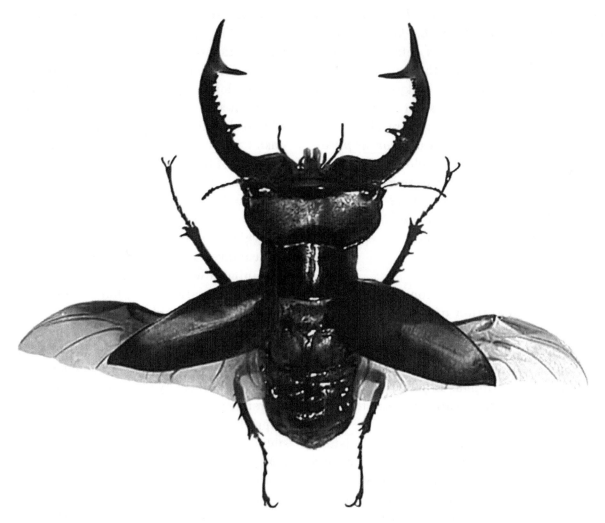

*LUCANUS ELAPHUS* 61MM F1 MALE WITH SPREAD WINGS

sitting where he had landed on a wall I had scanned three or four times in the last hour. My adrenaline pumped. There was no way I was going to try to knock him off with a stick, because he would fly off and I'd hate myself for years. I had my brother stand on my shoulders, no time to take off shoes or discuss alternate methods. Ryan is my little brother, but he weighs as much as a normal guy. Had I had time to think, I might have thought better, but the excitement of finding the elephant stag overshadowed the pain I hardly remember now.

This is still the only living male *L. elaphus* I've seen in the wild. I have seen many since, but all are captive reared or captive bred.

The next morning we woke up and dug through the camp's woods, uncovering *D. tityus* grubs, *Scolopendra* centipedes, grapevine beetle grubs, and more. At night we returned to our gas station and found more *P. capreolus* females walking along the pavement. At 10 p.m., as the first raindrops of a nightlong thunderstorm began to fall, I grabbed a small beetle from the pavement. On close inspection I knew it was not just another *P. capreolus* female. The apex of the elytra was slightly more pointed than round, there wasn't much of a red tint to the brown, and her femurs were black instead of yellowish. I had found a mate for my male. She was smaller than all but the smallest *Pseudolucanus* females.

I brought the pair home and set up a 2.5-gallon aquarium with rotten wood and dead leaves. The male and female weren't shy, and any eggs laid would certainly be fertile. In typical stag behavior, the female chewed up some of the wood and tightly packed it against larger chunks of wood. In each she laid an egg. There were three problems I wasn't aware of at the time:

The wood chunks were small and sparse, so only a few eggs were laid.

The moisture level was inconsistent because of excessive ventilation. Sopping substrate at the bottom and dry at the top contributed to the low number of eggs laid, and caused eggs to die and mold.

In excitement I disturbed most or all of the eggs. I didn't set them up in containers, but just put them back.

The male lived a month and the female continued on for two. If any eggs hatched they died shortly afterwards. Not one grub was produced.

A few months later, I happened to glance at the container of tiny grubs I had discovered a few hours and a few hundred miles before finding the male stag. I was amazed to see a large L3 stag grub peering at me through the side of the container. From the size of the grub and collection location, it had to be either *P. capreolus* or *L. elaphus*. This was the first big stag grub I had ever seen.

The 16-oz. container all six grubs had been placed in would have been huge if I hadn't mistaken the L1s for L3 larvae of tiny stags. (There is no way to tell L1 from L3 if the species is unknown.) The container was far too small for six L3 *Lucanus*. I dumped out the substrate and found four third instar grubs. Of course I wished I had known a month earlier that they would turn out to be the larvae of big stags. Still, the loss of two out of six was not bad. If I had waited another month, there would have been only one or two. Each of the remaining grubs was placed

in its own 16oz. cup filled with rotten wood. I decided to use only wood and not to supplement the larval diet with dog food because the risks outweighed the benefits. After all, there were only four grubs.

In early spring the following year—about nine months later—each of the larvae carved out an oversized, elongate pupal cell against the bottom side of each container. It was possible to see parts of each grub through the side and bottom. After two months the first one molted into a pupa. I tilted the container carefully to get a look at the head. The pupa wriggled and after a minute the face finally came to where I could see it. Wow! There was no mistake! The gigantic mandibles of a male elephant stag were there, folded down against the body.

This was incredible! I not only had elephant stag beetles, but I had reared them from hatchlings. As soon as the last grub pupated, I realized there was an insurmountable problem. All four were males. After a month I had four beautiful adult males with major head and mandible formation. They ranged between 45mm to 50mm. (The wild-caught male had been 48mm.) I kept them refrigerated at 55° F and held onto them for nine months, but couldn't find a female. I was surprised by the long adult lifespan (as the wild male had barely lived a month). I eventually sent them—still alive—to a friend who collects dead beetles.

The third time I found *L. elaphus* was in mid-August a few years later. There was an old log partly buried in the ground on a sloping, wooded hill. The log was five inches in diameter and eight feet long. At one end a pair of bess beetles (*Odontotaenius disjunctus*) were living with their grubs. At the other end were four L3 *Lucanus elaphus* grubs. The end with the stag grubs was more damp, solid, and half-buried in the ground.

The four *L. elaphus* grubs were brought home and placed in individual rearing containers. Sadly, three grubs were greatly stressed by the shipping or substrate change, and were dead within two days. The fourth grub grew and formed a pupal cell after a few months. The grub turned out to be a female. Since I didn't have any males, I put her in a mini-refrigerator outfitted with a thermostat and kept at 55° F. Sixteen months later she was still in perfect health and was placed in an egg-laying cage with a captive-bred male.

The fourth time I found *L. elaphus* was on July 3, 2003. I rolled back a log about eight inches in diameter. Below the log was an adult female elephant stag. She had chewed into a stretch of the log and apparently was at the task of laying eggs. I found an L3 nearby, which didn't survive. Both were kept in a small container in my pocket for three days. Sadly, the female was at the end of her life and only lived a week. There were no noticeable signs of egg laying. It was a wonderful surprise to unearth a male and three female L3s from the cage that November. All future adults and larvae would be captives.

Every *L. elaphus* collected was found in rotting hardwood only. (Even very rotted logs are easy to tell apart because pine branches grow in concentric, perpendicular rings. Hardwood branching is sporadic and often at forty-five degree angles.) I searched nearby areas, but the rotting logs were pine and contained very little insect life.

When driving along in the eastern U.S. it seems like there are thousands of miles of old hardwood forests. On inspection, it's all re-growth. If there are any truly old trees, there's just one, or they're in a straight line that once marked the boundary between fields. Every accessible inch of hardwood forests in the east was cleared for farmland in the late 1800s to mid-1900s. Even the mountainsides were cleared. Fields and pastures were later abandoned as productivity improved. Many areas were replanted with pine, though the original hardwoods eventually took over and started killing the pines. Even in older forests that have returned to hardwood, all the rotting logs are often pine. Despite extensive hiking, I've only seen two old growth areas (more than a hundred

feet across) and both were in the middle of new growth and near rock formations.

The elephant stag is difficult to find. It was probably very common before all the eastern forests were razed. This beetle is not exceptionally rare, but most hobbyists have never encountered a live one. As the re-established eastern forests continue to age and rotten pine is replaced with rotten hardwood, the elephant stag may become common again.

THE BEETLES

Elephant stags are sexually dimorphic to the extreme. The female is small with short, sharp jaws and normal proportions. The male is a monster with an oversized pronotum, plated head, and tusk-like jaws.

The female uses her compact jaws to carve up wood for egg laying. She drills tunnels through decomposed wood to hunt down and eat other beetle grubs and pupae. Small brush-like mouthparts sweep in food. She's able to chew the prey's skeleton, but only ingests the liquid portions, leaving behind the shell.

Male stags use the massive mandibles to fight for food and mating rights. They can puncture holes in large insects like hermit beetles, and slurp fluids from the wounds. However, they're not nearly as protein hungry as the female and will accept sugary liquids as food. *Lucanus* have minimal appetites compared to many stags.

Combat can be vicious. Males are heavily armored but can be damaged or killed in a fight. Males may be alternated for mating to prevent fights and insure females are fertilized. *Lucanus elaphus* are less aggressive than many stags and two or three males can coexist in a 10-gallon or larger breeding cage with some hiding areas.

The adult stage is the longest portion of the elephant stag beetle's life. In nature, most of that time is spent in the pupal cell. Adulthood normally lasts nine to twelve months, with males dying first. Wild-caught adults are nearly always at the end of the cycle and will live only a few days to a few months.

*LUCANUS ELAPHUS* FRONT VIEW

AVERAGE TIME FOR *L. ELAPHUS*
LIFE STAGES AT 70-74° F

Adult: 45 weeks
Egg: 4 weeks
L1: 4 weeks
L2: 7 weeks
L3: 24 weeks
Prepupa: 8 weeks
Pupa: 4 weeks

These beetles are built like tanks and can survive a few days of extreme dryness. Still, desiccation is not good for them and they should be kept on moist substrate. More than a few days of dryness will kill them, even if they don't die immediately.

Occasional handling doesn't bother these beetles at all. They aren't overly energetic and the claws aren't sharp, so they are easier to handle than most large beetles. *L. elaphus* males don't attack humans. Many male stags can inflict painful bites and draw blood if someone is foolish enough to put a finger between their jaws.

Elephant stag males lack interest in biting fingers, although they don't lack the ability.

Beetle jellies are a handy food, though they can be expensive in the U.S. They are designed for these beetles and are easy to use. Many foods spoil in a few days, but jellies can last over a month after being opened. *Lucanus elaphus* don't have much of an appetite, so one jelly a month feeds a cage with three females and a male. Beetle jelly formulations have changed in recent years and can become infested with grain mites, so fruit jellies without additives are preferred.

High protein foods given to females are thought to improve egg production (though more for voracious feeders like *Dorcus* and *Odontolabis* than *Lucanus*). In nature, females pin down prey in the rotten wood. Females are not designed to outrun food. They can overpower huge prey but are unlikely to catch food that can run away. Mundoworm (*Zophobas morio*) pupae are an inexpensive and readily acquired food source, but some forethought is needed since only larvae are sold. Mature mundoworms are placed in individual, empty cups and transform into immobile snacks (pupae) after a month.

Adults feed on a number of liquid and semi-liquid foods. Females can chew on more solid foods in order to slurp fluids. Various fruits work, but bananas are among the more readily accepted. Good liquid foods include 100% real maple syrup (mixed 1 part water, 1 part syrup) or brown sugar and water mixture (mixed 1 part brown sugar, 3 parts water). A few drops can be placed on the banana or pupa or poured in a small cup filled with paper towel. The paper towel prevents beetles from falling in and helps keep the liquid from pouring into the substrate when the container is tipped. (Fruit and sugar aren't natural foods.) The beetle's mouth can be placed on the food to induce feeding—a hungry beetle will stay. The visible mouthparts look like tiny orange brushes wiping in the fluid.

Elephant stags do not feed when they first become adults. They wait two to six months before feeding, mating, and laying eggs. The first months are spent in hibernation. Adults can be handled during this time. Ideally, they should be kept at 50°-65° F for two months after the molt to adulthood. A cool basement area works well.

Avoid high temperatures over 80° F that can yank them out of hibernation and severely shorten their lives. They will not mate during diapause, so it doesn't matter if males and females are left in their pupal cells or placed in a breeding cage. When adults begin to feed, they are ready to mate and lay eggs.

As adults grow older, loud buzzing sounds can be heard from the cage just after sunset. Elephant stag beetles have huge flying wings capable of taking them long distances. New keepers often don't realize these beetles can fly. They only fly at certain times. Otherwise, the translucent golden flying wings are neatly folded and hidden away under the elytra. Stags are strong fliers and are commonly found around the bright lights of gas stations, sometimes a mile or more from wooded areas.

Adults wandering around the cage (most commonly after sunset), flying, or mating indicates they have come out of hibernation. The beetles possess vast stores of energy and may survive seven or eight months at room temperature without food (much longer at cooler temperatures). However, it's important to offer food as soon as activity starts or they die early,

*LUCANUS ELAPHUS* PUPA

not having enough energy to mate or lay eggs. They don't have huge appetites and need to be fed only once or twice a week.

Following hibernation, males spend most of their time near the food dish. Mating usually takes place on or next to the dish. Never try to mate a pair in a small container with shallow substrate. Unlike rhinos and flower beetles, male stags can kill the female if she can't get away. There doesn't appear to be a mating ritual; the male simply climbs onboard.

Considering the sparse population and vast distances they must travel to mate in nature, pheromones are certainly part of the reproductive process. Both sexes are well equipped for flying and both have similarly developed antennae, so it's difficult to say which gender broadcasts pheromones. The related and similarly dimorphic rhinoceros beetles are known to broadcast a congregation pheromone. Like rhinos, the male stag is outfitted for battle and can't chase the female underground, so a similar strategy seems likely.

## EGG LAYING

Ova are off-white, small, round and just under 2mm in diameter. Freshly laid eggs are less than half that size. They absorb moisture and expand to full size in two to three weeks. As eggs expand they become less susceptible to damage, but are still comparable to tiny water balloons. Any puncture or excessive pressure destroys them.

Certain stag eggs, including those of *Homoderus* and *Dorcus*, nearly always die if handled, while others like *Odontolabis* and *Phalacrognathus* are rather sturdy. *Lucanus elaphus* eggs, as well as *Pseudolucanus* ova, are inbetween. It is best not to handle ova. If unearthed by the hobbyist or a female stag, place eggs on soft, damp mat in a small container. Put a few pinholes in the lid and set container back in the egg-laying cage (to maintain humidity). Wait a minimum of two days after hatching before transferring to a rearing cage.

The female can spend incredible amounts of time laying a single egg. She uses her jaws to cut

rotten wood into tiny pieces. She also collects moist mat from around the cage and mixes it with the wood. Commonly she packs the mix against the substrate just below the log. She may chew a shallow depression in the log and pack the wood-mat mixture a quarter inch deep. Sometimes she spends days chewing a four-inch tunnel through the log and packs the mix all the way to the entrance. As each egg is laid, she uses her retractable ovipositor to form a hollow around the egg. The hollow is a little larger than the (fully expanded) egg. Only one egg is laid in each prepared spot, though many prepared spots can be found along one small log. Over time, the female carefully deposits 20+ ova. Packed mat and tunnels through the wood are normal indications of egg laying.

The egg-laying cage should be at minimum a five-gallon aquarium. A ten-gallon or fifteen-gallon is preferable. Surface area is important in choosing the cage (so a 5-gallon bucket doesn't work well). Though eggs are usually laid in the top 3", the substrate should be 4"-6" deep to minimize eggs unearthed by tunneling females.

Logs used in the egg laying cage should be three to six inches in diameter. Sawdust from cut logs should be retained for the mat. Logs laid lengthwise (rather than vertical) are preferred for laying. Multiple logs in varying stages of decomposition will provide the largest number of possible egg laying sites. Most stags will only lay eggs in logs that are solid. If the surface of a log can't be scraped away with a fingernail it is too hard. *Lucanus elaphus* prefer damp logs and chew up a bit of wood for use in egg site construction. Still, females of this species do not like mushy, disintegrating logs, but choose logs that could be broken apart with a hammer and a little effort.

The lid should be solid glass or plastic. A few small holes or a thin gap between the tank and lid provide plenty of ventilation. A solid lid maintains a high and consistent moisture level throughout the cage, which is very important. If the top of the substrate dries out in less than a month, there is too much ventilation.

To prevent eggs and grubs from being eaten or damaged, there should be no more than one female per square foot of substrate surface area. Substrate preparation can smash previously laid eggs. Most stag beetle females will kill and eat other larvae they encounter while digging. Females have some ability to differentiate larvae of their own species, but not eggs or tiny grubs. When disturbed, larger grubs make noticeable noise—they stridulate by rubbing their last pair of legs against the middle pair. In nature, females can be dead before their own eggs hatch because they oviposit at the very end of their lives. However, L3 grubs from the previous year's females are often in the same logs and stridulation prevents them from being eaten.

Avoid using an egg-laying cage for more than one species. If different species are kept together, females spend most of their time hunting down grubs. This taste for grubs is likely to help remove competition in nature. Certain genera like *Lucanus*, *Pseudolucanus*, and *Odontolabis* stridulate, but others like *Dorcus* and *Phalacrognathus* do not. Females may not be able to identify specific species, so stridulating larvae might be protected from females of any stridulating species. Non-stridulating genera voraciously consume any grubs, including their own species.

The following setup type has been used successfully to collect eggs from both wild-caught and captive-bred *L. elaphus*: Begin with a 10-gallon aquarium and solid glass lid. Place a few firm but well decayed logs on the bottom. Fill around logs to 2 inches depth with compost manure. Add a few more logs and fill with 4 inches of crushed rotten wood or 2 inches coconut fiber and 2 inches rotten wood. Place a rotten log and large wood chunks on the surface.

## GRUBS AND PUPAE

Elephant Stags molt twice as larvae for a total of four moltings, including those to pupa and adult. Hatchlings or L1s molt after a month to L2s and in another six to eight weeks to L3s. The L3 grubs

molt into pupae around six months later. (The prepupa stage is a phase of late L3 and is not accompanied by a molt.) Another month and the pupa molts to adult.

*LUCANUS ELAPHUS* L3

Grubs are cannibalistic and should be kept separate. They aren't primarily predacious—unless they are starving. A dozen can live together in a small log, but only for as long as food is available. L1 and L2 grubs are tiny and nearly impossible to overcrowd, but L3 are very easy to overcrowd. Even if they don't kill each other they may bite each other's legs and abdomens. Some damage carries over to the adult stage. Abdominal damage is usually invisible on the adult. Leg damage will heal depending on its location. Large damaged areas will prevent proper molting and discourage successful development.

Unless the egg-laying cage was substandard or the female died prematurely, she should lay too many eggs to be reared in that cage. She wanders during laying in nature, but keeps returning to the same spots in captivity.

Grubs are dug up at L1-L2 and placed in separate rearing containers. It is difficult to safely

*PSEUDOLUCANUS CAPREOLUS*
HEAD CAPSULE

*PSEUDOLUCANUS CAPREOLUS*
FEMALE, OVARIES SHOWING

*PSEUDOLUCANUS MAZAMA* PUPA

remove grubs from hard, solid wood so some-times it's best to wait for more of the wood to be consumed. A plastic 16oz. container is suggested for each larva—a medium-size deli cup. The lid should snap on tightly and have 6-10 pinholes for ventilation. Clear containers make it easier to monitor food, growth, pests, etc. Each grub is reared to adulthood in this container. In smaller containers, humidity is difficult to maintain, food runs out quickly and larvae become stunted. Oversized containers eliminate the need for add-ing wood, but inhibit supplemental feeding and make checking on health difficult without dump-ing the container (as grubs can die from exces-sive handling). It is possible to rear two females in one 16oz. container, but two males together will turn out very small and can damage or kill each other.

High humidity must be maintained in the rearing container. The substrate should be very damp but not dripping wet. Excessive ventilation is dangerous. Holes in the lid are made with thin pins (not tacks or thick pins) to prevent drying. Larvae survive dry periods but will shrink. If moved to proper humidity, any survivors will become tiny adults.

In a pest-free 16oz. container, additional wood is normally not needed. Brown paste or powder replaces lighter colored, textured wood as it is consumed. The substrate level also drops. The top half of the substrate should be discarded and replaced if the grub is still feeding and 70% of the wood has been consumed. Replace all sub-strate if millipedes, roundworms, or earthworms are noticed.

The primary food of wood and mat can be used to grow large beetles. The degree of wood decomposition has a major affect on the size and health of the grubs. Dark brown, extremely rot-ted wood often used for rhinoceros and flower beetles is too rotten for stags. Stag grubs started on highly decayed wood normally become small adults and can experience high die-off. The wood must be decayed, but it is surprising how hard a wood the grubs can chew into.

*ODONTOLABIS STEVENSIS* FEMALE PUPA

Even if the mat and wood pieces are perfect, monster beetles are nearly impossible without supplemental nutrition. Substrate and supple-ments work hand in hand. Supplemental nutri-tion without quality substrate results in runts or deaths. Processed animal foods help to grow huge beetles. Most types high in protein and fat work well: dog food, cat food, fish flakes, ferret pel-lets (#1), turtle pellets, etc. Many pests includ-ing nematodes and mites relish supplements. Uneaten food can cause population explosions of these tiny creatures, which in turn irritate and stress stag grubs. Excessive rotting food can poi-son the air and suffocate larvae. It is better not to use supplements if overfeeding isn't avoided. For tropical fish, a general rule of thumb is "don't feed more than the fish will eat in 5 minutes." For stag larvae, don't feed more than the grub can eat in 2 days.

Grubs are tiny before L3, so feeding kibbled pet foods is difficult and can be harmful. L1 and L2 larvae are supplemented with a brown sugar and water mixture (1:3). Two normal droppers full (about 2 ml) are squirted into the substrate every two weeks. The sugar and moisture encour-ages the wood to mold, which may help grubs grow larger. High moisture is fine, but avoid water-logging the substrate.

Feeding L3s should occur once every two weeks. A small piece of the food (about one-third

*ODONTOLABIS STEVENSIS*

*PSEUDOLUCANUS MAZAMA*

the size of the grub's head) is placed in the tunnel near the larva. If the food is not placed nearby, the grub may not find it. A hole can be carefully made with a pencil, the food is dropped in, and the hole covered over with mat. Grubs eat food covered in white mold, but avoid later stages of mold (green, brown, or black). Remove and change food placement if it unnoticed by the larva within a few days.

Larval die-off is a normal part of rearing stags. Up to 10% of the grubs can turn black and die. Die-off is most common within a few days following major disturbances like shipping, removal from logs, or transfer to a new cage. The percent is variable, but die-off greater than 10% is the result of poor substrate quality, excessive pests, or low moisture. Keep a close eye on die-off. Dead larvae decompose quickly, so the only sign of a dead grub may be its head capsule. (A molt looks different because the head capsule splits into three sections.) Sometimes, dead larvae don't collapse and are covered in fungus growth. Do not reuse the substrate—discard the container or soak it in bleach and water.

If high die-off occurs, follow these steps:

1. Heat-treat the substrate.
2. Use 100% decayed hardwood substrate.
3. Maintain high humidity.

If performed in time, deaths will be eliminated though adults may still be stunted.

## ALTERNATIVE FEEDING METHODS

Log method: this technique is zero-maintenance and can result in extremely large adults. It can take months or years longer, and is better suited for genera like *Dorcus* and *Homoderus*, which lay eggs in solid decayed logs. One drawback is the progress and health of the larva can't be seen. It can take a few years to find out a larva died a few days after it was put it in the log. Leaving the last few larvae in the logs of the egg-laying cage is the log method, just with more space and less intent.

1. Submerge a small, solid, decayed log in water for 48 hours. Minimum log size is 3" diameter by 4" high.
2. Drill a 1.5" deep hole in one end of the log. The hole should be as wide as the larva is long.
3. Place 1 larva in the hole and carefully pack full of damp mat and cover (using tape or tacks and plastic).
4. Cover both ends of the log with plastic wrap. Hold in place with rubber bands.
5. Place in an area with limited airflow and moderate to high ambient humidity to prevent the log from drying out.
6. Wait up to 2 years.

The log method has also been used successfully for certain large longhorn beetles (Cerambycidae) that feed on rotten logs. Reared species include *Acrocinus longimanus* and *Prionus* species. The only difference is the logs can be kept a little drier.

Kinshi bags or bottles are commonly available in Japan. This method has produced the world's largest *Dorcus curvidens* stag beetles. Kinshi works well for species that prefer early-stage decayed wood like most *Dorcus* and *Phalacrognathus*. Other stags that feed on softer decayed wood like *Lucanus*, *Pseudolucanus*, *Prosopocoilus*, etc., do not do well on kinshi. They grow slowly, or stunted, and may die. All kinshi is not equal. Beetle-rearing kinshi is formulated with additives to help beetle growth, while kinshi used only to grow edible mushrooms is unlikely to result in impressive beetles.

Ground-up wood chips (usually oak) are mixed with various components like agar, MSG, sugar, and vitamins, then cooked in a pressure cooker. The most common and only necessary additive is 10% flour. The other components are not required; they are used to speed up fungal growth or in hopes of helping larvae grow better. The pressure cooker is used to destroy fungal spores that would compete with the chosen fungus. The mixture is cooled and inoculated with a small piece of the fungus. Fungus needs air to grow, so the open end of the bottle is covered with a microporous filter. Oyster mushrooms in the genus *Pleurotus* are recommended. Special filters and *Pleurotus* seed stock are available from mushroom supply companies. Also, oyster mushrooms are commonly available at large grocery stores in the U.S. To avoid contamination, inoculation usually takes place in a sterile bench or a trash bag that has been sprayed with peroxide solution to kill spores. It's important to avoid contamination because if contaminated they have to be thrown away. The added fungus can't be sterilized (or it would be dead), so some cultures may become contaminated no matter how careful you are. A good kinshi bottle turns completely white over the next few months as the fungus grows over the media. A contaminated bottle changes to green or brown.

Kinshi has some drawbacks. In its usable form, it has a very short shelf life and can be rapidly destroyed by fungus gnats and mold. Surplus kinshi can be dried to make it last years instead of weeks but estimating surplus and drying without contaminating is difficult. Homemade kinshi requires a bit of time and money—a pressure cooker is an especially large expense. Nevertheless, any hobbyist who has seen *D. curvidens* reared on kinshi will agree it's worth it. In the U.S., hobbyists may not find this method advantageous because our bigger species don't like kinshi. Still, it could be neat to try to grow a "monster" 30mm *D. parallelus*. (Many, but not all, *Dorcus* species do well on kinshi.)

There are inexpensive alternatives for making kinshi, but there's a good chance every bottle will become contaminated and have to be thrown away. These alternatives include using a microwave instead of a pressure cooker, 2″ layer of cotton instead of a microporous filter, and collecting seed fungus in the woods.

Accelerated fermentation is supposed to improve the nutritive qualities of rotten wood. Unlike kinshi, this can't be used successfully with fresh sawdust or woodchips.

1. Grind rotten wood into small flakes. Large pieces will not work.
2. Place in a sturdy trash bag. Even thick (1.1 mil) black trash bags allow for some air exchange, which is needed. On the other hand, thin bags not only tear easily, but provide too much air, which stops fermentation.
3. Thoroughly mix in 5-10% accelerator. Flour is normally used, but half flour and half sugar, or sugar only can be used. If desired, a small amount of powdered vitamins can be added (use powdered pet vitamins or crush a human multivitamin).
4. Add enough water to make the mix wet, not dripping.
5. Tie the bag shut.
6. Open the bag and mix the wood every third day until the smell is nearly gone—fermentation has a very strong smell. If it doesn't stink, part of the above procedure was left out or fresh sawdust was used. Accelerated fermentation takes 9-15 days and works quickest in a warm location. Even if the bag is placed in a cool area, fermentation can raise the temperature of the bag to over 100° F.

It's possible to determine the gender of grubs at L3. Mature male larvae are normally twice the size of females and the head capsule is larger, but sizes are not reliable. Locating the female's ovaries is more accurate, but they can be difficult to see. On either side of the dorsal abdominal surface, three segments back from the rear, there are two clear areas. Ovaries are not connected to the exoskeleton and move as the grub moves, but can be seen through the clear spots depending on how the grub is holding its body. They look like gray-brown beanbags for *L. elaphus*. It can take some time to see, but no matter how the male holds his body, nothing can be seen that looks like the ovaries. Ovaries are easier to locate on species

*PHALACROGNATHUS MUELLERI* MALE (© OLDRICH JAHN)

like *Dorcus curvidens* (ovaries are large yellow-gold beanbags) and *Odontolabis siva* (ovaries are a thin, light yellow, broken line).

L3 spend weeks constructing the pupal cell. The interior of the cell is oddly oversized and male cells are often ten times the size of the pupa. The walls are an inch or two thick and can consist of most of the substrate in the container. *Lucanus elaphus* usually form cells against the bottom corner of the container. Cells of this species are normally formed in June or July. Six to eight weeks after the cell is made, the grub transforms to a pupa.

By the time stag larvae are ready to pupate, they may have killed anything that could threaten them in the pupa stage. However, if all substrate was not heat-treated, carefully inspect for pests. Pupae are sensitive and should not be handled, but if any earthworms, wireworms, microworms, millipedes or centipedes are present—dump the container. Clean and place ½ inch of damp peat or coconut fiber on the bottom. Smooth out the substrate (a flat or lightly indented surface is best for molting—egg-shaped "rhinoceros beetle" cells cause wing deformities), place the pupa on top, and replace the lid.

Four weeks are spent as the adult develops inside the pupal skin. The eyes turn black and later the legs and mandibles begin to darken. The beetle breaks free from the shell and the elytra and flying wings are pumped with fluid as they expand to normal proportions. The elytra change from white to adult coloration within a few hours, but will not completely harden for weeks.

Entomophagous fungus can threaten healthy pupae. This type of fungus is rare, but can kill every pupa. By the time you realize there is a problem it is already too late. The pupa appears normal but never changes to an adult. Infected pupae feel hard, break in half like a cheese curl, and are white inside. Healthy pupae are full of liquid. This type of fungus is preventable, as it usually results from reuse of cages or substrate. If rearing containers are reused, they should be soaked in bleach water. Heat treatment doesn't kill fungus spores and would melt most plastic containers. Don't reuse uneaten substrate even when a healthy adult was produced. Keep in mind, while entomophagous fungus is a serious threat, it is extremely rare. 99% of the time, pupae overgrown with green or green-white fungus were poorly kept as grubs and died before the fungus grew.

## WOOD AND MAT MATERIALS

Color and hardness are useful indicators for choosing wood. Brown and dark brown wood is usable in the mat and is often very soft. Extremely dark or black wood should be avoided. Yellow or white wood is preferable, but it can range from hard as a rock to easily crushed by hand. The occasional wood overgrown with bright orange fungus also works. Crumbling yellow-white logs are good for feeding larvae, but logs should be more solid for egg laying. A hammer can be used to gauge the hardness of a rotten log. Give the log a good whack. Untouched wood is too hard. If the hammer is barely slowed down by the wood, it's too soft. If there's a dent, it should be good. Other indicators of proper quality include the presence of longhorn tunnels and mushroom or bracket fungi growth.

Good logs can be hard to find in city areas, but there are alternatives. Rotten branches fall from trees all the time. Even tiny branches are usable. Also, bark can be used even if the rest of the log is solid and unusable (as in most firewood). Branches and bark are chopped into one to two inch lengths and fed to grubs. Oak, locust, and beech work well, but any hardwood should be acceptable. Useful wood has been dead for years. Smash the branch into 1"-2" shards using a hammer. Branches are unusable if too hard to

be smashed. "Green" wood does not work. Again, the interior should be yellow, white, or light tan, not dark brown. Stag larvae prefer earlier stages of decay, wood that rhinoceros beetles have a difficult time with and flower beetle grubs can't touch. Any branches soft enough to be crushed by hand can be ground up and used as mat.

Larval food can be made from a seasoned oak log. Using a hole drill bit (1" bit), drill through the log and retain sawdust for the rearing cages. Avoid wood that is very difficult to drill. Also avoid logs if the bit goes through without resistance. Much of the log can be made into sawdust and leftover chunks buried in the mat.

Hardwood bedding can be purchased in bulk (normally aspen or poplar). Keep damp and age until it smells like mushrooms rather than sawdust. Aging takes a few months to more than a year. Wood will not decay if dry.

Mat should take up about a third of the container and fill spaces between the wood pieces. Mat helps maintain a constant moisture level. It is nearly impossible to adjust, determine, or maintain moisture with only wood chunks. Water or dry mat material can be mixed in to quickly adjust substrate moisture level. Grubs tunnel through the mat to move between logs and for leverage to chew into hard chunks of wood.

Common mat components include aged sawdust, rotten leaves, compressed coconut fiber, soft rotten wood, and compost. Aged sawdust and crushed rotten wood are best. Coconut fiber and ground rotten oak leaves are a close second. Peat, potting soil, and other materials that present little nutrition can be used as mat, but grubs might become stunted or die.

Compost is important in the egg-laying cage and is helpful as part of the mat. Avoid using more than 10% compost in rearing cages, because it makes a very poor primary food. Some compost seems to improve nutrition, but is most helpful in aiding formation of pupal and molting cells. Compost manure, mushroom compost, or leaf compost all work.

*HOMODERUS MELLYI*

PEST CONTROL

Unintentional guests often introduced with substrate:

*Mites:* Tiny white or tan arachnids from the order Acari. The most common are members of the Family Acaridae, known as storage mites because certain species commonly infest grain and food products. Mites are found in rotting plant matter everywhere. Unlike other destructive pests, they easily spread from cage to cage and may never be completely eradicated. (Dark-winged fungus gnats also get into caging, but barely reproduce on rotten wood.) Full-grown mites are much smaller than a grain of salt and often never grow bigger than the period at the end of this sentence. They tightly adhere to the larval skin and adult armor. They are looking for transportation and don't attach until food begins to run out, but then stay indefinitely. Removed mites do not leave scars on the larval integument, and adhere to indents rather than joints on the adult armor. Large numbers of storage mites correspond with high larval mortality because population explosions result from poor substrate and overfeeding. Storage mites don't feed on healthy beetles or larvae, but do eat the dead. Parasitic mites are far larger and only attach to the insect's joints, which are thin and easily pierced for feeding. Parasitic mites have not been observed on

*L. elaphus.* Removal: Most exposed mites can be removed safely from the adult beetle with a toothbrush. Some hobbyists recommend the use of a cotton swab and rubbing alcohol, but stay away from the spiracles and mouth. Drying is the only technique that will kill every mite, but it can kill the beetle with overuse. Place the beetle in an empty cup for one to two days. The mites dry up and fall off. The cup must be empty because any substrate or food will protect mites. Drying is a thorough removal method, but may be a little harder on the beetle. Don't put a clean beetle back in infested substrate. Heat treatment kills mites in the substrate. Do not attempt to remove or dry mites from larvae or pupae, because they are likely to die before the mites. Avoid freshly dead leaves and too much dog food to prevent mite population explosions.

*Nematodes:* These tiny roundworms live in the substrate and feed on rotten leaves and wood. They are usually 2-5mm long and a fifth of a millimeter wide. Nematodes don't directly attack stag larvae except in plague proportions. However, they rapidly reproduce and consume available food. Excessive numbers damage eggs and pupae. Nematodes may be the worst pest of all because the hobbyist usually doesn't notice them. Removal: Heat treatment. Cut down on the use of leaves and avoid excessive dog food to prevent population explosions. Nematodes hide in tiny cracks and under loose silicone in aquariums. Any reused aquarium should be filled with bleach water and left to sit for 24 hours, or set out to dry for a week or two.

*Earthworms:* Though large, these polychete worms are nearly invisible in rotten wood and leaves. Adult worms cover themselves in wood and mucus during dry periods. If a little water is added to seemingly lifeless wood, a number of adult earthworms can appear. Eggs and young are even harder to see. They eat the grub's food and the presence of large amounts of worm feces sickens stag larvae. Worms can rapidly destroy the usefulness of an egg-laying cage. Earthworms crush pupal cells, which kills prepupae and

*LAMPRIMA ADOLPHINAE*

pupae. Removal: Earthworms are easily killed by heat treatment. Large grubs like *Pseudolucanus* and *Lucanus* can eat earthworms in normal rearing containers like a 16-oz. deli-cup, but seldom encounter earthworms in larger containers.

*Wireworms:* These are not worms but grubs of click beetles (Elateridae). Most types resemble the common yellow mealworm. They do not bother stag adults or larvae. They eat wood, but gladly burrow through pupal cell walls right into the side of the stag pupa for lunch. Wireworms almost never occur in plague proportions like other pests, but a single tiny wireworm can kill the largest stag pupa with a single bite. Removal: Heat treatment. In appropriate-sized rearing containers, stag grubs usually kill large wireworms.

*Millipedes, isopods, centipedes:* Millipedes and terrestrial isopods eat the stag larva's food. Centipedes feed on millipedes, mites, etc. All three are usually harmless to stags, but if there are holes in the pupal cell, they can chew on the pupa and kill it. Removal: Heat treatment. Stag larvae don't eat any of these.

*Snails:* Tiny land snails eat wood, leaves, and dog food. They can reproduce quickly and eat some wood, but are insignificant compared to the above pests. Removal: Heat treatment.

*Springtails:* Extremely common and with minimal ability to jump containers, but these are completely harmless. Removal: Heat treatment.

Treating substrate for pests takes extra time but is worth the effort. Certainly, it's possible to be lucky and find materials without pests, but luck is not reliable. Substrate infested with pests becomes worthless and must be thrown out and replaced. When treated, less substrate is required. Cooking greatly reduces "mysterious" die-off and lack of egg laying. Worms can destroy an egg laying cage and the beetles may be dead long before the problem is realized. Not treating for pests is the number one reason for runts and death.

Cooked wood is not sterilized, just heat-treated. Mites, nematodes, earthworms, wireworms, millipedes, pillbugs, snails, and centipedes are completely removed with adequate heat treatment. Cooking removes these pests that compete for food, stress out, and kill stag larvae, but it doesn't eradicate fungi eaten by the grubs. Molds and fungus spores aren't killed by heat treatment, but time is required for fungi to regrow. New substrate added at any time during the process should be cooked before use.

In a short time there is more fungus in the wood than there was prior to cooking, because pests aren't eating it. Fungal regrowth is generally of no concern because a few days is insignificant to a stag's life cycle, grubs have fungi in their guts, and cooking is more likely to increase than decrease the initial food value. If cooking destroyed the nutritional content of food, Americans would be much thinner.

Substrate that is removed, heated, cooled, and replaced because of a pest infestation when a larva is in late L3 stage can cause premature pupation (resulting from either the change in consistency, moisture, sudden decrease or increase in food value, or the absence of live pests or molds). This technique works consistently for different genera and species, but only for older, yellow grubs. Also, it might not affect pupation if there isn't a pest problem to correct. Control groups under identical conditions waited months longer. Premature pupation isn't harmful, but the beetles will be smaller. This may be useful if the hobbyist is having trouble with females pupating long before males.

Mat and small pieces of wood can be cooked in the microwave oven. Fill a 1-gallon ice cream pail (drill some holes in the lid for venting) with substrate. Pour in ¼ cup of water and cook on high for 10-12 minutes. Carefully check the surface and cook longer if any pests are present. It will be hot! Don't handle until it has cooled to room temperature. Microwaves cook unevenly and it can be surprising how many things survive what seems a good cooking, especially if water isn't added. Microwaves usually aren't big enough to handle logs.

The conventional oven handles a lot of mat and large logs but takes more time. It works well to consistently kill accidental pests. It is important to cook the wood for long periods under low heat (two hours at 250° F). Unlike the microwave, water isn't required for heating. However, water should be added to dry materials to reduce the chance of combustion.

The hobbyist must be careful when cooking wood or mat. Hobbyists under 18 need to ask Mom or Dad first. Keep in mind the following considerations.

1. Do not cook dry substrate. Dry logs should be immersed in water for a day or two prior to cooking. Crushed wood or leaf mat can be hand mixed with water till moist.
2. Avoid pines—conifer wood catches fire at lower temperatures than hardwood.
3. Always use a timer.
4. High temperatures cause burns—use potholders. Be careful!

5. Cook leaves or crushed wood in a closed oven bag (available at grocery stores to cook turkey, ham, etc.), not on an open tray. More substrate can be cooked at a time and small pieces won't fall onto the oven's heating element.
6. Do not attempt to speed up the process by cooking at high temperatures.
7. Follow manufacturer's guidelines for oven use.
8. Cook when the spouse isn't home to avoid questions about the peculiar wet-wood smell.

Temperatures don't need to be extremely high to eradicate pests. If it's sunny and hot outside, you can throw a bunch of bags of substrate in the trunk. Park the car in the sunniest spots you can find for a few days. Also, the accelerated fermentation and kinshi methods eradicate pests.

## SUMMARY

The elephant stag beetle is one of the most spectacular U.S. insects and a wonderful pet. The adult is easy to care for, long-lived, and harmless. It is not a pest and the predacious females might even slightly reduce longhorn beetle populations. Hopefully this book will help advance the keeping of this magnificent native beetle.

Rearing may sound time-consuming because of the numerous variables. However, less than a few hours a year are required to raise dozens. Remember the following husbandry parameters:

1. Heat-treat all substrate prior to use.
2. Use white-yellow decayed hardwood.
3. Use supplements but do not overfeed.
4. Keep a constant high humidity for all stages.
5. Be sure to feed hungry adults.

With close attention, you may rear the first *L. elaphus* over 70mm. Good luck!

OTHER U.S. STAG BEETLES

## Dorcus parallelus

Maximum Length: 26mm. Found: Eastern and central United States This shiny, jet-black species, known as the antelope beetle, is considered very common, though it can be more difficult to happen across than *L. elaphus*. Adults are seldom, if ever, attracted to lights and spend most of their time underground in rotting stump roots. (I collected a pair next to a rotting tree stump in 1987 and found one male walking along the ground in 2001.)

While rotten wood is required, females prefer to lay eggs in wood that can barely be called soft. The female's mandibles are thin, widely spaced, and very efficient. She can chew holes through a log that can barely be dented with a hammer (though she cannot chew into freshly dead wood). If she carves huge galleries and tunnels through the wood, it is far too soft. She only lays eggs in very solid rotten wood. Egg laying is evidenced by small shallow pits (less than ½" deep) packed with "sawdust." A good egg-laying cage requires lead time. Place oak logs in a five- or ten-gallon aquarium. If possible, find logs with 1" or thicker bark on the side. Cover with extremely moist, crushed, well-rotted wood and place a glass cover on top. The logs should become decayed enough for egg laying in 3-4 months and will remain usable for a few years or until consumed. Eggs are laid in mid-summer.

*DORCUS BREVIS MALE*

Eggs shouldn't be disturbed. In mid-fall, carefully remove larvae from logs by prying apart wood with a screwdriver. Pupation takes place in February and the molt to adulthood in March. It then takes a month for the exoskeleton to fully harden. *Dorcus* sit in the pupal cells for months, but can be removed and placed in an egg-laying cage at any time. Still, adults won't begin eating or breeding until four months after the molt to adulthood.

## Dorcus brevis

Maximum Length: 20mm. Found: Central eastern U.S. This is our only other U.S. *Dorcus* species. It's very similar to *Dorcus parallelus* but can easily be differentiated because it has a small knob on the outer corners of each elytron. It's supposed to be more difficult to find. The male pictured was collected along with a number of larvae in January in South Carolina. Specimens were located in the underground, rotting stump roots of white oak, *Quercus alba*.

## Pseudolucanus capreolus

Maximum Length: 42mm. Found: Eastern and central U.S. and northeastern Canada. The red-brown stag beetle is the second longest U.S. stag. Adults are shiny and bright red-brown as the name suggests. This species is also commonly called the "pinch-bug" because it draws a little blood from curious children when they put a finger between its jaws. Major males can have larger bodies than major *L. elaphus*, but the mandibles are still short. Adult beetles are easy to tell apart at a glance, and even the females look different, as described in the collecting section. As mentioned in the background section, it is easy to differentiate *Lucanus elaphus* larvae from *Pseudolucanus* by the ratio of the length of the cranial suture. On the other hand, while there can be differences in shade or size, our *Pseudolucanus* larvae can't be consistently differentiated from each other. Males are commonly found around lights, often still on their backs the next day. Females are attracted to lights, but are long

*PSEUDOLUCANUS PLACIDUS*

gone by daybreak. Adults are normally collected in late June and early July. Some years they seem to be everywhere and other years it's hard to find one.

The set-up for egg laying is nearly the same as for *L. elaphus*. Well-decayed, rotten logs are buried in a mix of finely ground rotten leaves and wood. Eggs are laid low in the substrate so a

*PSEUDOLUCANUS MAZAMA* SPREADING WINGS

minimum depth of six inches is recommended. The egg-laying cage should contain almost as much mat as logs. Females produce 15-40 eggs. 16oz. rearing containers with wood substrate are used for each larva. Pupal cell formation begins in April. Cells are usually just a little bigger than the pupae. Adults molt out in late summer to early fall and wait till the following May to lay eggs.

### Pseudolucanus mazama

Maximum Length: 39mm. Found: South-central and southwestern U.S., into Mexico. *Pseudolucanus mazama* adults are dark brown, almost black, with a satiny finish. Females differ from our other *Pseudolucanus* and *Lucanus* in that they don't have a triangular extension between the jaws. Adults are attracted to lights and common.

Employ the same egg-laying setup as used for *L. elaphus*. *Pseudolucanus mazama* is the least picky in choosing egg-laying sites and an excellent species for a beginning hobbyist. Eggs are laid July-August. Pupal cell formation begins the following May-June. They spend a few months transforming to adult, but only eat and mate the following summer. (1 year is spent in development and 1 year as an adult).

*Pseudolucanus placidus*
Maximum Length: 32mm. Found: Michigan and Ontario, Canada, south to Louisiana and Alabama. Even dead specimens of this species are difficult to acquire in the hobby. Nevertheless, it is a common species represented by uncountable specimens in museums. Adults are dark brown and moderately shiny. Males have two inner teeth on the mandibles—our other two *Pseudolucanus* only have one inner tooth.

EXOTIC STAG BEETLES

*Dorcus titanus*
Maximum Length: 100mm. Found: Numerous subspecies are found across Asia, including Malaysia, Taiwan, Japan and the Philippines. Subspecies look nearly identical but can vary greatly in maximum size—some as small as 50mm.

This monster is closely related to the tiny U.S. *Dorcus* species, as well as to the most famous pet stag, *Dorcus curvidens binodulosus* from Japan. Large *D. titanus* males are the heaviest stag beetles in the world. This is a monstrous species with bulky, saw-toothed mandibles ending in a broad, inward curved tooth. The body is wide and flat and every part of the beetle is jet black. *Dorcus* are fast moving for stags, but most species open their jaws, pull in the legs, and remain motionless when disturbed. *Dorcus titanus* is an exception. It likes to attack and rarely adopts the stereotypical defensive posture. When handled, the male opens and closes its mandibles, while large males produce an ominous scissors-like sound. The jaws easily pierce skin. Males should not be kept in the same cage.

*DORCUS TITANUS*

Use the same egg-laying setup as for *Dorcus parallelus*. Egg to adulthood takes six to eight months, though larger males take an additional year if the log method is used. Adults live six to eight months. However, temperate subspecies, specifically *D. t. sika* from Taiwan, are supposed to survive two years if provided a cool period.

*Homoderus mellyi*
Maximum Length: 55mm. Found: Africa. *Homoderus mellyi* males are satiny-tan yellow with

*DORCUS TITANUS* PUPA

*HOMODERUS MELLYI* MALE

*LUCANUS MACULIFEMORATUS* SMALL MALE

*HOMODERUS MELLYI* FEMALE

a few dark brown markings. They have huge mandibles and a wide head and pronotum. Even large males have a normal head, but major males have an oversized head with a large scoop at the front between the mandibles. The little females are glossy dark brown with large yellow markings.

Eggs are laid primarily in logs partly buried or on the surface. Egg-laying logs should be kept

on the dry side of moist. Logs must be well rotted and slightly soft, but far too hard to break apart by hand. Females have efficient jaws resembling *Dorcus* and likewise lay eggs in shallow pits carved on the log's surface. In normal rearing cages, mature grubs begin by forming pupal cells from the outside and then burrow into the middle to form a cell just a little larger than the adult beetle. Larvae look normal, except large L3 males develop bulbous abdomens to resemble *Odontolabis* grubs. Egg to adulthood takes six to eight months and adults live another six to eight months.

*Lucanus maculifemoratus*
Maximum Length: 85mm. Found: Asia, including Taiwan and Japan. This species is similar to *L. elaphus*, but is much larger and has a fuzzy appearance due to numerous yellowish setae on the carapace. Care is the same as for *L. elaphus*, but individual rearing containers should be 32oz. and larvae eat a ton of rotten wood. *Lucanus maculi-femoratus* takes a few months longer to

*ODONTOLABIS DALMANNI INTERMEDIA* MAJOR MALE

*HEXARTHRIUS* SPECIES FROM MALAYSIA

*ODONTOLABIS DALMANNI INTERMEDIA* MINOR MALE

*PHALACROGNATHUS MUELLERI* FEMALE

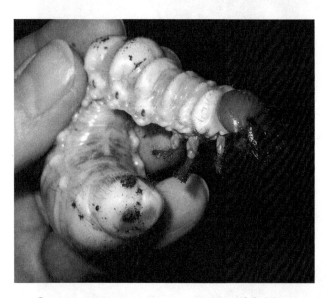

*ODONTOLABIS DALMANNI INTERMEDIA* L3 MALE

*PHALACROGNATHUS MUELLERI* MALE

reach adulthood but the adults are ready to breed around the same time. Adults live 4-5 months.

*Odontolabis dalmanni intermedia*
Maximum Length: 106mm. No logs are needed in the egg-laying cage. A ten-gallon tank with four or more inches of damp, compactable mat works well. Female *Odontolabis* species compact substrate against the bottom of the container and lay eggs inside the clumps. Eggs are hardy for Lucanids, and careful handling doesn't kill them.

Larvae of members of this genus have a peculiar shape to them. They look different from most other stags even as L1 because the end of the abdomen is huge and bulbous. They form outside-in pupal cells like *Homoderus*. Egg to adulthood takes 12-18 months.

*Odontolabis stevensi*
Maximum Length: 80mm. Found: Indonesia. *Odontolabis stevensi* adults are glossy black with a wide yellow margin along each side of the

elytra. *Odontolabis* are active, energetic, and behave like a ground beetle. They don't conform to the plodding, methodical movements of many stags. This species may have the loudest of all Scarabaeoidea larvae. Their stridulation can be heard from thirty feet away. Mat should consist entirely of ground rotten wood. Compost or ground leaves may seem satisfactory in the substrate, but most (if not all) beetles will end up dying in late L3 or during pupation. Adults live six to ten months.

### *Phalacrognathus muelleri*

Maximum Length: 60mm. Found: Australia. This is one of the most exquisitely colored stags in the world and certainly earns its common name, rainbow stag. It entered Japan and Europe in the late nineties as one of the most expensive beetles ever. However, it turned out to be one of the easiest to breed and the price for a single grub plummeted from $1,000 to as little as $6 within two years.

Females are not picky and lay eggs in the different setups used for *Lucanus, Homoderus,* and *Dorcus.* Larvae have elongate, tapering abdomens, which gives them a very different look from normal lucanid grubs (*Lamprima* also have this odd shape). *Phalacrognathus muelleri* larvae grow well on normal wood but tend not to get very big that way. Kinshi or the log method work better to produce large adults. Six to eight months is taken from egg to adulthood. The beetles live four to twelve months, but usually six to eight.

*CYCLOMMATUS METALLIFER* SMALL MALE

# 6
## DARKLING BEETLES (TENEBRIONIDAE)

This chapter is written in hopes of inspiring others to keep and rear some of the spectacular beetle species in this family. While many hobbyists presently rear *Tenebrio molitor* and *Zophobas morio* to feed reptiles and other insectivores, few keep darklings as pets. The information provided here should offer a new possibility for keepers who are trying to decide which beetles to rear.

Long adult life and endearing personality should make this group among the most appealing to the beetle enthusiast. Adults of most species live a few years, which far surpasses a few months for many pet beetles like flower scarabs and rhinoceros beetles. They don't have sharp claws and can hardly pinch or bite. The beetles are curious, active, and commonly explore their captive habitat while energetically waving antennae. Some beetles collect and store seeds, dig burrows to collect dew, or display curious social behaviors. The immatures are energetic and inquisitive.

Most U.S. beetle enthusiasts pass over this family because the most impressive natives are difficult to come across and the truly gigantic exotics can't be imported live. Even dead specimens of the largest tropicals are difficult to locate and are relatively expensive. (The most expensive dried specimen costs nearly three hundred dollars for a single beetle of moderate size.) It seems strange there's no darkling hobby to speak of in Europe or Japan, since they occasionally import various spectacular species from Africa and the Middle East. Though we have some very nice species here in the states, there are dozens of truly spectacular, giant tropical species that would make amazing pets.

A DARKLING AND FRIEND

My introduction to the beauty of darkling beetles was in 1994 at a Bugfest presented by a nature center about thirty miles from my home. One of the displays included a dozen large *Eleodes* walking around on a sand substrate. I had long been familiar with mealworm beetles, but was amazed with these long-legged, bulbous

146

*PHLOEODES DIABOLICUS*, IRONCLAD BEETLES

*ALOBATES PENNSYLVANICA*

monsters measuring in at almost an inch and a half. Next to the display was a glass beer bottle filled with a few dozen dead darklings with a sign explaining that this bottle was found containing all these dead beetles, as it had acted as an accidental pitfall trap. The sign went on to say that littering is deadly to large numbers of these handsome creatures as they wander their desert home. The display gave me a desire to locate some of these creatures in order to keep them as pets and to learn how to reproduce them. Rearing information was distinctly lacking, but through trial and error I was able to rear some to adulthood and keep them continuously for fifteen years.

U.S. native giant darklings have gained a small amount of popularity as pets, science projects, and displays since the early 1990s. Some of the large southwestern *Eleodes* species have been kept and bred in recent decades since they are common, make impressive displays, and can be easy to raise. Our most sought after pet species, the blue death-feigning beetle, had been difficult to acquire till recently and it had been falsely rumored they wouldn't lay eggs in captivity. The large *Eleodes spinipes* and *E. suturalis* are attractions at a few insect zoos (though insect zoo specimens are 100% wild-caught). *Zophobas* and *Tenebrio molitor* are often kept for children's science fair projects as a display of metamorphosis.

The instructions outlined in this chapter are based on experiences rearing a few dozen North American species, as well as partial captive reports for one from Israel and one from Africa. The methods outlined here have proven successful and repeatable with the listed species, but there is much to be learned and with the large variety of species a truly complete guide to rearing darklings could fill libraries (or a decent hard drive). There are numerous tiny species that are easy to rear, but the emphasis here is on giant darklings.

This chapter attempts to follow the most accurate taxonomy, but darkling taxonomy can be trying. There are a number of subfamilies some

BLUE DEATH-FEIGNING BEETLE

taxonomists like to elevate to family status, often with different persons viewing only a few of these as subfamilies. There are multiple trains of thought. Zopherinae is the only debatable subfamily mentioned in the text because it's the only one with species of interest to the hobbyist. Some tenebrionid genera like *Eleodes* can have many similar species of uncertain status or multiple synonyms. Lastly, there can be generic changes or moves like *Asbolus* for *Cryptoglossa* and *Neomida* for *Hoplocephala*. Two genera mentioned in this chapter have names that sound similar to the names of other insects. *Asbolis* (similar spelling) is a butterfly genus and *Taurocerus* (similar spelling) is a true bug genus, while *Tauroceras* (same spelling) is a generic synonym for bullhorn acacia.

### DARKLING BEETLE BACKGROUND

Members of this huge family come in any color you want, as long as that color is black. There are exceptions, but even the "colorful" species tend to be black and white or black with a colored metallic sheen. (While it would seem the name *darkling* refers to their coloration, it is actually a reference to behavior.) Darklings make up for their lack of color with a vast array of body shapes and textures. They can be long and cylindrical, round and bulbous, or have long or curved legs. A number of small species resemble and move like ants. New World *Embaphion* and Old World *Endustomus* have large flattened extensions, while others such as *Blaps* and *Eleodes* have elytra extended into a rear sword that can be used for sparring over mates. *Prionotheca* is surrounded by spines and covered in hairs. The body surface may be wrinkled, punctate, striate, dentate, costate, hirsute, granulate, or a combination of textures. A few even change color: gray and blue *Asbolus* exoskeletons become nearly black when wet and return to normal coloration when dried.

Darkling beetles are members of the superfamily Tenebrionoidea with a dozen or so other families, including the very similar ironclad beetles (which are usually listed as part of the family Tenebrionidae but have been removed and replaced by numerous authors). There are 17,000-20,000 species worldwide depending on subfamily designation and new discoveries. About a thousand occur in the United States.

ORDER COLEOPTERA
SUPERFAMILY TENEBRIONOIDEA
FAMILY TENEBRIONIDAE

Names for these beetles and larvae are legion, though common usage is darkling and mealworm. The root of the common name for the family *Tenebrio* means "lover of darkness." This name results not from their prevalent dark coloration, but from *Tenebrio*'s habit of hiding in dark crevices during daylight hours. Darkling is a fairly common name for the majority of species, though a few exceptions are colorful and a number of large desert species could be considered day-active. Another commonly encountered name is "false wireworm" in reference to the beetle larvae. Wireworm is the common name for larvae of click beetles—family Elateridae—since they are long, thin, and cylindrical like a piece of wire.

*BLAPS HISPANICA* (© DORTE BENGTSSON)

(There is no specific character useful in definitively telling every larvae of the two orders apart, but wireworms tend to have a wedge-shaped head with a small, fixed labrum and more uniform, less pronounced legs. Larvae of the Perothopidae are even more difficult to discern from tenebrionids. Perothopidae adults look like click beetles that can't click, but are not to be confused with false click beetles, false darkling beetles, or false wireworms.) Some elaterids vary greatly from the wireworm name and look like a giant ant lion larva or a three-dimensional string of geometric diamonds. Although few darklings naturally feed on meal, larvae of the most well known species, *Tenebrio molitor,* are commonly known as mealworms, and since the name is so well-established and the appearance rather consistent, it is appropriate to call all larvae in this family mealworms.

Though a unique family, some can be confused with other beetles. A number of species are hyperactive and difficult to discern from ground beetles (family Carabidae). Most darklings move deliberately and are generalist feeders, but some are highly energetic and predatory like ground beetles. The tarsi structure can be used to tell them apart since darklings have five segments on the front and middle feet, but only four on the back pair of tarsi. In the same way you can tell fungus darklings from similar looking pleasing fungus beetles (family Erotylidae). The African *Calognathus* has huge jaws and looks a lot like a stag beetle. *Taurocerus* and males of the common grain pest species in the genus *Gnatocerus* also have notable jaws, while *Bolitotherus cornutus* has thoracic horns like a tiny rhinoceros beetle. They're easy to discern from stags and rhinos because the antennae are usually made up of eleven segments and look like a string of beads (moniliform). Some are clubbed at the end, but the segments aren't flattened, and there is no elbow as in Scarabaeoidea. Other common darkling features are elytra covering the abdomen, usually covering the sides, the first tarsal segment always being longer than the second on the rear tarsi, and not having fleshy tarsal pads. Some of the tiny species can be difficult to tell from other families without magnification because the miniscule size makes it hard to see any features.

Darkling beetles are harmless to humans but have some defensive capabilities. Their primary protection from predators is a very tough exoskeleton (rarely fitted with spines) that most animals can't bite or chew, and is the reason adults are rarely used as feeders. A less universal but common defense is the ability to excrete quinones from the end of the abdomen or behind the head. Adults have strong biting jaws, but with few exceptions they have a large labrum covering their jaws, so they do not attempt to bite in self-defense.

The powerful defensive secretions some darklings are capable of emitting vary in intensity, form, and use. The fluid contains powerful organic acids known as quinones that smell strongly and can temporarily stain skin with high enough concentration. The fluid doesn't hurt unless it gets in the eyes or an open wound. The volume and concentration is generally weak so that it doesn't cause skin discoloration like the secretion of giant round millipedes. Most species that use this defense release it from the pygidial gland at the tip of the abdomen and don't excrete enough for it to be visible as a fluid. It is broadcast as a very strong smell. A few, notably *Zophobas* and relatives, also release fluid from a gland in the pronotum. Use of quinones is variable in potency, specific acid content, and use. Some species possess extremely weak secretion ability or don't spray unless handled roughly. The few highly defensive species can be "trained" with regular handling but can "forget" if not handled for a few days.

*NEOMIDA BICORNIS*

Species that have defensive glands at the end of the abdomen use the glands in different ways. Some exude an odor or spray with no visible sign. Others extend the abdomen to expose the lighter-colored pygidium during use. The most impressive are eversible glands that look like gelatinous horns or tentacles shooting from the end of the abdomen. Eversible glands expose their content as they are turned inside out, which is directed by the gland itself or movements of the rear legs.

All defenses can be thwarted. *Eleodes* are often called head-stander beetles because they stick their rear up in the air to offer the least pleasant aromatic area for eating. The grasshopper mouse in the desert southwest has learned this trick and sticks *E. longicollis* beetles rear-first into the

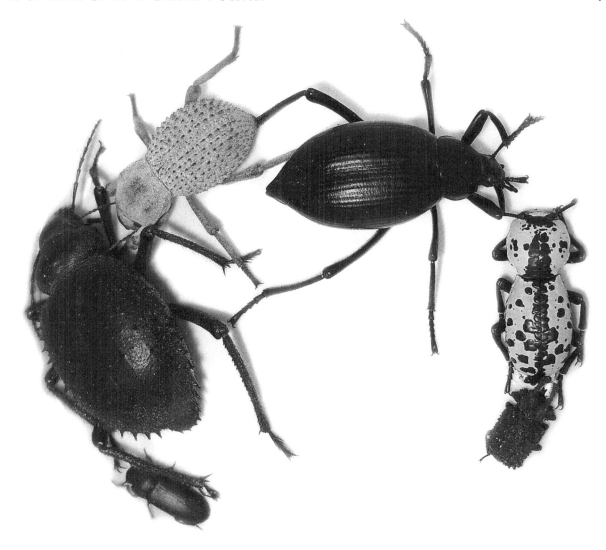

A VARIETY OF DARKLING BEETLES

sand, eating only the front half. The large defensive glands and shell are left in the sand.

Mimicry is associated with common darkling defense. The large *Moneilema* cactus beetles have no defensive glands, but when disturbed stick their large black abdomens up in the air just like *Eleodes* darklings. A defenseless June beetle, *Phyllophaga cribrosa*, is a darkling mimic. *Diploptera punctata*, the Pacific beetle mimic cockroach, looks like a brown darkling complete with fake elytra suture, but isn't defenseless, as it produces a quinone that even smells the same as some darklings. Some big black darkling species stick their rear in the air like head-standers but have no defensive glands.

Head-standing behavior was associated with a creation story of the Cochiti Pueblo of the southwestern U.S. It so happened that *Eleodes* was assigned to place the stars but dropped them, which resulted in our disorganized galaxy. To this day the beetle is ashamed and hides its face when anyone approaches.

A Mayan myth about a prince turned into an ironclad beetle has resulted in a long history of using the living beetles as jewelry in Mexico. Ironclads resist desiccation and some species survive months without food. For this reason

*Megazopherus chilensis* survives long periods of being decorated with gems and used as living jewelry tied to a little chain.

Darklings are first among venerated beetles. The radiant sun beetle, *Prionotheca coronata*, has been found wrapped inside mummies in five- to six-thousand-year-old Egyptian tombs (even before the famed sacred scarabs). These darkling beetles were made into amulets thought to protect the dead on their journey to the underworld.

Darklings are famous for their mastery of desert habitats but they are common in forests as well. In many desert areas across the world, darkling trails and adult darklings are the primary sign of animal life during the day. The greatest morphological variation, largest sizes, and most number of species are found in the world's deserts. Forest species tend to be flattened and smaller, since they're most common under loose bark (and don't need to keep their bodies away from hot desert sand). Even large species like *Alobates pennsylvanica* are two-dimensional in comparison to their rotund desert cousins, and although the legs are relatively long, they are held out to the sides.

The rotund body of most desert species is hollow, as flying wings have been traded in for a moisture retention system. They breathe in and out of this cavity to limit moisture loss due to respiration. Large size reduces surface area to volume and is another adaptation to reduce moisture loss. Most get moisture from morning dew, while some collect it on their own bodies, standing so it drips towards their mouths. The physical structure of the body and surface texture are specially formed for this function.

Darkling beetles have a tiny little stripe of an eye, as though eyesight were an afterthought. The eye seems black and lifeless since it lacks the reflective surface, see-through upper layers, and prismatic characteristics found in many insect eyes. However, these compound eyes usually have hundreds of facets and at least provide decent motion detection. Other commonly kept beetles like stags and rhinos have huge, glistening, globular eyes that can make up half the mass of the head. Humans often associate large eyes with cuteness, which could be a significant reason for limited interest in this family. Tiny eye bands are truly less familiar and more alien.

An incredible variety of darklings are found across the globe. Handsome U.S. species include horned fungus beetles, death-feigning beetles, and ironclads. The largest North American species are in the genus *Eleodes*, a huge genus with very different looking species. South America boasts some handsome, two-inch *Nyctobates*, spectacular horned *Tauroceras*, and large, metallic-green, spider-like forest species. In Europe members of the genus *Blaps* (commonly called cellar or graveyard beetles) resemble *Eleodes* but can grow even larger and are among the largest beetles found in northern Europe. The Namib desert in Africa is famous for its many large, active, and strange species. The African continent boasts dozens of species that exceed 50mm in length, as well as the large, rotund tok-tok beetles (also known as tok-tokkies, usually *Psammodes* species) which are famous for using their bodies as drums by beating them against rocks to make noises to attract mates. I once owned a specimen from Africa that came in with some giant ground beetles. It looked like a big black *Anthia* with the head and striate elytra of *Eleodes*, and was two and half inches long. I was never able to learn the genus. (I sent it back to the collector so he would know what to look for, so I could purchase more specimens. Like the dog dropping his bone in the water trying to get a bigger bone held by his reflection in the water's surface, I never saw it again.) One of the strangest species, *Helaeus perforatus* from Australia, resembles other dish-shaped darklings, but the "dish" (elytra) is filled with two strips of long, brown "hair." The large, black-and-white *Sternodes caspius* hails from central Asian deserts. The world's longest darkling comes from tropical Asia. *Pheugonius mjoebergi* from Borneo looks like a giant *Tenebrio* with enlarged rear legs similar to a frog beetle. It's not as massive as some shorter

*ZOPHOBUS MORIO* (TOP),
*MYLARIS* SPECIES FROM EL DORADO,
ARGENTINA (BOTTOM)

*ZOPHOBUS MORIO* SHOWING
EVERSIBLE GLANDS

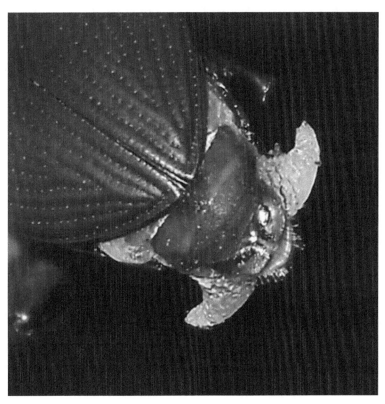

African species, but it is long and can grow up to 79mm.

## COLLECTION

Darkling beetles are very rarely caught in bait or light traps, but they are highly susceptible to pit-fall traps. Beetles are hunted by checking under tree bark and flipping rocks. The bracket fungi feeders are the easiest to find, since their homes can be seen from far away. Larvae of various species are commonly encountered inside the wood of rotten logs.

## BEETLE HUSBANDRY AND EGG LAYING

Adult lifespan is long compared to most beetles and varies greatly by species, but is seldom as long as some reports. Most will live a year or two under reasonable conditions. Adults can't molt to mend damage, so older animals are often missing a few tarsi or part of an antenna. Wild beetles are usually in good shape, so old specimens are likely an artifact of captivity. Males tend to be the longest-lived. A few reports claim a male *Eleodes* survived twelve to fifteen years in captivity, but I've only observed a few odd individuals surviving as long as four years. *Asbolus* may be the exception, with adults reported to commonly exceed a decade, but documentation is lacking.

Darkling beetles are famous for their resistance to dryness, but though the majority of species are found in desert areas, they still require moisture on a regular basis. Most of the desert species are more sensitive than grain pests and may die if there is no access to water for a few days. Conversely, species that survive dryness the best are also the most susceptible to dying from too much humidity when combined with limited ventilation.

Adults should have access to a water dish or a damp area of the substrate. (In nature they can drink water from the settling dew many mornings.) The water dish should be very shallow or filled with gravel to prevent drowning. A slice of fruit or potato is an alternative, but must be replaced regularly to limit an infestation of mites or flies.

Ventilation requirements for darklings are much higher than for other pet beetles. (Restricted ventilation reduces the risk of dehydration for stags and scarabs.) The beetles may survive a few months with restricted ventilation and damp substrate, but it will kill them prematurely. The lid should be metal or nylon screen to allow for good airflow, though most large species can't climb glass and have no flying wings, which makes a lid unnecessary.

In desert areas the beetles are normally found under rocks and boards, but occasionally can be seen running here and there on a hot sunlit day. Nocturnal behavior is likely an important way to avoid natural predators, but the hot sun is probably the major risk in desert areas. Desert species are known to emerge in mass on cloudy days. Species found in forests are never seen in the sunlight. Although desert darklings are more active at dusk, they commonly walk around terrariums in captivity at all times of day. They nearly always emerge to drink when the cage is watered and will come out for food if it's something they like. They can be seen chewing on dog food or cricket carcasses all times of day.

Hiding spots provided in captivity are used with zeal, but don't measurably improve health or longevity. Nevertheless, hide spots do provide a limited level of protection against desiccation if the keeper forgets to add water to the dish or cage. Any flat board or rock can be used, but the coconut huts and cork bark sold at the local pet store work great, and their light weight reduces the chances of smashing or pinning animals. Small cork bark tubes are a favorite hangout. Smooth objects should not be used, since darklings cannot climb them.

Occasional handling doesn't bother the beetles at all. They aren't overly energetic, don't try to pinch or bite (they have capable, strong jaws, but don't use them in defense), and the claws aren't sharp, so they are easier to handle than most large beetles. If they're dropped on the floor now and then, they do fine. Depending on the species' chemical defense, handling is more likely to annoy the keeper than the beetle.

Darklings are omnivorous scavengers and eat items from rotten leaves to dead animals in nature. In captivity they'll feed on a variety of fruits, vegetables, and pet foods like dry dog or cat food. They also cannibalize pupae. Dead crickets or other soft-bodied dead insects can be offered, but aren't necessary. Adults do not have huge appetites, so it could take a beetle several months to eat a piece of food as large as itself. It's difficult to say with certainty which foods are best for adults because the effect on them isn't externally visible and the relation to egg production is difficult to judge. Most commonly kept beetles are short-lived, so larval care determines most adult functions. (Many stags and rhinos lay just as many eggs if they're not fed.) Darklings are long-lived beetles, so feeding is likely an important factor in egg laying and longevity.

Most species are extremely tolerant of temperature changes that would kill most other animals. The tropical *Prionotheca coronata* pictured here survived a power outage and subsequent freeze that killed every other animal at a reptile importer. Temperate species commonly undergo winter diapause as beetles. Sometimes beetles are seen streaking across the desert (disturbed by a predator?) on a hot day that would shortly exhaust an animal of lesser construction. In captivity, room temperature (70°-75° F) is recommended, though hotter temperatures or cycles could possibly be necessary to initiate egg laying in some species.

Many species have given up the ability to fly. Most, if not all, of the largest species not only can't fly but also have no hind wings. In these species the front wings develop separately in the pupa and fuse together during the molt to adulthood—the fused joint is so strong that elytra from a dead specimen snapped in half often break through the elytra rather than the fused suture. Most of the small species (5mm or less) have wings. All of the grain pests and feeder species

fly very well. Even so, genera that have well-developed hind wings like *Tenebrio* and *Zophobas* are almost never observed trying to fly in captivity.

There may be exceptions but none of the species I've worked with have exhibited the ability to climb vertical glass or smooth plastic. Lack of tarsal pads is a family feature. They can climb rough surfaces, but generally avoid climbing as they have little desire to move vertically.

Sexual dimorphism is apparent in many genera, including *Eleodes*, as the males are much less rounded in shape. When the sexes aren't easily discerned by shape, the males tend to be notably smaller. Wild-caught adults can range greatly in size and it can be even more difficult to determine gender with captive-reared animals due to variable stunting. Species in which only males possess a mucro (caudal process) only have definitive mucros in large males. When genders look similar it can be impossible to determine sexes because adult genitalia is usually well concealed. However, sometimes they'll distend their abdomen to expose genitalia when lifted in the air, which makes for an easy check.

Mate selection can include chemical, auditory, and visual cues. Pheromones are certainly part of the reproductive process but many flightless species congregate naturally and it's hard to say what exactly lures them to the same hides. You'll often find a small group of them under one rock or piece of wood in an area and find them under a different rock the next time. As mentioned, the African tok-tok beetles are famous for using sound to lure in mates. They hit the bottom of their abdomen against rocks to make a knocking pattern. Given their eye structure it would seem unlikely that vision could play a major role in mate selection, but males can usually pick out females of the same species with little trouble. Males can often be tricked into going after larger, unrelated beetles in captivity, as they mistake them for a super female. Males love big females since it's a sign they're healthier and capable of producing more eggs.

Males fight over females and it's not rare to find a pile of males trying to hitch a ride on one female. Mating behavior can be used to tell gender (females are on the bottom), but males and females may hitch rides on the same gender when other genders are absent. The male to female ratio is not especially important, but large numbers of males to a single female may cause the female stress or curtail egg-laying behavior.

Copulation occurs for a short period, though a male may stay on the female's back for days or weeks. Beginners often mistake males hanging on for mating, but during actual mating the beetles are actually joined at the end of the abdomen. Normally a female will not lay eggs if she has not mated in the last few weeks.

*BLAPS HISPANICA* EGG (© DORTE BENGTSSON)

The egg-laying cage should be at minimum a 2.5-gallon aquarium (1 gallon = 4.55 liters) with a substrate depth of two to three inches (52-77mm). A five or ten-gallon cage is preferable for large species. Surface area is important in choosing the cage, so a 20-gallon extra tall with the footprint of a 10-gallon would be equal to a 10-gallon. Substrate depth greater than a few inches is unnecessary. Avoid using an egg-laying cage for more than one species, especially if one is more prolific or has more aggressive larvae. If breeding is successful, you won't be able to tell which species the larvae came from.

Females can lay hundreds of eggs each year, usually in spring or summer, but getting females to lay eggs can be the most challenging aspect of husbandry. The number of ova depends on health, nutrition, and suitable egg-laying areas. A number of species are quite picky about the substrate composition and humidity level and won't lay a single egg without specific conditions. Ground-up hardwood leaf litter helps to induce egg laying when placed on a few inches of moist substrate. Larval molting hormones also provide a stimulus for egg laying. Early instar larvae can be placed in the substrate to stimulate females. One or two yellow mealworms per cage can be employed for this purpose, but larvae of the same species or a member of the same genus is best.

Unless the egg-laying cage was substandard or the female died prematurely, she should lay too many eggs to be reared in the cage. She wanders during laying in nature, but keeps returning to the same spots in captivity. Larvae readily disperse over a large area in nature, but can't in a small aquarium.

Most females dig an inch or two down, so a "missing" female is a good sign of egg laying. Cannibalism of eggs by adult females is unlikely. Larvae may eat some eggs, but usually when laying occurs the large numbers produced suggest eggs are not cannibalized. Movement from large numbers of larvae can cause eggs to surface and dry out, but females of most species refuse to lay eggs in crowded conditions.

Commonly, eggs are never seen because of their very tiny size, but if a female is found buried, the eggs can be easy to locate nearby if the soil is dark in color. Eggs laid near the surface are covered in a sticky secretion and become invisible as they become coated in substrate during laying. Tiny tunnels against the glass and movement of small larvae are easy to observe, so these are the most common signs of reproduction.

Ova are yellow or white, small, cylindrical, and commonly 1mm or less in length and far more narrow. Though not easily damaged by handling, they are tiny and difficult to locate. Some species have eggs that are highly resistant to desiccation, but moist substrate is recommended for any but the grain pests. Eggs hatch after a few weeks into incredibly tiny mealworms.

## MEALWORMS

Mealworms are far more famous than mealworm beetles. The number of TV shows and movies that depict a bowl or object full of writhing *Tenebrio* or *Zophobas* larvae is legion. When in a bowl it's often meant to be eaten by the ghoul holding it and sometimes they really are eaten by the star or contestant. They are available from any shop that sells fishing bait or insect-eating pets. Children can pick out a nice one to compete in mealworm races. These races have become popular at bug festivals that have popped up around the country in recent decades. Large candy suckers containing a mealworm or little packets of dried, spicy larvae are popular novelty items. They're also found in some brands of Mexican tequila as imposter mezcalero worms (a moth caterpillar). When I visited Cancun, Mexico, every brand I found had one *T. molitor* in the bottom of the bottle.

Larval body design varies little relative to the intense shape variation of adults. Even the pie-dish-shaped *Embaphion* and most massive, rotund *Eleodes* come from larvae that are barely discernable from the common yellow mealworm. The exact coloration is different for nearly every species, but unless you're familiar with a certain species most of them look the same. The terminal body segment is usually cone-shaped, but can be flattened like a paddle or concave. Various genera have two spines at the end of the cone, such as in *Gonopus*, or multiple spines on a

paddle as in *Nyctobates*. Some members of the subfamily Pimeliinae like *Asbolus* and *Prionotheca* are unusually hairy beneath the head and thorax. In most species the front pair of legs is double the size of the rear two pairs. Despite all

(TOP) *ZOPHOBAS MORIO*, (RIGHT) *TENEBRIO MOLITOR*, (CORNER RIGHT) *EMBAPHION MURICATUM*, (CORNER LEFT) *ELEODES SUBNITENS*, (LEFT) *ELEODES SPINIPES*

the variations just listed, they still all look rather similar.

True ironclads (not the various non-zopher-inae tenebrionids that are often called ironclads) have different-looking larvae, which is the reason they are sometimes moved to their own group.

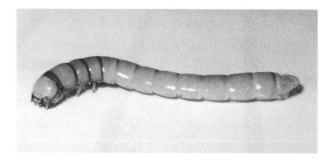

*ASBOLUS* LARVA

Although adapted for a primarily subterranean life, mealworms are agile and hard-bodied. If food is placed on a log or piece of wood, the larvae easily scale to the top with their sharply clawed feet. They climb with more agility than adults, but likewise do not climb smooth surfaces. The exoskeleton is rather thick compared to most beetle larvae, even a number of terrestrial and arboreal grubs. Mealworm body coloration is normally tan to dark brown, which would likely be clear or white if they spent no time in the light.

Larvae have distinct upper and lower body plates with a joining pleural region like centipedes. This type of body segmentation occurs in a number of beetle families, but is vastly different from the commonly kept scarabs and stags.

Sex in larvae is difficult to impossible to determine in most species, since the exoskeleton is opaque and reproductive organs cannot be viewed externally. (Reproductive organs can be seen through the exoskeletons of scarab and stag larvae.)

Mealworms apparently make great food for a variety of insectivores, but they do try to defend themselves. When handled they can extrude paired appendages from the bottom end of the abdomen, which are used in physical defense. Many species eject clear liquid (blood) from the sides of the body if sufficiently bothered. Some large mealworms, like *Eleodes spinipes* and *Zophobas,* can give a little pinch with their jaws.

Larvae are cannibalistic but the exoskeletons are tough and there's little need to keep them separate. The round shape also makes it difficult for them to bite each other. They generally don't eat each other—unless one dies or they are starving. Of course there are exceptions, such as with members of the African genus *Gonopus,* whose larvae are predaceous and will hunt down and eat all of their tank mates.

*ALOBATES* LARVA

As they develop, the hard exoskeleton is shed ten to sixteen times. It can be difficult to see the difference in size between early molts and there may not be any measurable increase in size in the last few molts. The shed is commonly eaten (though *Tenebrio* never seem to eat their exuvium) and the white mealworm returns to normal coloration within a few hours. Unlike most beetles, mealworms molt under the substrate without carving out a molting cell first. The number of total instars doesn't appear to be fixed. In some species larvae that aren't yet full-grown can be isolated for pupation and within a few weeks will become prepupae. This sets them apart from other pet beetles—with only three instars—and makes it more difficult to follow larval development.

Size is relative to individuals of the same species, but not to other species. A large *Tenebrio* mealworm will produce a larger adult than a small one. However, an *Embaphion* mealworm of the same size as *Tenebrio molitor* will produce a beetle twice as big with much longer legs. Mass is not lost but is used differently in the development of different body types, including hollow or flattened elytra. This isn't restricted to different adult types—an *Eleodes longicollis* larva will become a bigger beetle than an *Eleodes subnitens* of the same size. One drastic example is that mealworms of the gigantic *E. spinipes* rarely grow as big as feeder *Z. morio* mealworms.

*ELEODES SPINIPES* LARVA

Temperature affects development. Yellow mealworms used as food are usually kept in the refrigerator to prevent them from feeding or changing into beetles. Desert species may withstand cold for a time, but tropicals like *Zophobas* die quickly. Temperature affects speed of growth but (within reason) has limited affect on adult size. However, temperatures in the lower 70's F tend to favor larger beetles since high temperatures can speed up development without allowing enough time for maximum feeding and growth.

The goal of the beetle hobbyist is to rear the biggest, most impressive creature possible through proper care of the mealworms. Even if the substrate and rearing conditions seem optimal, it can be difficult to grow mealworms to maximum wild size, let alone true monsters. Genetics play a role—especially male versus female size—but rearing conditions and food quality determine the final adult size. Even under similar conditions larvae can give rise to substantially different-sized individuals. The first to hatch often grow largest because increased competition and contact with mealworms and frass stunt later hatchlings. It's possible to raise all monsters one year and all runts the next without explanation. Substrate composition, supplemental foods, and optimal space work hand in hand, but growing big beetles is an art as much as a science.

Use of hormones to grow monster darkling beetles is in the realm of science fact rather than fiction. "Giant mealworms" commonly available as feeders are simply *Tenebrio molitor* fed a tiny amount of artificial insect growth hormone in order to produce oversized larvae for feeding. This hormone was created to disrupt normal insect development and prevent larvae from reaching adulthood, but it doesn't seem to bother *T. molitor* at all the way it is administered. The hormone is called a juvenile hormone because it encourages larval molts and growth while inhibiting the pupal molt. Despite reports, the larvae have a very high success rate reaching maturity and are fertile. The likely reason they are able to survive the hormone is the very low dosage rate combined with the naturally unfixed number of instars. The following generation are not as big, though are larger than usual (likely due to larger egg size rather than residual hormone), but by the third generation they are back to normal size. The method of administration is a guarded commercial secret, so it is possible something other than or in addition to the artificial hormone is used. Lastly, it's curious that feeder-breeding companies haven't fed hormone to *Zophobas* superworms to produce superduperworms.

This is the only growing stage, so the way mealworms are fed and treated will determine how big and healthy later stages become. The pupa is a transformative stage that does not feed, and adult beetles do not grow. Poorly kept larvae can become covered in black sores, be too weak to make it to or through pupation, or result in deformed pupae and adults.

Larvae of most species can be kept on a few inches of substrate in a plastic creature cage, plastic box, or aquarium, since they can't climb. If a lid is used it should have numerous vents or a full screen lid. Good ventilation is important. The nuances of substrate qualities and associated pests is covered in the following section.

## Food Substrate and Pest Control
Grains and processed animal foods help to grow healthy beetles. Rolled oats and cracked corn are the most commonly used and available inexpensive grains. Many types of processed animal foods such as dog food, cat food, chicken mash, fish flakes, ferret pellets, and turtle pellets are useful foods. Cabbage or lettuce and pieces of apple, potato, pumpkin, and melon provide nutrition and moisture. Many pests, including nematodes and mites, relish all the above foods if there is enough moisture. Uneaten supplements can cause population explosions of these tiny creatures, which in turn irritate, partially suffocate, and can kill mealworms. These items should be kept on the dry side of the cage to prevent mold and reduce pests. Mealworms readily locate food sitting on top. If the humidity is high it may be necessary to place a 40-60 watt incandescent light bulb over the area to keep the food from spoiling.

Alternative food additives such as yeast and protein powder have been used. Yeast is supposed to grow larvae quicker, but a pinch added

to substrate doesn't seem to make any difference. There may be an application methodology for yeast that is kept secret. Protein powders can be very successful in improving growth, but usually cause split wing cases that make the beetles look like a fat man that can't fit in his suit coat. The larger size doesn't compensate for deformities.

Various fungus beetles like *Bolitotherus* and *Neomida* feed only on bracket (or shelf) fungi. The bracket fungi must be collected from old logs or firewood. Adults will feed on thin bracket fungi and various foods, but only lay eggs on large fungus brackets that are at least ¾" (19mm) thick. These can be dried for long periods to reduce pests and competing darkling or weevil species. Keep in mind that spongy species like chicken bracket fungi will rot and smell horribly for days or weeks after being removed from the wood. The rotting uses up oxygen and quickly kills beetles and larvae if there's a lid on the container.

Common substrate components include aged sawdust, rotten leaves, soft rotten wood, and compost. Hardwood sawdust (including the popular aspen or poplar animal bedding) and crushed rotten leaves are helpful to induce egg laying and improve larval growth. Peat, coconut fiber, potting soil, and other materials that present limited or zero nutrition are often used as the primary substrate component since they do not spoil or attract pests. Compost manure, mushroom compost, and leaf compost are useful, but prone to some pest issues. Keep in mind that certain soils or composts adhere to the beetle's bodies and obscure their good looks or even build up enough to restrict movement, and for this reason should be avoided. Decomposing leaves and wood of nearly any rotten hardwood can be used as the primary food for the majority of larvae, even the yellow mealworm, which is why grains and animal foods can be considered secondary or supplemental.

The substrate should be moist to damp and never dripping wet. Larvae tend to survive limited ventilation that would kill adults, but they'll do well in surprisingly dry conditions as long as

*ELEODES SUBNITENS* TENERAL MALE, EVIDENCED BY PROFEMORAL SPINES AND NARROW ELYTRA

*ELEODES SPINIPES* PYGIDIUM AND MUCRO

moisture is available in part of the substrate. Too much moisture is deadly to larvae of most desert species, including many *Eleodes*. There should always be a dry section of the substrate because larvae can't escape excess water like adults that sit on the surface. Even with a dry area, if the surrounding substrate is very wet, larvae can develop brown or black spots on the exoskeleton. Larvae affected with more than a few small spots are doomed, but their tank mates can be saved with reduced moisture. Larvae of species from forest areas such as *Alobates* and *Zophobas* don't need a dry area, but can still be harmed by extremely damp substrate.

Grains and pet foods can also attract and cause pests to proliferate. Natural components, primarily rotten leaves and wood, can also have damaging hitchhikers. The following accept varying levels of dryness and are of primary concern. (Pests that are less commonly a problem in darkling husbandry are mentioned in the stag chapter.)

*Mites:* The problematic species are members of the family Acaridae, known as storage mites because certain species commonly infest grain and food products. These mites, relatives of the human itch mite, are found in rotting plant matter everywhere. Unlike other destructive pests, they easily spread from cage to cage and may never be completely eradicated. Full-grown mites are much smaller than a grain of salt and seldom grow bigger than the period at the end of this sentence. The hypopus (dispersal) stage mites tightly adhere to the beetle larval skin and adult armor, often around the spiracles where they can restrict breathing. They are looking for transportation and don't attach until food begins to run out, but then stay indefinitely. Removed mites do not leave scars on the larval integument, and adhere to indents rather than joints on the adult armor. Large numbers of storage mites correspond with high larval mortality because population explosions, resulting from too much moisture and rotting foods, increase the amount of restricted spiracles. Storage mites don't feed on healthy beetles or larvae, but consume the dead. Parasitic mites aren't seen in captive tenebrionids. Removal: Drying is the only technique that will kill every mite and is well suited to darklings. Place the beetles or larvae in an empty cup for one to two days. The mites dry up and fall off. The cup must be empty, because any substrate or food will protect mites. Don't put a clean beetle back into infested substrate. Heat treatment kills mites in the substrate, but may lead to a new outbreak if conditions remain the same. Mite paper can be used as a barrier to prevent introduction of mites (where an uninfected cage is placed on the treated paper). Do not attempt to remove or dry mites from pupae, because they will die before the mites. Avoid freshly dead leaves and wet dog food to prevent mite population explosions. *Tenebrio molitor* cultures often become infested with these mites but since the substrate is solid meal they coat all nearby surfaces and never enter the hypopus stage. Ventilation must be increased, ambient humidity lowered, and no moisture added.

*Grain moths:* these can be troublesome pests, as they require almost zero moisture and can be attracted from outside by the food. The most common grain moth encountered in food storage is the Indian meal moth (*Plodia interpunctella*) though the ones I usually see are a similar, monotone gray moth, and the much larger *Pyralis farinalis*. Fortunately they don't bother large darkling larvae but should be removed and controlled because they can eat all the food and riddle the substrate with silken tubes. Removal: Heat treatment for light infestations, complete removal of substrate for large numbers.

*Drugstore beetles: Stegobium paniceum* gets its name from its ability to feed on most drugs, though it can get nourishment from a variety of stored products. It's found worldwide and is a member of the Anobiidae family, which includes deathwatch beetles. Larvae are C-shaped, fat, and white. Moisture is generally never added. Pupal cells are formed near the top of the medium in silken cocoons. Development takes about two

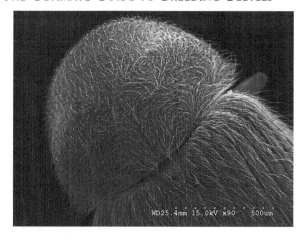

*DRUGSTORE BEETLE*

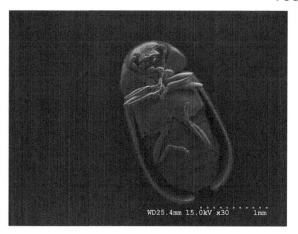

*DRUGSTORE BEETLE*

*RED FLOUR BEETLE*

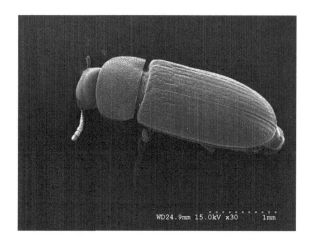

*RED FLOUR BEETLE*

months and then adults live a month or two. They are small (often listed at 2.5mm, but usually from 1-2mm) and softer than most beetles (and can be smashed during handling).

*Flour beetles:* The red flour beetle (*Tribolium castaneum*) is a red-brown, flat, hotdog-shaped beetle that can range from 2.5 to 4mm in length. The smaller, brown *T. confusum* is usually less commonly seen. *Tribolium* are common grain pests found worldwide. They are members of the family Tenebrionidae. They can infest dry flour, oatmeal, and dog food, and so can be difficult to eliminate from darkling cages.

## PUPATION

Large darkling species normally require just under a year from egg to maturity, so larvae will be full-grown after eight to ten months and ready to construct pupal cells. A week or two after it has formed a pupal cell the larva enters the prepupa stage. This stage lasts about a month and is evidenced by an inability to use its legs and staying in a curled or S-shape. The membrane between the upper and lower segments usually stretches out. Prepupae can flip over like pupae, but lose normal locomotion.

Pupal cells are just tiny caverns carved in the dirt. They are very primitive scrapes, as the walls aren't reinforced by any secretions and aren't even very smooth. They are much larger than the pupa and have little curvature of the bottom. Lack of specialization makes it easy for the hobbyist because most flat surfaces work in place of a pupal cell.

Mature larvae or pupae should be removed to isolate them from active larvae or adults. Pupae are usually sturdy and hold up well to careful handling, but if earthworms, wireworms, microworms, millipedes, centipedes, or mealworms are present, they may chew a hole in the pupa. Even a tiny hole will result in death. This stage is different from larvae and adults because even minor physical damage invariably leads to death.

*ELEODES SUBNITENS* PUPA

Pupae are not entirely defenseless despite appearances. Abdominal plates and terminal spines offer some defense. The wriggling movements not only allow them to knock away small predators, but also to maim them. Body segments have spaces in between that open and close as the abdomen is twisted in the characteristic circular movement curve.

Isolation pupation is unique to keeping darklings. Mature larvae can be isolated in small, empty cups and will enter the prepupa phase in a few weeks to a month. Larvae that are not completely mature can usually be forced to pupate early. If larvae are too immature they'll have to be placed back in the rearing cage if they don't show signs of pupation after a month. Like many other beetles, larvae postpone pupation (sometimes for very long periods) when kept in crowded conditions. However, forced early pupation cannot be successfully employed in other pet beetle families.

Pupae of *Zophobas* and *Tenebrio* can sit out safely in the low humidity and high airflow of a normal home, but most other species will desiccate within a few days. Contact with moist substrate can kill pupae. Even a tiny film of standing water in the bottom of the isolation cups will usually result in death. Mature larvae and pupae in isolation cups should be placed in an incubation chamber. An easily constructed chamber consists of a 10-gallon aquarium covered by a solid glass lid with an inch or two of soil or coco fiber on the bottom. Substrate should be damp but never wet enough to cause any condensation inside the isolation cups.

Many darkling species can be placed in a cage with deep, damp substrate for pupal cell formation. They'll dig down six inches or more and carve out a large hole. If larvae density is high they'll collapse each other's holes and refuse to pupate, or pupate surrounded by dirt and become deformed. This would be a great standard methodology for pupation, except that it takes a lot of room and the high moisture required to keep the substrate from collapsing can kill developing stages. Even in shallow substrate, if the prepupa becomes buried, the pupa will not be able to properly expand the legs. If it doesn't die earlier, it will become a rather deformed adult.

Pupa gender is usually impossible to discern. The genitalia are inside the abdomen (rather than a distended coil found in male pupae of some beetles). In beetles like *Eleodes* with differently shaped females, the pupae are not shaped differently. Even darklings with massive differences in shape and size may not have sexable pupae, because growth can be highly variable in captivity. Male *Eleodes spinipes* pupae, though, are easy to identify by the presence of a spine on the front femur.

*ELEODES SPINIPES* ELYTRA FAILURE

Four weeks are spent as the adult develops inside the pupal skin. The eyes turn black and later the legs and mandibles begin to darken. (If another portion of the body turns black, it is dying or dead.) Pupae normally lay on their backs and flip over before molting. They can be manually turned over when the claws turn black since a small number may not flip on their own. If they remain on their backs the elytra will become dented or severely deformed. The beetle breaks free from the shell and the elytra and flying wings (if present) are pumped with fluid as they expand to normal proportions. The elytra change from white to adult coloration within a few hours, but will not completely harden for weeks.

Dents can be made in the elytra at this time, so handling should be strictly avoided. If the beetle isn't on its feet during the molt it will have large dents or become grotesquely deformed. Dents made in the elytra in subsequent hours are harmless but permanent. (Dents are also seen in wild-caught specimens.) Those made in the first day generally can't be fixed without severe damage, but dents made over the next few days can usually be popped out by the keeper. After a week or two the hardened elytra can't be dented.

In globular species the manner in which the elytra expand is amazing. The abdomens aren't fat, the pupae look just like other darklings, but the elytra expand out like a balloon enveloping a large air cavity. They also fuse at this time and the suture becomes nearly as strong as the solid surface of each elytron. It's hard to understand how they can form in this way, but it likely results from structure and high fluid pressure. Total elytra formation failure is extremely rare.

It is very important to remove new adults and place them in a cage with good ventilation, as they can no longer tolerate the humidity required by the pupae. The lack of ventilation in the incubation chamber will kill adults within a few weeks. Within a day or two the elytra will darken to the black adult coloration, but a week or so should be given before removal.

*ELEODES SPINIPES* TENERAL
(NOTE TINY ABDOMEN INSIDE ELYTRA)

DARKLING BEETLE SPECIES
Large or popular U.S. species are listed, as well as common or spectacular species from around the world.

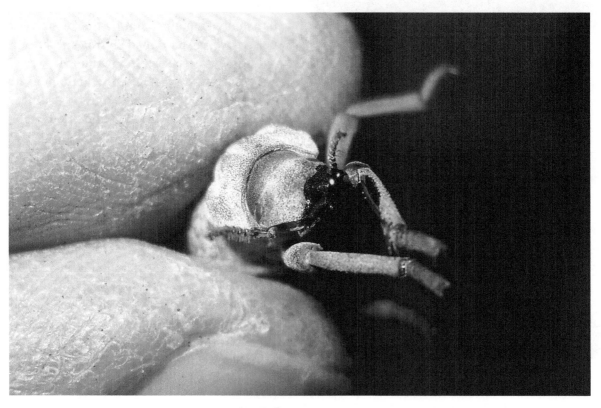

*ASBOLUS* WITH BLACK SPIT

*BOLITOTHERUS CORNUTUS*, MAJOR MALES, MINOR MALE, AND FEMALE

*Alobates pennsylvanica*

This large species (ranging from 20-26mm) is common in northeastern U.S. forests. Adults are usually found under loose bark that's relatively dry and at least a few feet above the ground. They are commonly found in groups of two to four. Defensive fluids are not observed with normal handling. The mealworms tend to be found singularly in damp, rotten logs partly buried in the ground. Larvae are pale, almost white, and more grub-like and moisture-dependant than the usual mealworm. They are midway in size between *Tenebrio* and *Zophobas*. Adults and larvae are supposed to be predatory, but larvae seem too frail.

*BLAPS GIGAS FROM HAMMAMET, TUNISIA, 1988*

reported success getting and growing larvae recently, but so far in low double-digit numbers. In the U.S. this species lives in California and Arizona. *Asbolus laevis*, the "dune bug," was also moved from *Cryptoglossa*. It is black and smooth and similar in care and behavior.

*Blaps mucronata*

The churchyard or cellar beetle is a familiar U.K. species that has become rare in cellars due to modern pesticides and food storage. The species name refers to the mucro, which is a usual feature of this genus, though often more pronounced

*ASBOLUS* PLAYING DEAD

*Asbolus verrucosus*

The blue death-feigning beetle is one of the best-known pet species (often listed as *Cryptoglossa verrucosa*). Beetles are very long-lived in captivity. A decade or more is commonly reported, but dated evidence is lacking. They have no rear defensive secretion or odor, but occasionally produce black spit if death feigning isn't producing adequate results. Adult males, around 15mm, are much smaller than females, 20-25mm. The baby blue coloration turns nearly black with moisture. Unlike other beetles that change color with moisture (i.e., *Dynastes* and *Gymnetis*), dry coloration takes hours rather than minutes of drying. The larvae have white faces and a paddle-shaped terminal segment. (See image of captive-produced mealworm.) A number of hobbyists have

*BLAPS HISPANICA* MATING PAIR
(© DORTE BENGTSSON)

on large males. (In *Eleodes* the mucro is only found on large males of certain species.) Like *Eleodes* it raises its rear into the air and exudes a foul smell when disturbed. Larvae have no special features to set them apart from other mealworms. *Blaps hispanica* is a related large species that has been kept in captivity. *Blaps mortisaga* is a mainland European species whose scientific name references its occurrence in graveyards. Many similar looking species are found in southern Europe, while others are found in the Sahara and deserts of central Asia. One of the largest is *B. gigas*, which grows up to 50mm. (*B. mucronata* is 20-30mm.)

### Bolitotherus cornutus

The forked fungus beetle is one of those strange species that looks very different from the usual

*ELEODES LONGICOLLIS* HEADSTANDING

darkling. Males have a pair of spectacular thoracic horns and a tiny forked horn on the head. Females have only tubercles on the pronotum and look like an ironclad. (Most ironclads resemble a chunk of dirt.) Adults feign death when disturbed, but can employ small, orange, eversible defensive glands if annoyed. The back legs are rubbed against the glands to flick small droplets. Colonies can be difficult to find, but when located, there are dozens of them. Larvae feed only on dead or dying hard shelf fungi and probably can't be adapted to anything else. Colonies can be kept in a deli-cup with pinholes for ventilation, with shelf fungi added a few times a year as it's consumed. (Limited ventilation is needed and constant drying is not acceptable.) Development time at 73° F is nearly a year. Fungus feeders like this and *Neomida bicornis* don't mind high humidity and limited ventilation. Unfortunately this spectacular creature only grows to 14mm. It occurs across the eastern U.S. and adjacent Canada.

### Eleodes longicollis

This skinny, long species is highly variable in size, 18 to 35mm in the wild (rarely more than 25mm in captivity). Specimens approaching maximum size are females. Smaller specimens

*BOLITOTHERUS CORNUTUS* PAIR

*ELEODES SPINIPES* MOUTH

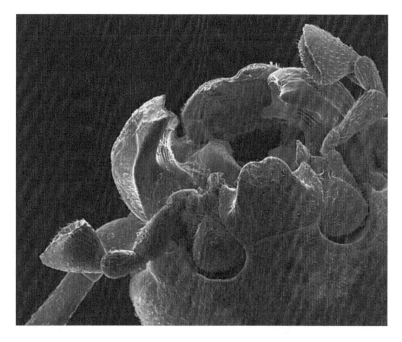

*ELEODES SPINIPES* ANTENNA AND EYE

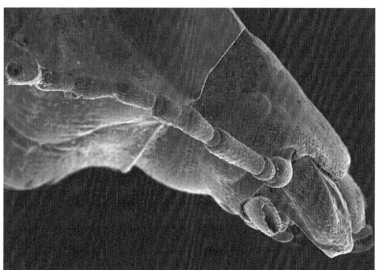

*EMBAPHION MURICATUM* FRESH MOLT

*ELEODES SPINIPES* PAIR

success. If conditions are perfect, the majority die—otherwise, they all do. (After three or four generations in captivity the survival rate increases greatly.) This species comes from Texas and is among the hardest to acquire. It may occur in neighboring states.

## Eleodes subnitens

This species from Arizona is the easiest darkling to rear outside normal feeder species. Eggs are laid in shallow, lightly humid substrate as well as deeper, damp substrate. The mealworms survive minimal feeding and can grow on dry pet foods or rotten leaves and wood. Larvae are similar but a little bigger than *T. molitor*. Larval frontal head

*ELEODES SUBNITENS* PAIR

can be either sex. Like most *Eleodes*, the adults live up to a few years. There is minimal die-off during the larval and pupal phases, but females seem to lay dozens rather than hundreds of eggs. Mature larvae should be separated into cups and kept humid but not moist. This species is found in Arizona.

## Eleodes spinipes

The beetles are the largest of the U.S. darkling beetle species, with exceptional specimens reaching near 40mm. A few others rarely approach the same length but are long and skinny. Males have a long mucro at the end of the elytra, but it is only very notable in large specimens. Even tiny males have a spine on the front femur. Females lay hundreds of eggs and larvae grow well, though they are very sensitive to excessive humidity (but can't be kept dry). Larvae are easily produced and reared, but getting them from mature larva to adult is difficult. Prepupae need to be removed and set up in a minimally humid environment for

*ELEODES SUTURALIS*

*EMBAPHION MURICATUM*

color is as light as the body, which makes it easy to tell from most other *Eleodes*. Mature larvae need to be removed and isolated if kept in shallow substrate or crowded conditions, since prepupae don't surface like *Tenebrio*. The beetles commonly excrete a defensive odor when handled, but it's a relatively faint odor without visible associated liquid. Adults are 18-25mm in nature and 15-20mm in captivity.

*Eleodes suturalis*
Adults such as the female pictured, from New Mexico, can reach 35mm and are rather thick-bodied and heavy. Males are similar but less broad. This is a common, widespread, and handsome species, but there are smaller species labeled *E. suturalis* which look similar but don't have side ridges on the pronotum and elytra. It is confused with others of the 120 U.S. *Eleodes*, primarily *E. obscurus* and *E. acutus*. There is normally a red band of color on the elytra surrounding the suture (similar red markings occur on other *Eleodes*) that's very notable with sunlight or flash photography, but is vivid in any light on some specimens. Beetles can produce a strong defensive smell but usually don't when handled gently. Females dig down a few inches to lay eggs in damp substrate.

*Embaphion muricatum*
Despite the incredibly different adult shape, larvae are similar in size and shape to *T. molitor*. Females produce large numbers of eggs and rearing is relatively simple, though fresh adults are highly susceptible to dying from limited ventilation. Mealworms are easy to rear, but require damp substrate for good survival. Beetles are difficult to acquire. Fully sclerotized adults do not last many months with high humidity, but live two or three years when kept drier.

*Gonopus* sp.
These odd-looking beetles live a year or two and are very sturdy. The strong front arms and tiny pronotum make them reminiscent of a little gorilla. They produce no noticeable defensive chemicals. Females seem to lay a lot of eggs, but larvae are extremely predatory and cannibalistic, which makes rearing difficult. They're a yellow mealworm color but are wider and have a forked

*EMBAPHION* SPECIES, MADIERA CANYON, ARIZONA

*MERACANTHA CONTRACTA*, FROM *VINTON CO.*, *OHIO*

*NYCTOBATES GIGAS FROM ENTRE RIOS*, *ARGENTINA*

terminal segment. The adult beetles show up on price lists in Europe now and then.

### Meracantha contracta

The copper bead beetle has globular elytra and no flying wings, like many desert species, but is found in eastern North American forests. This rotund, handsome species is considered common but is difficult to collect in numbers. If you find one, it will be the only one you find that day. Beetles are black with a metallic bronze sheen and grow to 12-16mm. A single female will produce a few hundred eggs, but stops producing after a few months without a male. Adults only live six to eight months. Larvae grow easily, but the survival rate through pupation is low.

### Nyctobates gigas

Giant darkling beetles from South America have been kept with some success by native hobbyists and are probably similar to *Zophobas* in rearing requirements. The larvae are colored like yellow mealworms, but have notable, short, black spines on the terminal segment.

### Prionotheca coronata

The radiant sun beetle is found throughout much of the Middle East. This monster is many times the size of the largest U.S. species, and is one of the few species ever to make it to the hobby from Israel. They are massive with gigantic heads,

though they're more bulky than long, 30-45mm. Adults live about two years in captivity and possess no defensive chemicals. Females lay eggs readily and larvae are normal looking mealworms with yellow bodies and dark gray heads. Larvae were observed hanging out exclusively in the driest areas of the substrate, which is a behavior not observed in other species. Unfortunately, an over-watering error (which killed another easily reared species at the same time) killed the mealworms when the largest were less than two centimeters, so the difficulty of rearing and pupation is unknown. Full-grown mealworms may have a unique structure on the terminal segment, though nothing unusual was observed on the immature ones.

*PRIONOTHECA CORONATA*

*PRIONOTHECA CORONATA* MALE

*PRIONOTHECA CORONATA* FEMALE

*Tarpela micans*
The spectacular, metallic rainbow beetle is a rare exception to the lack of color in darklings. Beetles grow to 17mm in length. Groups of adults are

*TENEBRIO MOLITOR, NORMAL ADULT AT TOP, HORMONE-FED ADULT AT BOTTOM*

usually found under loose bark of oak logs. It's reportedly a widespread and common species in eastern North America, but has been unavailable to the hobbyist.

*Tenebrio molitor*
The yellow mealworm is the most familiar and widely cultured beetle in the world. It can be reared like other darklings, but also does fine on a bed of dry oatmeal or other grain. This is the only species where pupae are often kept with larvae, though some are cannibalized. Normal beetles are 12-15mm, while hormone-fed are 18-22mm. The abdomen is usually distended to release a defensive odor during handling. With modern pest control it's almost never found as a pest, and is even uncommon in the wild, where adults are sometimes found under dry bark.

*Zopherus nodulosus haldemani*
This species is associated with rotten cottonwood and probably can't be reared on anything else. Adults vary in size from 15-28mm. They feed on small lichens found on tree bark. Despite what seems to be warning coloration, there's no defense other than death feigning and the very thick

*PRIONOTHECA CORONATA* MATING

*ZOPHERUS* PLAYING DEAD

*CRYPTOGLOSSA VARIOLOSA*

shell. White areas of the exoskeleton turn dark gray when wet. As with other members of its subfamily the larvae reportedly look more like a buprestid than a mealworm. Nobody has reared this species because it's not easy to acquire specimens and even tougher to convince them to lay eggs. There are eleven *Zopherus* species in the United States and only thirty-five total ironclads.

*ZOPHERUS HALDEMANI* FEEDING ON LICHEN

### Zophobas morio

These are the common pet store superworms (*a.k.a.* king mealworms or mundo-worms). The black-headed mealworms have dark brown bands but can be mostly dark brown ranging to pale white-tan overall. Larva coloration relates primarily to food but varies by individual. Full-grown larvae placed in cups for pupation do not require humidity above levels found in a normal home. Adults are easily disturbed and release a very potent, milky-white secretion between the head and thorax, along with scent from the pygidial gland. Beetles are 24-28mm and usually don't live much more than six months. Females lay eggs in substrate such as compost or compost and leaves. Larvae can then be fed grains or dog food as it is eaten. Small larvae will die if kept as dry as *Tenebrio*, but chicken mash substrate (unmedicated) with lettuce or cabbage for moisture is an alternative.

### FEEDER USE AND CONCLUSION

Use of surplus darklings as feeders is important in maintaining healthy cultures. If egg laying is successful, there are often too many to rear optimally, so the excess can be fed off to ensure adequate space. Some pupae and adults will be deformed, and it's nice to have a use for these. Adults can vary greatly in size, so runts can be fed off (assuming the difference between male and female is recognized). For those raising feeders, it is more interesting to keep *Eleodes subnitens* than the common mealworm. Rearing requirements are different but nearly as simple. It is similarly productive and has similar mealworms, but adults are larger and more handsome. Of course, more difficult species offer limited opportunities to provide feeders for predatory inverts and herps.

*ZOPHOBAS MORIO*

Many large darkling beetles make wonderful pets. Large species are flightless, lack stabbing claws, and can't climb normal caging. They are easy to care for, long-lived, and full of personality. Death-feigning beetles, especially, are a safe and beloved pet for children. Since few enthusiasts keep this family, it's easy to learn something new, be the first to rear a species, or to perfect its husbandry.

# 7
# OTHER BEETLES

## Introduction

The order Coleoptera is the most varied and complex of all world orders of living creatures. Members occupy every niche and feed on every imaginable organic substance. The following groups are those that are kept to some degree or another by hobbyists. (There are countless other families and subfamilies, but they are simply not cultured.)

## Family Scarabaeidae: Subfamily Euchirinae
## Long Arm Scarabs

Euchirine scarabs are incredible, giant, Old World species found mostly across tropical Asia. There are only a few genera and a few dozen species. There are no North American species and specimens rarely, if ever, show up at U.S. insect zoos. As the name suggests, males have gigantic, elongate front legs that are outfitted with a few large spines. All the euchirine beetles have double claws that end in two large points, rather than one like other scarabs. These beetles hang tightly onto skin and the claws can be more painful than much larger rhinoceros beetles. Larvae are easily differentiated from all other scarabs because the anus has a V-notch in the middle. (Other scarabs and passalids have a straight horizontal slit, while the stag anus is vertical.)

Larvae live in tree hole habitats and so can be fed a mix of rotten wood, compost, and decomposing leaves in captivity. Even beginning hobbyists have little trouble rearing grubs to maturity, but getting a decent number of eggs from captive-reared adults is difficult. Also, they are slow growing.

*Cheirotonus* Grub

The genus *Euchirus* contains the largest species, *Euchirus longimanus*, at three and a half inches in body length. This may not sound terribly large unless you consider they have no horns and are wide and thickly built. *Euchirus* are brown and somewhat homely. Members of this genus are more difficult than the others and take three to four years to mature.

*Cheirotonus* are large but rarely exceed three inches, though they are beautifully colored and spectacularly formed. The strange pronotum is purple and metallic green with a number of marginal spines and a thick coat of ventral setae. The elytra are black with yellow markings.

*CHEIROTONUS* CAPTIVE-BORN MALE

*PROPOMACRUS BIMUCRONATUS*
(© OLDRICH JAHN)

The various species look similar, but the elytra markings can be used to recognize some species, though the arrangement of spines on the male's front arms is the usual method. They are commonly kept in Japan and Taiwan, but probably aren't kept past the F1 generation very often. The survival rate of larvae is extremely high, but development usually takes three years and captive females rarely lay more than a few dozen eggs. Wild females lay 30-50 eggs. Male pupae have a large horn in the middle of the pronotum, but the adults have a large depression.

*Propomacrus* are the smallest euchirine scarabs at barely two inches. Members of this genus range into southeastern Europe and so are commonly kept in captivity on that continent. Only members of this genus are capable of reaching maturity in one year in captivity. In nature they likely require two years and often take that long in captivity.

## FAMILY PASSALIDAE
This family of large, subsocial beetles is most common in the tropics, though a few species range into North America. Members of this group are generally large at one and a half to over three inches. Grubs have a unique appearance and

*ODONTOTAENIUS DISJUNCTUS* LARVAE

*ODONTOTAENIUS DISJUNCTUS* LATE STAGE PUPA

*ODONTOTAENIUS DISJUNCTUS* FRESH-MOLTED ADULT

*ODONTOTAENIUS DISJUNCTUS* ADULT

*CHEIROTONUS* CAPTIVE-REARED ADULT MALE AND FEMALE

*ODONTOTAENIUS DISJUNCTUS* ADULT AND L3

seem to only have four legs, as the hind pair is greatly reduced and used in stridulation. Larvae and adults of the common and well-known *Odontotaenius disjunctus* have an advanced language with over a dozen different noises for different purposes. Despite this, passalids are considered subsocial since their social behavior is different from the complex societies of some ants and wasps. There are a few U.S. species, but only *O. disjunctus* is widespread. It is commonly used in classrooms, and has been reared in captivity.

## Odontotaenius disjunctus
### BESS BEETLE

Bess Beetles are great specimens for classroom use since specimens vary rarely attempt to bite and can be handled readily. The claws do not hold on tightly and cause no pain. College students may be asked to look after beetles as an assignment, or specimens are used in strength experiments since they can lift and tow many times their weight.

This is a common beetle throughout much of the eastern and central United States. Northern specimens are usually much smaller. (For example, specimens from Ohio are much smaller than those from Virginia, and both of those are dwarfed by specimens from southern Louisiana.) There are a few rarely encountered similar-looking species in the extreme south.

Collection is usually done by excavating rotten logs in wooded areas. Adults are attracted to lights in late summer, sometimes in good numbers, but do not fly most nights of the year. Attempts at flight are unheard of in captivity.

Adults and larvae feed exclusively on rotten wood. They eat any rotten wood that is soft and easily broken by hand. They are usually found in rotten logs that are brown (rather than light brown or black-brown). It's nearly impossible to get the beetles to eat anything else. Grubs will eat a ton of dog food in captivity, but it doesn't seem to have any positive effect on growth.

Ova are unique in that they are dark brown, which is quite unusual for a beetle egg. Females usually produce one to two dozen in the spring. A cool winter period is needed to induce egg laying in captivity. Eggs are laid in April, hatch, go through three instars, and begin to form pupal cells in early August. They grow very fast for such a large beetle. Under natural conditions pupal cell formation occurs inside one of the feeding tunnels, but in captivity they often do not make pupal cells and must be placed in fake pupal cells as they become immobile. In two weeks they transform to adults, but it takes a few months for them to fully sclerotize and transform from orange to dark black.

Handling adults regularly seems to have no ill effects, but handling larvae is not recommended, and gentle handling of pupae and fresh adults can result in their death.

## FAMILY CERAMBYCIDAE
### LONGHORN BEETLES

These beetles are named for the long antennae and though some have enlarged mandibles or cephalic tubercles, they don't have horns. There are legions of large and colorful species in the U.S., many of which are attracted to lights. The longest beetle in the world may be the South American *Titanus giganteus*. It looks somewhat like our *Prionus* species that grow to over three inches, but this species is said to reach eight inches. (Most dead specimens are under six inches.) Larvae of various species are uniform in appearance: white, elongate, ribbed body with a small, triangular brown head, and barely visible legs.

The Cerambycidae is one of the largest beetle families, but it holds very little interest for beetle culturists. Reasons for the lack of interest include negativity regarding the pest status of various species and negative aspects of the animals themselves. A number of the large species can't be kept in the same cage, or they bite each other's legs and antennae off. The adults of our largest genera like *Prionus* and *Ergates* live only a few weeks, but take years to mature. Rearing is generally difficult and slow, and larvae often die if they are handled.

Many of our prettiest native longhorns attack live plants as larvae and it's difficult or impossible to rear them without a large, living specimen of the specific host. Adults do fine on cuttings, but early stages do not, and developmental periods are many times the longevity of cuttings. In nature, larvae move down the branch during feeding, but in captivity they need to be manually transferred as soon as the cutting dies. Transfer can lead to death, and dying food will lead to extreme stunting if any survive.

Members of this family are rarely seen at insect zoos, with only a few exceptions. The western cactus longhorn beetles have long been used as display animals because they live a long time and are easy to feed, and pose no threat to other plants. (*Moneilema* is also our only genus with much of a culturing history.) The Cleveland Zoo displayed monstrous *Batocera rufomaculata* longhorns from Malaysia around 1995-2005, while the Cincinnati Zoo reared *Acrocinus longimanus* a decade or so ago.

*Moneilema gigas*
CACTUS BEETLE

Our six *Moneilema* species are some of our strangest-looking beetles, as they are reminiscent of a big, black, southwestern lubber grasshopper. However, they are thought to be darkling beetle mimics because they copy the behavior of *Eleodes*. They likewise raise the abdomen up in the air when disturbed, but don't produce a defensive smell or fluid. There are six species that range from Texas to California, and one that ranges as far north as western Canada. *Moneilema gigas* is our largest at 28-38mm. The sturdy antennae and thick black legs make them look even bigger. They can live a year or two as beetles and make great display specimens.

Cactus beetles earn their name because they live among and feed on cactus. In the southwestern U.S. they feed primarily on cholla (*Cylindropuntia* spp.) and prickly pear (*Puntia* spp.) cacti.

*MONEILEMA* SPECIES

*MONEILEMA* GRUBS

This feature made them a savior in Australia, as introduced prickly pear cactus was turning square miles into impenetrable, useless land. Their introduction to control this cactus is a major success story in biological pest control. Starving adults can be convinced to eat carrots and some other vegetables, but may not live very long and much prefer their natural food.

Food is easily grown. Prickly pear cactus is an odd cactus in that some species grow outdoors even in the far northern U.S. Of course it doesn't grow during cold winters, but it has no trouble withstanding below freezing temperatures. A

*DENDROBIUS MANDIBULARIS FROM THE SOUTHWEST*

drawback of this food is that irritating small prickles break off (though large spines are easy to avoid). Pads can be cut from a plant and should be manipulated with tongs. It is not a good idea to dig through or handle the substrate with bare hands.

*Moneilema* females lay dozens of large, oblong eggs (5mm) cemented near the base of cacti inside a thick secretion that mixes with sand to form a protective cocoon. Eggs will hatch in a week when watered, but can stay inside the egg for weeks to months if kept dry. Larvae do not leave the egg without moisture. They should be fed live cactus and will become adults in six to ten months. Most larvae cannot find cactus pads placed on top of the substrate, since they use the root system to locate and enter pads. There is some captive die-off for this reason, but if the pads are given time to establish roots, it remedies this problem. Holes can be cut in the pad and larvae set inside, but the pads may melt down—larvae do very poorly if transferred more than a few times. Development time from hatching to

full-grown grub is only about four months. Mature larvae make extremely thick pupal cells in the sandy soil, mixing dirt with secretions, and cannot leave them until becoming adults and chewing their way out.

*Acrocinus longimanus*
HARLEQUIN LONGHORN BEETLE
This beautifully marked, sexually dimorphic longhorn is probably the most well-known longhorn beetle. Dead specimens are common, popular, and inexpensive (and are usually males, since they have the impressive, oversized front legs). This species is commonly used to illustrate the phoretic relationship with pseudoscorpions. Those tiny arachnids use these large beetles to find mates and disperse. The pseudoscorpions also enjoy a fertile hunting ground for hypopus stage mites that are also hitching a ride under the beetles' elytra.

*PRIONUS IMBRICORNIS FROM VIRGINIA*

Husbandry consists of rearing larvae using the log method. Females deposit large, cylindrical eggs under or in cracks of rotten logs in the laying cage. An aged, slightly decayed but very solid, hardwood log is submerged in water for a few days to ensure adequate moisture. A small hole is drilled in the log and an egg placed inside. The hole is filled back in and covered with clay or duct tape. Usually three eggs are placed

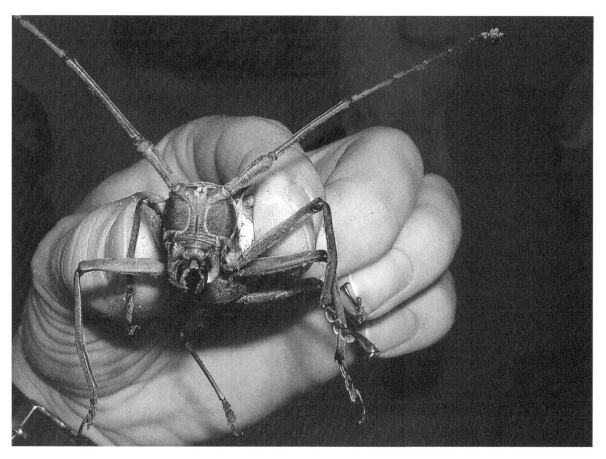

*BATOCERA RUFOMACULATA* FROM MALAYSIA

*MANTICHORA* MATING, NOTE INSERTION

in different spots on an 18″ long by 6″ diameter log. Next, plastic is wrapped over both ends and held on with rubber bands or rope. Finally, wait two to four years, and hopefully a few beetles will emerge.

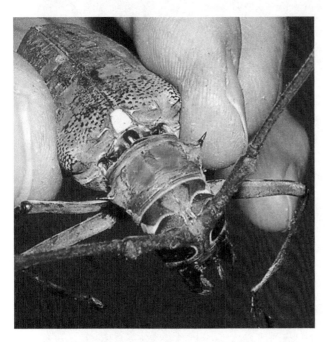

MALAYSIAN LONGHORN BEETLE

## FAMILY CARABIDAE
### GROUND BEETLES AND TIGER BEETLES

The most famous and spectacular species are the enormous ones from Africa like the *Anthia* ground beetles and *Mantichora* giant tiger beetles. (Tiger beetles used to have their own family.) Some genera have reproduced in captivity, but so far the impetus for egg laying is poorly understood, and the number of adults reared tends to be far fewer than the number of adults bred. In the United States our most spectacular ground beetles include the colorful *Calosoma scrutator* and the monster *Amblycheila cylindriformis* (which was originally described in the genus *Mantichora*).

### Calosoma scrutator

The fiery searcher is one of our most common, widespread, colorful, and largest ground beetles. Beetles come to lights in the summer. They are found north into Canada, but are usually only really common along the southern half of the country.

The adults live one to two years in captivity with minimal care. If temperatures drop below 68° F for long periods, they'll bury themselves and can remain without food for up to six months. The cage should be well-vented. Beetles can be kept in groups safely, but only if given adequate food and space. No more than four or five should be placed in a habitat measuring 10″ x 18″ floor space. I've reared a few to adulthood, but the larvae are weak and the stimulus for egg laying is uncertain. Eggs were laid in a 70-gallon terrarium with a bunch of leaf litter and an active orange *Porcellio* (Isopoda) culture. Larvae are black and look similar to *Necrophila* larvae, but are not as energetic. They feed on isopods, but will also eat pre-killed crickets (since they had no ability to catch active prey).

*PASIMACHUS* SP., 33MM

### Pasimachus spp.

These handsome predators have large, curved jaws and are sometimes confused with *Pseudolucanus* stag beetles. Adults are long-lived at one to three years. Various species have huge jaws and are jet black, but some species have metallic green or metallic purple margins. Adults will hibernate for six months around winter in captivity when given deep substrate. Eggs and larvae have not been noted in captivity.

*MANTICHORA* MALE

*CALOSOMA SCRUTATOR*

*CICINDELA* SPECIES

*Amblycheila cylindriformis*
The biggest U.S. tiger beetle is also active, hardy, and long-lived. Specimens normally measure in at 1.5″ (37mm), but can vary slightly. Despite its gigantic size, few enthusiasts know it exists, since it is rare and popular books don't contain photographs, line drawings, or descriptions of this species. It is found in a number of western and central states, but specimens are uncommon. There are a few other U.S. *Amblycheila* species that are extremely rare but very similar.

Adults are voracious predators that tear crickets apart. The beetles are hyperactive when disturbed but usually sleep during the day. Specimens are extremely hardy and survive up to two years in captivity. Adults don't harm each other, but the longer they live the greater the chance they'll lose a claw or antenna.

Unfortunately dead specimens are far more valuable than live (as very few dead specimen collectors have this species in their collection) and predatory beetle culture is a hobby that

doesn't yet exist. Larvae are predatory obligate burrowers that should be easy to rear, but as with many predatory beetles, the impetus required to get adults to lay eggs in captivity is unknown.

*Cicindela* spp.
There are countless, small, colorful members of this genus found throughout the U.S. Some subspecies and species with very limited natural ranges are threatened, but most are wide-ranging and extremely common. It's unlikely the average collector would encounter a threatened species, but it's a good idea to be familiar with the local fauna just in case. Permits are required for contact with protected species.

Many species can be collected near lights at dusk in summer, or found hibernating under the loose bark of large fallen trees in winter and early spring. Most are active during the day, though that's usually the most difficult time to collect them. A few species have been reared in captivity.

The beetles are short-lived compared to other carabids, and depending on species will live less than a month to half a year. Most live two months or less outside of hibernation.

Getting females to lay eggs can be difficult. Females will not lay eggs if soil properties are

*AMBLYCHEILA CYLINDRIFORMIS*

incorrect. Some properties are universal: the substrate for egg laying should be a sand and soil mixture and kept damp. Some requirements are species-specific: one protected species that has been reared in permitted labs, *Cicindela nevadica lincolniana*, requires a brine solution added to the substrate, or eggs are never deposited.

Hatchlings can be removed and reared separate, but are often kept in large cages together. Substrate should be 6" or better for burrow construction. They are kept in sandy soil where they like to bury all but the tops of their heads to wait in ambush for prey. Unlike adults, larvae can live a long time in nature, often two years. In captivity, the larvae mature in well under a year if fed daily. 1st instar larvae are tiny and can be fed springtails, while even full-grown 3rd instar are only large enough to eat ¼" crickets.

## *Mantichora* spp.

A manticore is a mythical creature with the body of a lion, a horned human head, and a scorpion tail. The real *Mantichora* are just as peculiar, but much more pleasing to the eye. These massive-jawed, globular tiger beetles look quite different from their elongate, cylindrical relatives. Both genders have oversized, uneven, and bent jaws, but the male's jaws are even larger, making it easy to tell from a female. They live a few years in captivity with minimal care. The beetles form an underground cell and hibernate six to eight months each year if provided deep substrate. However a hibernation period doesn't induce egg laying. Egg laying seems to be a result of drought and monsoon cycles and is probably influenced by day length, temperature, and prey availability. The only successful documented breeding report from the Bristol Zoo in England took two years and seven months, multiple attempts at recreating monsoon cycles, and 11 adults to produce only 10 larvae. After six months, the larvae seemed to refuse to pupate under the provided conditions (Roberson and Spencer, 1997).

## FAMILY SILPHIDAE
## CARRION BEETLES

These are among our most interesting beetles, due to rapid growth, bright colors, and decent size. They do produce rather unpleasant defensive odors when molested, are infested with mites, and feed on dead animals. Our largest species, the American burying beetle, *Nicrophorus americanus*, is endangered. It used to be common across much of the country, but now occurs in just a few states. The cause for its decline is unknown. It's barely different from many other *Nicrophorus*, which are all still very common. At a maximum of 45mm, it's the largest U.S. member of the genus. Permitted institutions had a good record of reared specimens in captivity as far back as two decades ago (Creamer, 1992). The very different but similar sounding *Necrophila americana* may be the only species that has been reared by more than a handful of beetle enthusiasts.

## COLLECTING

Beetles can be baited with dead animals or rotten bait. I've baited *Nicrophorus orbicollis* with

*CARRION BEETLE* ADULT AND LARVA
(© LINDSEY PYNE)

*NECROPHILA AMERICANA* (© LINDSEY PYNE)

food, but females must be given meat such as a chunk of hamburger or a pinky mouse to induce egg laying. The eggs are laid just a millimeter below the surface of the soil. Each ovum of this small beetle is almost the size of a *D. tityus* ovum. Eggs hatch in less than 48 hours. Larvae are black, smooth, and spindle-shaped. Larvae go through three instars in a week and then carve out a pupal cell.

*Nicrophorus orbicollis* and other members of this genus require a much higher level of care and are far less accepting of cage mates than the above. In this species, the male and female can usually be distinguished by the shape of the red markings above the mandibles (rectangular for male, triangular for female). Groups of adults can be kept together as long as males and females are kept separate, but they still cannibalize if not fed for a few days. Adults feed on mealworms and dead crickets. Adults should be kept on damp substrate or they desiccate rapidly.

For breeding, a pair is placed in a cage with three to four inches of soil, and some leaf pieces, while a large mouse or small rat carcass is placed on top. They partly bury it and cover the rest with the leaves. Like the above species and many other beetles, larvae go through three instars, but this is difficult to observe because early disturbances will likely cause adults to eat young larvae. Adults feed larvae with digested meat, but eat some larvae if there isn't enough food for them all. The male should be removed as soon as he surfaces, and a few days later the female should surface and be removed. It takes about ten days from egg to mature larva, but then a month and a half before new adults emerge.

a fermented molasses and beer mixture. It's good to make sure you can recognize the red markings on the head and pronotum of *Nicrophorus americanus*, in case one were accidentally baited, but it is listed as endangered because the chances of finding specimens are incredibly low. The various related species look similar but have different markings. Members of this genus are usually not found under larger carcasses of raccoons or possums, while *Necrodes* and *Necrophila* are. Rotten watermelons can also attract a variety of genera (primarily those that used to all be *Silpha*).

*Necrophila americana* is probably the easiest to find and rear. Since it is yellow and black and close to an inch, it is said to resemble a bumblebee in flight, though I've not seen one fly in the daytime.

All silphids carry large mites under the legs in nature. These need to be removed in captivity. It can be difficult, since the beetles stink terribly when disturbed, are very flexible, and do not like to be messed with. The mites are harmless, but are an extreme nuisance, and reproduce to cover the beetles' entire bodies. (The excess would fall off when the beetles fly in the wild.)

Adults, eggs, larvae, and pupae can be kept in the same cage without cannibalism. There should be an inch or two of damp soil for egg laying and pupation. Beetles and larvae will eat dog

## FAMILY PHENGODIDAE
### GLOWWORMS

When I hear the name glowworm I still think of the late 1980s stuffed-animal toy caterpillars with light-up rear ends. Real glowworms are brightly colored and lack a cute face. Otherwise

WESTERN GLOWWORM FEMALE, POSTULTIMATE MOLT

TINY ADULT MALE WESTERN GLOWWORM

times, but these can only be seen in extreme darkness.

Predation is oddly specific. Prey much less than half the phengodid's size is generally ignored, and it will not attack anything but millipedes. I've offered various feeder insects and crustaceans with no response. The glowworm wraps itself around a chosen millipede and bites in just below the head. Next it enters headfirst, and stretches its body up to seven inches inside the millipede's shell like a hungry, monster pipe cleaner. During feeding the entire contents are consumed, but the exoskeleton is untouched.

The females never change into beetles, but look like a larva their whole lives. They are an exception to the insect rule that sexually mature adults never molt. (Even mayflies with the odd pre-adult stage don't molt after maturity.) In captivity, mature females will molt one to three times a year, depending on how well they are fed, and may live more than three years. They can survive six months without food. Males never grow as big—they are short-lived after they become a frail beetle with giant candelabra antennae.

### Zarhipis integripennis
WESTERN GLOWWORM
This particular species specializes in North America's longest millipedes from the genus *Orthoporus*. It will accept other giant millipede species in captivity. (A defective *Narceus gordanus* is being consumed in the photo.) Supposedly the glowworm can give humans a decent nip, but I have never tried to force a bite by holding one in a closed hand for a long time. Specimens just curl up when held.

known as millipede hunters, the glowworm beetles do not resemble the cute, toddler dolls. Members of the family Phengodidae are frighteningly powerful predators that prefer to attack and kill animals larger than themselves and do so with ease. Also, their butts don't light up. They have concentric bands and spots that glow at all

### FAMILY DERMESTIDAE
Dermestids are easier to identify by the larva than the adult. Adults are small, nondescript, oval beetles covered in scales. They have clubbed antennae that fit neatly in grooves. They often retract all appendages when disturbed. The larvae have thick armored segments and evenly

FEMALE WESTERN GLOWWORM BITING IN UNDER THE HEAD OF A MILLIPEDE

FEMALE WESTERN GLOWWORM

*DERMESTES LARDARIUS*

spaced tufts of long setae that somewhat re-semble cactus spines in arrangement. They are wide at the front and narrow toward the end. Overall they look a little like a fuzzy, brown cat-erpillar.

This is a family of beetles even most beetle lovers can't stand, as they consume and destroy prized, dried beetle specimens. They are pests of stored products and require little to no moisture. Collectors of dead specimens must guard against the larvae by keeping specimens in pest-tight containment. There are a few "large" species that are commonly reared for cleaning bones in taxidermy. (One quarter to one third of an inch is huge for a dermestid.) The larger species are capable of eating dead insects, but the chance of finding an infestation in a specimen box is near zero. The following species has a definite pref-erence for dried meat, is easy to contain, and is not overly productive.

### Dermestes lardarius

At 7-9mm this is a veritable dermestid giant. The beetle is handsomely marked in black and yel-low-gray, while the larva is brown with spectacu-lar long setae like the average dermestid grub. The beetles fly, so a lid must be used. Window

screen easily contains them, since even minor adults are too big to escape.

Adults and larvae can be fed corn-based dog food in captivity, though egg and larva produc-tion of any merit requires some meat. Hot dogs and salami slices both work well. Mature larvae drill into moderately hard wood or an object of similar density to pupate. All stages should be kept dry, though a small dish filled with foam and water or a wet corner of the substrate can be offered. Moisture is not a bad thing, but if they can't escape to a dry area they eventually die. The beetles will feed on almost anything.

Larvae mature in just 6-8 weeks, but take about that much longer to develop to adults. Beetles live a year or two. Females are said to lay up to 100 eggs, but small colonies rarely produce that many larvae. Large colonies, of course, pro-duce quite well, though production per female is not very high.

*Dermestes maculatus* is the species com-monly used for cleaning bones, since it repro-duces much more rapidly, but it is also more likely to escape its cage and become a nuisance. It averages a little smaller and is black. Speci-mens are often found in boxes of feeder crickets.

### FAMILY DYTISCIDAE
### PREDACIOUS DIVING BEETLES

These handsome beetles make a favorite display at a number of invertebrate zoos and a few spe-cies have been captive-reared. The adults are long-lived, day-active, and energetic. They breathe air contained under the wing covers and swim with paddle-like legs.

Males and females look similar at a glance, but a feature that's common for water beetles is the sexually dimorphic structure of the front tarsi. Male tarsi are flattened and equipped with pads or suction cups to hang onto the female. Differences in these pads can also help with spe-cies or genus identification.

Diving beetles are masters of air as well as water. This comes in handy when temporary

*DERMESTES LARDARIUS*

WATER BEETLE

pools dry up. It's not all good, as uncountable numbers end up dying in swimming pools every year. They often do not fly in captivity, but a lid is still necessary because males can use the front suction pads to swing themselves up the glass.

Unlike water scavenger beetles that eat everything, these leave aquarium plants alone, but will eat fish food pellets, dried krill, and a variety of live aquatic and terrestrial prey. Feeding consideration is related primarily to keeping the water from fouling. Adults and larvae breathe air, but rancid water from overfeeding still leads to an early demise.

The beetles are much sturdier than larvae. These are predatory, but like most beetles, healthy adults usually can't kill each other. The larvae, commonly called water tigers, don't have such a thick skeleton and some species are prone to cannibalism, especially when crowded and underfed. Adults can survive poor water conditions for a time, while larvae are highly sensitive to bad water quality and low oxygen content. Larvae look like delicate little dragons and glide slowly through the water as they dog paddle. In some species, larvae have long abdominal gills.

GIANT WATER BEETLE MALE

Egg laying and pupation take place on emergent areas, so captive habitats must reflect this fact. Successful culture setups exist but are rare. Aquariums should be large (40 gallon or better) and filled 2/3rds with water. Small aquariums and shallow water usually result in zero egg production. The water can be filtered with an air-powered sponge filter. Along one side there must be an emergent area with an inch of soil and small, flat rocks or wood. Glass or Styrofoam may be glued or anchored to create the base structure. The water level should be kept constant to avoid drying out or drowning the emergent area. Eggs are usually deposited in soil just above the water line, though some species scatter eggs or insert them in plant stems. Adults should be removed when eggs or small larvae are observed. Water tigers usually float, upside down, near the surface, and can be fed isopods, dried krill, or crickets. Food should float. After a few weeks of feeding the larvae crawl onto the soil and carve out a pupal cell beneath the flat rock or wood provided.

Smaller species usually live a year or two in captivity, while our largest species in the genera *Dytiscus* and *Cybister* live two to four years. These large beetles, from 25-38mm, may be found at lights in the evening. The two genera can

*THERMONECTUS MARMORATUS*

*THERMONECTUS NIGROFASCIATUS*

WATER SCAVENGER BEETLE WITH CHARACTERISTIC SILVERY AIR BUBBLE TRAPPED ON THE UNDERSIDE

*THERMONECTUS MARMORATUS*

be difficult to tell apart, but *Cybister* larvae do not have cerci and the male's tarsal pad lacks the two large basal suction cups. *Cybister fimbriolatus* is probably the most commonly encountered, large, eastern species.

*Thermonectus marmoratus*, the sunburst diving beetle, may be the most familiar U.S. species, as far as captivity is concerned. This small species has been displayed in zoos throughout the U.S. and is usually wild collected from southern Arizona, though it is common throughout the southwest. It is one of the few dytiscids with a successful culture history (Morgan, 1992).

## FAMILY HYDROPHILIDAE
### WATER SCAVENGER BEETLES

These can be confused with the preceding group, but are different in many ways, though only a few of the characteristics affect husbandry. As the name *scavenger* suggests, they eat almost anything organic. They breathe head first rather than rear first, and carry air under the outside of the body rather than under the wing cases. They even move their legs differently when they swim. Larvae are less cannibalistic and less sensitive to dirty water. However, adults are more sensitive

to dirty water and are messier feeders. Larvae usually don't have gills and look like giant, gray maggots (were those outfitted with big mean heads with jaws). Not all species live in water, as there are numerous small dung-feeding beetles, including the introduced dung scavenger (*Sphaeridium scarabaeoides*). The largest aquatic U.S. beetle (below) is from this family.

### *Hydrophilus triangularis*

Size: 35-40mm. The giant water scavenger beetle can be found almost anywhere in the continental U.S. As with various water beetles, the males have specially adapted front tarsi to hold onto the slippery females. Adults will eat most aquarium plants, carrots, and romaine lettuce, as well as crickets and aquatic vertebrates. Females produce eggs year round in captivity. Impressive floating eggcases are formed that superficially

*HYDROPHILUS TRIANGULARIS*

resemble mantis oothecae. The adults usually don't eat the oothecae, but will eat larvae. (If it's a mixed tank with dytiscids, the eggcase will be attacked and eaten quickly.) Each eggcase contains 100 or more eggs, which hatch out in three or four days. Larvae aren't as interested in vegetable matter as adults, and can be fed dead crickets and dried shrimp. Cannibalism is not bad if there is decent space and feeding. Larvae go through three instars like many beetles, and are full-grown in about three weeks. Pupal cells are formed in damp dirt, so an emergent area should be provided. The adults may live much longer under some conditions, but usually don't last more than a few months.

## FAMILY COCCINELLIDAE
### LADY BEETLES

Lady beetles, commonly called ladybugs or ladybirds, are small beetles that are usually predatory and are famous for their habit of eating aphids, mealybugs, and scale insects. These may be the most famous beetles in the U.S. today. Uncountable t-shirts, costumes, movie characters, toys, and candies approximate the lady beetle likeness. A lady beetle is the official state insect of six states, including my own. They are often reared in classrooms from kits that come with a certificate for living larvae. A few species are produced in huge numbers for biological control and can be purchased by the bucket-full.

In recent years the Asian multicolored lady beetle (*Harmonia axyridis*) has become a nuisance pest across much of the U.S. Large numbers try to hibernate in buildings and houses in many areas. Although harmless, it also likes to bite humans. Supposedly the U.S. Department of Agriculture tried to introduce this species numerous times between 1916 and 1982, but it only became established accidentally in 1988 (Eaton and Kaufman 2007).

Oval yellow eggs are glued to leaves or stems. Larvae are active, diurnal, and fast growing. They are spindle-shaped, with long legs, and are usually covered in spines. Most are black with yellow or orange markings, while others appear to mimic the mealybugs they eat. After less than a month of feeding, they glue themselves under a leaf to anticipate pupation. The pupa is exposed and hangs from the tip of the abdomen. A few more weeks and the adults emerge. The beetles are normally long-lived, and can be kept in the refrigerator for many months.

## FAMILY BRUCHIDAE
### PEA WEEVILS

These are not considered true weevils and do not resemble them in adult appearance, only in habit and larvae. This small family of tiny, unassuming beetles would hold no interest except that one is commonly cultured as a lab and feeder insect.

### *Callosobruchus maculatus*

Cowpea weevils feed on cowpeas (also known as black-eyed peas), as the name suggests. Few other beans or peas can support growth of the larvae. It's not a pest the average beetle enthusiast would ever run into inadvertently, and it is intolerant of cold temperatures. It is a lab-cultured species that is used for experimentation and for insectivore food.

BRUCHIDAE FEEDING ON CANTELOUPE

Cowpea weevils are kept in a deli-cup with a few pinholes or a paper filter lid. Metal screen should never be used as undersized adults can walk through the holes. (Adults are 1.5-4mm long and much more narrow.) An inch or two of cowpeas are added as the medium. Some sources suggest soaking the cowpeas in water for a day, but even with extremely low ambient humidity, pre-soaking is totally unnecessary.

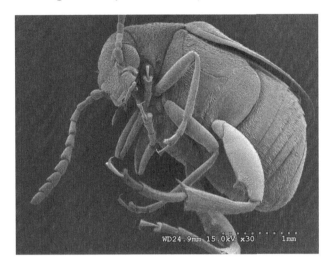

Male Cowpea Weevil

The eggs look like nearly microscopic, clear raindrops glued to the cowpeas and edges of the container. Eggs look the same a year after they hatch as they did the day they were laid. Hatchling grubs supposedly have long legs and spines, while later instars are fat, wrinkled, pale, and legless like true weevils. Adults live a month or so and don't need to feed. They'll eat small pieces of fruit or sugary liquids, but it doesn't seem to make a difference on productivity and has limited effect on longevity. The exoskeleton is thick compared to many beetles their size, but they can be useful food for small reptiles, spiderlings, orb weavers, and water bugs. (Centipedes, whipspiders, and mantids usually won't touch them.) This species flies when disturbed after it climbs to the lip of a cage. It's necessary to keep knocking them down while feeding to predators, and the predator's caging must be adequately secured.

Male and female beetles are extremely different in shape. Females have a huge abdomen that, in some specimens, sticks out past the elytra almost as far as the elytra are long. The males have a compact shape and the elytra cover the abdomen. They possess enlarged rear legs outfitted with a pair of inner femoral spines.

## Family Elateridae
### Click Beetles

Members of the family Elateridae are known as click beetles because of a mechanism they use to right themselves when they get stuck on their backs. The mechanism can also be used to startle predators—keepers too—when the beetle is grabbed. There is a second common name for this family, used for the larvae: wireworms. The larvae of most species earn the name because they look like a piece of wire (or a streamlined version of a mealworm). However, many larvae are not wire-like and at least one species looks like an unreal geometric train.

Wireworms molt a dozen or so times and, like mealworms, the number of molts doesn't appear to be fixed. Larvae eat the shed exoskeleton, and the growth between each molt is minimal, so documentation of molting periods is extremely difficult.

The larvae of most species feed on rotten wood and old leaves, but will scavenge on almost anything living or dead. Larvae won't pass up a chance at protein and will feed on a variety of egg and pupae of other insects. Most are kept similar to darkling mealworms. They cannibalize if overcrowded or starving, but do not bother each other if adequately fed. However, some species, specifically members of the genus *Alaus,* are obligatory carnivores that will starve to death without live prey and cannot be kept together.

### Collection

Click beetles are rarely found at lights and usually cannot be baited. Half a dozen specimens of one of our biggest and brightest species from

*ALAUS MYOPS*

*ALAUS MYOPS*, NOTE THE
CLICK MECHANISM

*DEILELATER PHYSODERUS*
GLOWING CLICK BEETLE, 15-20MM

Texas was once baited with orange slices, but it's unlikely this catch could be repeated. Larvae and adults are usually collected from cavities inside rotten logs in summer and adults in winter to early spring.

EYED CLICK BEETLES
*Alaus* species
Members of this genus are the largest, longest-lived, and most spectacular U.S. click beetles. It is also the only genus reared by more than one or two people. There are half a dozen species, similar in life cycle, but which vary in coloration and maximum adult size. (Each species ranges widely in size.) All have two black eyespots on the pronotum and begin life as big-headed larvae with wide bodies that do not resemble the common wireworm form.

ALAUS LUSCIOSUS FROM TEXAS,
BAITED WITH ORANGE SLICES

Beetles feed on sugar water and orange slices. They overwinter inside logs and live four to six months after becoming active. Ova are .0625" long, cylindrical, and off-white in color. They resemble mealworm eggs and hatch in three to four weeks. The larvae are wide-bodied with large jaws and are highly predatory and cannibalistic. A combination of mealworms and isopods or incapacitated crickets has been successfully employed as food in captivity. They are highly aggressive predators, but active crickets can usually jump to avoid capture. One to two inches of potting soil is kept lightly damp to keep

larvae from drying out. The developmental period and adult lifespan are both approximately ten months.

ALAUS CLICK BEETLE LARVA (© SARA PAGEL)

*Alaus* wireworms have incredibly strong jaws capable of chewing through any plastic—even hard, thick plastic can be drilled through in a few days. They should only be kept in glass or metal containers. The ability to chew through caging grows with each molt, and culminates in the full-grown wireworm.

Mature larvae seek out solid, slightly rotten logs to hollow out pupal cells within. A small log should be placed in the cage or the larva will wander unceasingly. In nature they're usually found in stumps or logs 20" or better in diameter, but 3" logs will work in captivity (only one per small log). The log should not be soggy or excessively dry. They will eventually settle down and pupate without a log, but care must be taken to watch for prepupae. Pupae become deformed if surrounded or covered by substrate. Place prepupae on top of a slightly concave layer of damp substrate.

# GLOSSARY

**Allometry:** Disproportionate symmetry associated with armature of the head, pronotum, mandible, or leg relative to total size and usually associated with the male beetle.

**Anaerobic:** Without oxygen.

**Apex:** Point furthest from the point of attachment.

**Cephalic Horn:** Large projection of the exoskeleton located on the head of a beetle.

**Clypeus:** Shieldlike front of the beetle's face, before the labrum.

**Coleopterist:** Person who studies beetles, order Coleoptera.

**Commensal:** Term describing an organism which lives on or with another organism, which it does not directly harm or benefit.

**Costate:** Presence of elevated veinlike ridges on the elytra.

**Dentate:** Bordered with a row of small teeth.

**Denticle:** Tiny horns or large bumps that originate off of a larger horn.

**Desiccate:** To dry out.

**Diapause:** Hibernation, or period of inactivity.

**Dimorphism:** Literally, two forms. In dung beetles there is male dimorphism and sexual dimorphism.

**Diurnal:** Active during the day.

**Eclose:** To emerge from the pupal skin, molt to adulthood.

**Elytra (*singular*, Elytron):** The hardened outer front wings of a beetle, or wingcases.

**Endocroprid:** Dung beetle which lays eggs inside or just below the pat.

**Entomophagus:** Literally, insect-eating.

**Eversible:** Able to be turned inside-out.

**Extant:** Currently living species.

**F1, etc.:** Used to refer to the generation removed from wild-caught. F1 are the offspring of wild-caught, while F2 are the offspring of F1. (If wild-caught are crossed with later generations, the result would be no designation or F1.)

**Femur:** Normally the largest leg segment, located between the trochanter and tibia.

**Frass:** Beetle solid waste or excrement.

**Granulate:** To appear covered in small grains (numerous small, flat elevations).

**Hirsute:** Covered in long hair.

**Hyphae:** Filamentous matter that makes up fungi.

**Instar:** Stages between larval molts.

**L1:** Hatchling grub, first instar. The "L" comes from the German word *Larven-stadium*, that means instar in English. (It is always capitalized because it is a noun.)

**L2:** Grub that has molted once, second instar.

**L3:** Grub that has molted twice, third instar.

**Labium:** The lower lip.

**Labrum:** Upper lip that covers mandibles and forms the roof of the mouth. This is a pronounced facial feature of darkling beetles and mealworms.

**Larva:** The immature growing stage of an insect, prior to the pupa stage and after the egg.

**Major:** A male with well-developed horns, armature, or size.

**Mandibles:** The main upper chewing mouthparts, or jaws.

**Margin:** Border or edging.

**Mat:** Finely ground wood flakes or soil-like mixture used to fill in space around pieces of rotten wood.

**Maxilla (*pl.*, Maxillae):** Lower, secondary jaw.

**Maxillary Palpi:** Segmented antennae-like part of the maxillae, upper pair of palpi.

**Minor:** A small, runt male dung beetle with small or no horns or other reduced armature.

**Molt:** Process by which an arthropod sheds the old exoskeleton that is replaced by a new exoskeleton located underneath, the cast off shell or exuvium.

**Molting Cell:** Smooth-walled chamber built by the grub prior to shedding the exoskeleton.

**Moniliform:** Beadlike, made of round segments. Construction of most darkling antennae.

**Mucro:** A sharp, pointed projection, such as at the tip of darkling elytra or the end of a leaf.

**Nidification:** Nest construction.

**Ovum (*pl.*, Ova):** Egg.

**Palpus (*pl.*, Palpi):** Short, segmented appendage on the maxillae and labium.

**Paracoprid:** Dung beetle which buries dung in a tunnel deep below the pat for egg laying.

**Pat:** Pile of dung from a large herbivore, commonly refers to cow dung.

**Prepupa:** A stage of development prior to pupation, this is the terminal larval stage when the larva's legs and jaws become immobile.

**Pronotum:** Top middle segment of a beetle's body, or enlarged surface structure of prothorax.

**Punctate:** With pits or punctures.

**Pupa:** Intermediate mummy-like stage of a beetle's life cycle, between the larva and adult stages.

**Pupal Cell:** Large, smooth-walled chamber in the earth carved out by a mature grub prior to molting into a pupa.

**Pygidial Gland:** Organ located at the dorsal end of the abdomen that produces defensive odor or fluid.

**Pygidium:** Terminal dorsal segment of the abdomen when exposed beyond the abdomen, generally covered by elytra on darkling beetles and stags. The shape of this segment is useful in gender determination for many scarabs.

**Sclerotization:** Process by which the arthropod exoskeleton hardens.

**Setae:** Hair-like exoskeleton projections often used as sensory organs, to keep sections of the body free from debris, or to strain liquid food.

**Sexual Dimorphism:** Gender-related differences in body and appendage shape.

**Sexual Dichromatism:** Differently colored genders, a form of sexual dimorphism.

**Spiracle:** Breathing pore on the sides of the darkling abdomen (visible on larvae but hidden by elytra on beetles).

**Sternite:** Ventral abdominal segment.

**Stria (*pl.*, Striae):** Depressed line or line of punctures on a body part or extending the length of the elytra.

**Striate:** Marked with parallel impressed lines, or possessing striae.

**Stridulate:** To create noise by rubbing together body parts, usually specialized legs or wings. Common in Passalidae, most Lucanidae larvae, and some Scarabaeidae.

**Substrate:** The material placed in the rearing cage for egg laying and as food for the larvae.

**Suture:** Line indicating the junction of the elytra.

**Tarsus (*pl.*, Tarsi):** Foot, or segment following the tibia. The adult scarab foot is usually composed of five small segments and two claws.

**Telecoprid:** Dung beetle which rolls dung a distance away from the pat and buries it shallowly for egg laying.

**Teneral:** Refers to the period when an adult insect first ecloses and is still soft.

**Tergite:** Dorsal abdominal segment.

**Thoracic Horn:** Large projection of the exoskeleton on the pronotum of a beetle.

**Tibia:** Segment between the femur and tarsus.

**Trimorphism:** Term for three distinct male forms of a species within a single wild population and based on thresholds of larval development.

**Tubercle:** Tiny hornlike prominence.

**Vibrotaxis:** An organism's detection and response to mechanical vibrations.

# BIBLIOGRAPHY

Allard, Vincent. (1985) *The Beetles of the World. Vol. 6: Goliathini 2.* Sciences Nat., Venette, France.

Allard, Vincent. (1986) *The Beetles of the World. Vol.7: Goliathini 3.* Sciences Nat., Venette, France.

Arnett, Ross, Jr. (1993) *American Insects: A Handbook of the Insects of America North of Mexico.* The Sandhill Crane Press, Inc., Gainesville, FL.

Arnett, R. Downie, and H. M. Jacques. (1980) *How to Know the Beetles*, 2nd ed. Wm. C. Brown Co. Publishers, Dubuque, Iowa.

Barney, S., and O. McMonigle. (2012) *The Complete Guide to Rearing the Rainbow Scarab and Other Dung Beetles.* Elytra and Antenna, Brunswick, Ohio.

Bily, Svatopluk. (1990) *A Colour Guide to Beetles.* Treasure Press, Artia, Prague.

Busching, Milan K. (1995) Captive breeding and display of the Hercules beetle *Dynastes hercules* at the Insect World, Cincinnati Zoo. 1995 *Invertebrates in Captivity Conference Proceedings.*

Creamer, Karen D. (1992) Natural history, husbandry & display of carrion beetles (Coleoptera: Silphidae) 1992 *AAZPA Regional Conference Proceedings.*

Creamer, Karen D. (1993) Husbandry and display techniques of the American burying beetle *Nicrophorus americanus* (Coleoptera: Silphidae). 1993 *AAZPA Southern Regional Conference Proceedings.*

Dillon, E., and L. Dillon. (1972) *A Manual of Common Beetles of Eastern North America.* Dover Publications, New York.

Eaton, Eric R., and Kenn Kaufman. (2007) *Kaufman Field Guide to Insects of North America.* Houghton Mifflin, New York.

Edmonds, W. D. (1980) Dung beetle nesting behavior. *Scarabaeus: A Newsletter for Those Interested in Scarabaeidae.* No. 2, June 1980.

Edmonds, W. D. (1982) Observing dung beetle nesting behavior. *Scarabaeus: A Newsletter for Those Interested in Scarabaeidae.* No. 6, September 1982.

Evans, Arthur, and James Hogue. (2004) *Introduction to California Beetles.* University of California Press, Los Angeles, California.

Evans, A., Bellamy, C., and L. Watson. (1996) *An Inordinate Fondness for Beetles.* Henry Holt and Company, New York.

Eisner, T., Eisner, M., and M. Siegler. (2005) *Secret Weapons Defenses of Insects, Spiders, Scorpions and Other Many-Legged Creatures.* Harvard University Press, Massachusetts and London.

Fincher, G. T. 1996. (BCH-3810) *Biological Control of Dung-Breeding Flies Affecting Pastured Cattle.* Food Animal Protection Res. Lab., USDA, ARS, College Station, Texas.

Grandcolas, Phillippe, and Cyrille D'Haese. (2001) The phylogeny of cockroach families: Is the current molecular hypothesis robust? *Cladistics* 17: 48-55.

Jahn, Oldrich. (2003) *Odontolabis. Invertebrates-Magazine* 2(3).

Hanski, Ilkka. (1991) *Dung Beetle Ecology*. Princeton University Press, Princeton, New Jersey.

Hellweg, Michael. (2009) *Raising Live Foods*. TFH Publications, Inc., Neptune City, New Jersey.

Jahn, Oldrich. (2002) Buffalo beetles in breeding. *Invertebrates-Magazine* 1(Sept., 4).

Jahn, Oldrich. (2004) *Mecynorhina oberthueri*. *Invertebrates-Magazine* 3(June, 3).

Janssen, Peter. (2006) Thai scientist promotes dung-beetle farming. *Monster and Critics Science Feature*.

Johnson, Sylvia A. (1982) *Beetles*. Lerner Publications Co., Minneapolis, Minnesota.

Jones, Richard A. (2001) *Blaps* Perhaps. *The Bulletin (Amateur Entomologists' Society)* 60 (435).

Kishida, Isao. (1971) *Beetles*.

Krikken, J. (1984) A new key to the suprageneric taxa in the beetle family Cetoniidae, with annotated lists of the known genera. *Zoologische Verhandelingen* (210): 1-75.

Lai, Jonathan, and Orin McMonigle. (2001) *For the Love of Rhinoceros and Stag Beetles*. Morning Star Press, Taiwan.

Lai, Jonathan, et al. (2008) *For the Love of Rhinoceros and Stag Beetles*, 2nd ed.

Lachaume, Gilbert. (1983) *The Beetles of the World. Vol. 3: Goliathini 1*. Sciences Nat., Venette, France.

Lachaume, Gilbert. (1985) *The Beetles of the World. Vol. 5: Dynastini*. Sciences Nat., Venette, France.

Levinson, H., and A. Levinson. (1996) *Prionotheca coronata* Olivier (Pimeliinae, Tenebrionidae) recognized as a new species of venerated beetles in the funerary cult of predynastic and archaic Egypt. *Journal of Applied Entomology* 120: 577-585.

Lowenberg, Arndt. (1999) *Exotische Käfer Pflege und Zucht von Rosen- und Riesenkäfern im Terrarium*. bede- Verlag GmbH.

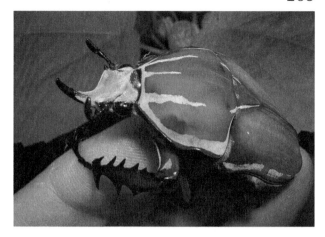

*MECYNORHINA TORQUATA X UGANDENSIS* HYBRID

*ODONTOLABIS DALMANNI INTERMEDIA*

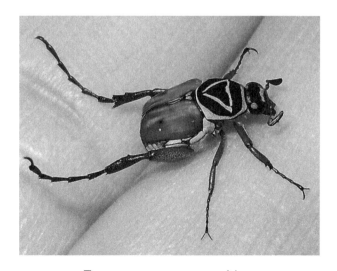

*TRIGONOPELTASTES DELTA* MALE

Marshall, Stephen A. (2006) *Insects: Their Natural History and Diversity with a Photographic Guide to Insects of Eastern North America.* Firefly Books, Buffalo, New York.

McGavin, G. C. (2000) *Insects, Spiders and Other Terrestrial Arthropods.* Dorling, Kindersley Limited, London.

McMonigle, Orin. (1999) *The Complete Guide to Rearing Grant's Rhinoceros Beetle.* Elytra and Antenna, Brunswick, Ohio.

McMonigle, Orin. (2001) Giant skunk beetles. *Invertebrates-Magazine* (Dec. ).

McMonigle, Orin. (2004) *The Complete Guide to Rearing the Elephant Stag Beetle.* Elytra and Antenna, Brunswick, Ohio.

McMonigle, Orin. (2004) *Ghosts of the Trees.* Elytra and Antenna, Brunswick, Ohio.

McMonigle, Orin. (2006) *The Complete Guide to Rearing Flower and Jewel Scarabs.* Elytra and Antenna, Brunswick, Ohio.

McMonigle, Orin. (2008) *The Complete Guide to Rearing the Eastern Hercules Beetle.* Elytra and Antenna, Brunswick, Ohio.

McMonigle, Orin. (2011) *The Complete Guide to Rearing Darkling Beetles.* Elytra and Antenna, Brunswick, Ohio.

Mizunuma, Tetsuo. (1999) *Giant Beetles. Euchirinae . Dynastinae.* Tositsugu, Endo, Japan.

Morgan, Randy C. (1992) Sunburst diving beetles: Living jewels brighten rippling waters. *Backyard Bugwatching (Sonoran Arthropod Studies, Inc.)* (No. 14.)

Morgan, Rancy C. (1998) Giant water scavenger beetle *Hydrophilus triangularis* Say (Coleoptera: Hydrophilidae) natural history and captive management. 1998 *Invertebrates in Captivity Conference Proceedings.*

Morón, Miguel. (1984) *Escarabajos 200 Millones de Anos de Evolucion.* Museo de Historia Natural de la Cuidad de Mexico.

Morón, Miguel-Angel. (1990) *Rutelini 1: Chrysina—Chrysina—Chrysophora—Pelidnotopsis—Ectinoplectron.* Sciences Nat., Venette, France.

Papp, Charles S. (1984) *Introduction to North*

*DELTOCHILUM GIBBOSUM FROM CITRUS CO., FLORIDA*

*GOLIATHUS ALBOSIGNATUS*

*DYNASTES HERCULES PUPA*

*American Beetles.* Entomography Publications, Sacramento, California.

Powell, Jerry, and Charles Hogue. (1979) *California Insects.* University of California Press, Berkeley and Los Angeles, California.

Preston-Mafham, Rod, and Ken Preston-Mafham. (2005) *Encyclopedia of Insects and Spiders.* Thunder Bay Press, San Diego, California.

Rigout, J., and V. Allard. (1992) *The Beetles of the World. Volume 12: Cetoniiini 2.* Sciences Nat., Venette, France.

Robertson, Matthew, and Warren Spencer. (1997) *Breeding South African Tigers, Mantichora krugii, (Coleoptera: Cincindelidae) at Bristol Zoo.* Bristol, Clifton and the West of England Zoological Society, Great Britain.

Rowland, Mark, and Douglas Emlen. (2009) Two thresholds, three male forms result in facultative male trimorphism in beetles. *Science* 323 (February 6).

Stanek, V. J. (1969) *The Pictorial Encyclopedia of Insects.* Hamlyn Publishing Group Ltd., Svoboda, Prague.

Streit, Barney D. (2006) Collecting necrophiliacs. *Scarabs* (November, 17) 2006.

Streit, Barney D. (2008) Notes on four species of *Phanaeus. Scarabs* (September 31).

Warner, Bill. (1991) Scatalogical ramblings. . . . A scarabologist's guide to dung trapping or "Los Hermanas de Caca." Scarabs (2)

Werner, F., and C. Olson. (1994) *Insects of the Southwest.* Fisher Books, Tucson, Arizona.

White, Richard E. (1983) *A Field Guide to the Beetles of North America.* Houghton Mifflin Company, Boston.

Wilson, C. B. (1923) Life history of the water beetle *Hydrous triangularis* and its economic relation to fish breeding. *Bulletin of Bureau of Fisheries.* 39: 9-38.

Yoshi, Kenji. (1995) *Stag Beetle & (Rhinoceros) Beetle Japan.*

Zidek, Jiri, and Svatopluk Pokorny. (2008) Illustrated keys to palearctic *Scarabaeus* Linneaus (Scarabaeidae). *animma.x* 27: 1-28.

*Dynastes granti*

*Eupatorus gracilicornis* Pupa

*Chalcosoma moellenkampi* Pair

# ABOUT THE AUTHOR

The author formulated and tested a repeatable captive husbandry methodology for *Strategus antaeus* in 1988. Further discoveries based on husbandry parameters for *Dynastes tityus* and *Cotinis nitida* formed the basis for the only documented successful methodology ever used to rear the genus *Goliathus* through multiple generations. Works include dozens of published articles on beetle husbandry from 1996 to present and the original complete guide to rearing beetles series from 1999 to 2006. He co-authored a large, hard-cover text on beetle husbandry released in combined Chinese and English released in Taiwan in 2001 and an additional chapter in the 2008 second edition. In 2011 he authored a manual on breeding darkling beetles and co-authored a dung beetle husbandry manual in 2012. Even with a quarter century of experience studying rearing methodologies the author required the cooperation and experiences of many dozens of amateur and professional coleopterists to bring you the ultimate guide to breeding beetles.

*DYNASTES TITYUS* FINDS A FRIEND

# Coachwhip Publications
# CoachwhipBooks.com

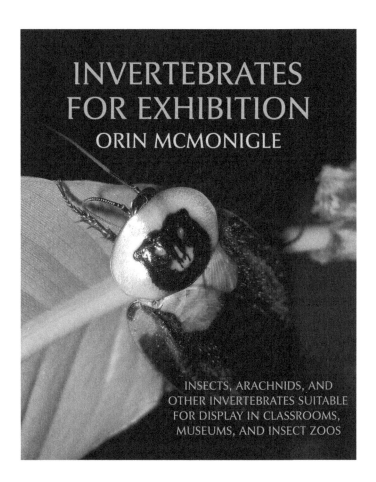

## Invertebrates for Exhibition
## Orin McMonigle

ISBN 1-61646-105-5

CPSIA information can be obtained at www.ICGtesting.com
Printed in the USA
LVOW010906070912

297796LV00002BA/1/P

9 781616 461324